Think linearities: smooth transitions from dictatorship to democracy; the implications of economic globalisation for educational systems; the wise advice of international agencies about how to reform teacher education; the beneficial results of investing more money in the improvement of educational systems; the advantages of decentralisation. Now read this book about Argentina, Brazil, Chile, Colombia, Mexico, and Peru and see how expected linearities become non-linear and solutions to problems become unpredictable. An excellent addition to the literature: a theory shock for practical people and a practical shock for theoreticians.

Robert Cowen, Emeritus Professor, University College London Institute of Education

Latin America has been a laboratory of global education policy for decades. Nonetheless, joining the global policy conversation is not a synonym of meaningful and effective policy change, as this book brilliantly shows. In their chapters, the authors reflect on the main challenges of enacting policy instruments and sustaining policy change in different instances: from official discourses and public regulations to classroom practices. This ambitious and perfectly-executed joint research initiative covers a wide range of relevant policy trajectories in a carefully selected sample of countries from one of the most unequal and politically polarized world regions. Must-read for scholars, students, policy-makers and social activists trying to understand recent policy trends in Latin American education, but also how to advance equitable educational change in increasingly globalized policy spaces.

Antoni Verger, Professor, Department of Sociology, Universidad Autónoma de Barcelona

There has been no comprehensive, up to date overview of educational change in Latin America – there is now. This book offers us a set of accessible, research informed insights into the complex, contradictory and controversial agendas of education reform in major Latin American countries. It explores, critically and reflexively, the tensions and struggles between neoliberalism and social justice that inform and incite the processes of reform. It examines the tensions and struggles between local initiatives and the global education reform movement. This will become the standard text to which researchers, students and policy analysts interested in Latin American turn.

Stephen J Ball, Emeritus Professor of Sociology of Education, University College London

Axel Rivas and his colleagues offer us an outstanding volume of interdisciplinary research to understand and act on the long-standing – and seemingly increasing – educational inequalities in Latin America. This is an exceptional book, bringing together 19 scholars from six Latin American countries, who creatively and rigorously avoided ineffective rigid ideological analysis, while considering local nuances and regional commonalities, to develop an original and comprehensive framing of educational policies in Latin America. A timely contribution, much needed to understand and transform some of the most unequal and unfair educational systems in the world.

Gustavo E. Fischman, Professor, Arizona State University | Mary Lou Fulton Teachers College

I warmly welcome the book edited by Axel Rivas, *Examining Educational Policy in Latin America: Comprehensive Insights into Contemporary Reform*. It is a collection of essays that add valuable insights to the study of educational reforms of this century in Latin America. With clear and concise prose, sound arguments, and a solid empirical base, the distinguished authors illustrate the complexities of educational policy in Argentina, Brazil, Chile, Colombia, Mexico, and Peru. They pay attention to the global context and each country's political and economic vicissitudes. It is an outstanding book, a must-read for those interested in comparative and international education.

Carlos Ornelas, Professor of Education, Universidad Autónoma Metropolitana, Mexico City

Examining Educational Policy in Latin America

This book synthesizes and analyzes the complex map of educational reforms in Latin America in the first two decades of the 21st century. The book offers insights into the agendas, processes and political economy of educational reforms in Argentina, Brazil, Chile, Colombia, Mexico and Peru.

Written by renowned contributors from each country, chapters present systematic, critical and reflective accounts of an intense period of education reforms. The book fills a gap in educational research and provides a systematic study that compares the cases analyzed. The first broad, comparative collection of its kind, the book is well-suited to courses in international and comparative education policy.

Axel Rivas is Professor, Researcher and Dean of the School of Education of the Universidad de San Andrés, Argentina, Academic Director of the Center for Applied Research in Education San Andrés (CIAESA), author of multiple articles and 14 books on comparative education and education policies, and Associate Editor of the Journal *Education Policy Analysis Archives*.

Examining Educational Policy in Latin America

Comprehensive Insights into Contemporary Reform

Edited by Axel Rivas

NEW YORK AND LONDON

Cover image: Claudio Gallina

First published 2022
by Routledge
605 Third Avenue, New York, NY 10158

and by Routledge
4 Park Square, Milton Park, Abingdon, Oxon OX14 4RN

Routledge is an imprint of the Taylor & Francis Group, an informa business

© 2022 selection and editorial matter, Axel Rivas, individual chapters, the contributors

The right of Axel Rivas to be identified as the author of the editorial material, and of the authors for their individual chapters, has been asserted in accordance with sections 77 and 78 of the Copyright, Designs and Patents Act 1988.

All rights reserved. No part of this book may be reprinted or reproduced or utilised in any form or by any electronic, mechanical, or other means, now known or hereafter invented, including photocopying and recording, or in any information storage or retrieval system, without permission in writing from the publishers.

Trademark notice: Product or corporate names may be trademarks or registered trademarks, and are used only for identification and explanation without intent to infringe.

Library of Congress Cataloging-in-Publication Data
Names: Rivas, Axel, editor.
Title: Examining educational policy in Latin America : comprehensive insights into contemporary reform / Edited by Axel Rivas.
Description: New York, NY : Routledge, 2022. |
Includes bibliographical references and index.
Identifiers: LCCN 2021035663 (print) | LCCN 2021035664 (ebook) | ISBN 9781032126975 (hardback) | ISBN 9781032126951 (paperback) | ISBN 9781003225782 (ebook)
Subjects: LCSH: Education and state--Latin America. |
Educational change--Latin America. | Education--Political aspects--Latin America. | Education--Economic aspects--Latin America.
Classification: LCC LC92.A2 E93 2022 (print) | LCC LC92.A2 (ebook) | DDC 379.8--dc23
LC record available at https://lccn.loc.gov/2021035663
LC ebook record available at https://lccn.loc.gov/2021035664

ISBN: 978-1-032-12697-5 (hbk)
ISBN: 978-1-032-12695-1 (pbk)
ISBN: 978-1-003-22578-2 (ebk)

DOI: 10.4324/9781003225782

Typeset in Galliard
by Taylor & Francis Books

Contents

List of Illustrations		ix
Acknowledgments		x
List of Contributors		xi

1 Introductory Study: A Comparative Analysis of Educational Reforms in Latin America 1
   AXEL RIVAS

2 From "Spray and Pray" to "Reform without Spray": The Two Stages of Education Policy in Argentina 39
   BELÉN SÁNCHEZ AND AXEL RIVAS

3 From Structural Reforms to Controversial Changes: The Education Policy Landscape in Brazil 58
   FILIPE RECCH, VINÍCIUS BAPTISTA SOARES LOPES AND LUCAS HOOGERBRUGGE

4 Educational Policies in Chile: Between the State, the Market and Accountability based on Academic Achievement Tests 75
   CRISTIAN BELLEI AND GONZALO MUÑOZ

5 From Political Intentions to Structural Interventions: A Review of Two Decades of Education Policy Reforms in Colombia 96
   JORGE GRANT BAXTER AND MÓNICA CRISTINA LEÓN CADAVID

6 The Educational Policy Agenda in Mexico (2000–2020): A Time of Continuities and Political Shocks 109
   JUAN C. OLMEDA AND VALENTINA SIFUENTES

7 The Slow Development Process of Educational Policies in Peru 130
   MARÍA BALARIN WITH THE COLLABORATION OF MANUELA DE SZYSZLO

8 The Changing Spatial Dynamics of Education Policy in
   Latin America   150
   JASON BEECH

   Index   157

Illustrations

Figures

1.1	Presidential terms of the six Latin American countries, 2000–2020	4
1.2	Moderate and extreme poverty (percentages), and GDP per capita (constant in 2011 international dollars). Latin America and the Caribbean 2000–2018	5
1.3	Evolution of expenditure in education compared to GDP. Selected countries, 2000–2017	23
1.4	Evolution of the percentage of students in private schools per education level. Selected countries, 1999–2018	28
2.1	Graphic summary of the national agendas of education policy of the period 2003–2019	53
4.1	Evolution of institutional designs and educational policies in Chile	89
5.1	Different periods of education reform in Colombia	105
7.1	Different periods of education reform in Peru	146

Tables

1.1	Summary of economic and social indicators of selected countries. Circa 2017 and circa variation 2000–2017	7
1.2	Policy instruments related to the governance turn and the extent to which they were implemented in the studied countries	31

Acknowledgments

This book is the result of a collaborative research project coordinated by the San Andrés Center for Applied Research in Education of the University of San Andrés (CIAESA), Argentina. The overall title of the project was "The keys to education" (Las Llaves de la Educación) and it contains different publications on the educational systems of Latin America. The project was possible thanks to the support of Instituto Natura and the work of 19 researchers from six countries. The project was also supported by the following academic institutions: the Center for Advanced Research in Education of the University of Chile (Chile), the University of the Andes (Colombia), El Colegio de México and the Development Analysis Group (GRADE, Peru). The statistical analysis of the introductory study was carried out by Martín Scasso, Emilia Larsen was the project assistant and Ignacio Barrenechea oversaw the final editing of this book. We also thank them for their dedicated effort in this project.

The cover art is by Claudio Gallina.

Contributors

Axel Rivas (Universidad de San Andrés, Argentina)

School of Education Director at the Universidad de San Andrés, teacher and researcher. Academic Director at the Center for Applied Research in Education San Andrés (CIAESA). Regional Advisor for UNESCO in Latin America.

PhD in Social Sciences, UBA, Argentina. Master's Degree in Social Sciences and Education, FLACSO, Argentina. Bachelor's Degree in Communication Sciences at the UBA. Doctoral Studies at the Institute of Education of the University of London.

Author of 14 books about education policies. His most recent articles are: "Race to the classroom: the governance turn in Latin American education. The emerging era of accountability, control and prescribed curriculum" (2020), in *Compare: A Journal of Comparative and International Education*, and "Low stakes, high risks: the problem of intertemporal validity of PISA in Latin America" (2019), in *Journal of Education Policy*. Editor for South America of the magazine *Education Policy Analysis Archives*.

Belén Sánchez (Universidad de San Andrés, Argentina)

PhD Candidate in Education (Universidad de San Andrés), Master's in Education and International Development (Institute of Education, University College London), Bachelor's Degree and Teacher in Education Sciences (Universidad de San Andrés).

Doctoral Fellow at CONICET. She was executive Coordinator of the project "Pedagogical governance of the Argentinean educational system: a provincial comparative study" as a doctoral fellow of the Universidad de San Andrés at the Center for Applied Research in Education San Andrés (UdeSA/ACEESA). She teaches for the Master's Degree in Education and the Bachelor's Degree in Educational Sciences at the Universidad de San Andrés.

She was the Coordinator of the Education Program of the Center for the Implementation of Public Policies for Equity and Growth (CIPPEC) and consultant for government agencies and international organizations. She has also served as Head of Practical Works at the Universidad Nacional de San Martín.

xii *List of Contributors*

Filipe Recch

Filipe Recch holds a PhD in International Comparative Education (Stanford University), an MA in Political Science (Stanford University) and an MA in Public Administration (Fundação João Pinheiro-FJP/MG). He also holds a Bachelor's in Social Sciences (Federal University of Minas Gerais). In addition, he is a postdoctoral researcher at the Lemann Center for Entrepreneurship and Educational Innovation in Brazil at Stanford University.

Vinícius Baptista Soares Lopes

Vinícius Baptista Soares Lopes is a PhD candidate in Political Science at Federal University of Minas Gerais (UFMG). He holds an MA in Political Science and a Bachelor's in Social Sciences (UFMG). Currently, he is a member of Centro de Estudos em Gestão e Políticas Públicas (PUBLICUS – UFMG) and of Rede de Estudos em Implementação de Políticas Públicas Educacionais (REIPPE).

Lucas Fernandes Hoogerbrugge

Lucas Fernandes Hoogerbrugge holds an MA in Education (Stanford University) and a Bachelor's Degree in Administration (UNICAMP). He is the leader of government relations in Todos Pela Educação and advisor to the State Council of Education of Minas Gerais. In addition, he held various leadership positions in the Ministry of Education in Ceará and has worked as a consultant for the Omidyar Network World Bank, Movimento Colabora Educação, and other NGOs and foundations.

Cristian Bellei (Universidad de Chile)

Sociologist from the University of Chile, Master's in Educational Policy, and PhD in Education from Harvard University.

Since 2006 he has worked as Lecturer of Sociology at the University of Chile and as Associate Researcher at the Center for Advanced Research in Education at the same university; and since 2018 as a lecturer at the Universidad Austral de Chile.

Previously, he worked as a professional advisor to the Ministry of Education (1994–2003) and as head of the education area of UNICEF in Chile (1998–2003).

His research and publications deal mainly with educational policy, school quality and improvement, educational equity, segregation and the market in education.

Gonzalo Muñoz (Universidad Diego Portales, Chile)

Sociologist; Master's in Sociology from the Catholic University of Chile. He is currently studying for his PhD in Educational Sciences at the University of Granada, Spain.

Academic of the Faculty of Education at the Universidad Diego Portales.

He was head of the General Education Division of the Ministry of Education of Chile between 2014 and 2016. He worked as a member of the Board of the Education Quality Agency, Director of Studies of the Center for Innovation in Education of Fundación Chile, Head of Studies of the General Education Division of the Ministry of Education and Associate Researcher of Asesorías para el Desarrollo. He has been a researcher and consultant in different national and international institutions and has collaborated with educational change processes in countries such as Uruguay, Paraguay, Panama and Honduras. He has published several books and articles in his areas of expertise: educational policies, school improvement and educational leadership.

Jorge Grant Baxter

PhD in International Education Policy, University of Maryland. Director of Center for Educational Research and Training and Associate Professor at the Faculty of Education, Universidad de los Andes. Jorge was Regional Director for Latin America for Sesame Workshop, a Specialist in Education at the Organization of American States (OAS); Adjunct Professor at George Washington University; and Professor at the Monterrey Institute of Technology in Colima and Guadalajara, Mexico.

Mónica Cristina León Cadavid

Master's degree in education emphasizes public policy, education management and school life, Universidad de los Andes, Colombia. Education research professional. Specialist in Education Institutes Management, Universidad del Tolima, Colombia. Mónica also has a Degree in Basic Education emphasizing Artistic Education from District University Francisco José de Caldas, Colombia.

She has worked as a research professional with qualitative methods (design, application of instruments and data analysis) at the School of Education, Universidad de los Andes, particularly in education programs assessments. In addition, she has teaching experience in preschool, basic and secondary educational institutions within the private sector.

Juan C. Olmeda

PhD in Political Science from the Department of Political Science at Northwestern University, USA (2013), in which he also obtained a Master's degree in Political Science. He previously obtained a Master's degree in Ethics, Politics and Public Policy from the University of Essex, UK (2001).

He is a professor-researcher at the Center for International Studies of El Colegio de México and a National System of Researchers (SNI) member, Level 1. Since March 2017, he has also been the editor of the journal *Foro Internacional*.

He specializes in comparative politics with a focus on Latin American federal countries. During 2017 and 2018, he coordinated the research project "Case studies to identify factors associated with the conformation of monitoring and evaluation systems in the federal entities" funded by the National Council for the Evaluation of Social Development Policy of Mexico.

Valentina Itandehui Sifuentes García

PhD in Social Science with a major in Sociology from the Colegio de México. She holds a Master's degree in Political and Social Sciences and a Bachelor's degree in Communication from the Universidad Nacional Autónoma de México.

Her line of research focuses on educational inequality and young people, and she is the author of several articles on the subject. Her doctoral thesis was recommended for publication by the Colegio de México. In addition, she has participated as a speaker in national and international conferences.

María Balarin (Group of Analysis for Development, Peru)

PhD in Educational Policy from the University of Bath (UK), MA in Psychoanalytic Studies from the University of Essex (UK) and BA in Philosophy from the Pontificia Universidad Católica del Perú.

She is Principal Investigator and Research Director at the Group of Analysis for Development (GRADE). Her research agenda is both academic and applied and focuses on education and social policy issues. Her applied work focuses on analyzing and qualitative evaluation of public policies, specifically from a process and implementation approach. Since her academic work, her interests have focused on analyzing the relationships between education, the state and society.

She is a member and part of the Grupo Sofía's Promotion Group.

Jason Beech

Jason Beech is Senior Lecturer in the Faculty of Education at Monash University and visiting professor at Universidad de San Andrés. He has researched for more than 15 years about the globalization of knowledge and policies related to education, and is also interested in exploring the link between cosmopolitanism, citizenship and education. He is senior researcher of the National Council for Scientific and Technical Research of Argentina (CONICET), and Associate Editor of *Education Policy Analysis Archives*. He has taught in several universities in the Americas, Europe and Australia.

1 Introductory Study

A Comparative Analysis of Educational Reforms in Latin America

Axel Rivas

Introduction

The turn of the 21st century marked the beginning of a complex era in Latin America. During the 1990s, many Latin American countries were still recovering from the traces of military dictatorships. The health of the democracies was still weak as many countries were still experiencing the aftermath of brutal coups d'état. Concerning educational policies, many Latin American countries, during the 1990s, received the attention of several international agencies that tried to implement neoliberal reforms in the education field and other public goods. This context contributed to a relatively homogeneous landscape in Latin American education reforms.

Nonetheless, during the first years of the 21st century, there was a more intense, diverse and contradictory agenda of reforms. Governments of different ideologies followed similar steps towards standardized accountability and, at the same time, diverse strategies promoting educational justice. The notable economic growth of the new century's first decade allowed more room to implement a wide range of educational policies. The agenda became more complex, and policy trajectories suffered several reconfigurations as governments changed (in some cases radically).

This book aims to map the educational policies that were implemented in the region in this significant and intense period. This book offers a critical and reflexive analysis of the different educational policies implemented between 2000 and 2020. The main theoretical framework aims to unveil policy discourses, changing ideologies and identities, and educational reforms enacted in the realm of the classrooms.

The idea of mapping educational reforms during this period has been so far elusive, unlike what happened with the educational reforms of the 1990s. This book develops the first integral and comparative map of the educational policies in Argentina, Brazil, Chile, Colombia, Mexico and Peru during this period. We analyzed the education policy agendas from a systemic perspective in a shared and collaborative research project, allowing us to offer a genuinely comparative study of the trends, convergences and divergences in different domains of educational policies.

DOI: 10.4324/9781003225782-1

The book is the product of a large project that recruited some of the region's most notable scholars. Each author/group of authors specialized in one country, but the team followed the same guidelines and analytic lens. All researchers used the same comparative framework to analyze the educational agenda during the period 2000–2020. The team worked together in building the common theoretical and analytical dimensions and cross-read each chapter. The compactness and fidelity of all the authors' methodological approaches contribute to offering a valuable comparative study of the region. In tackling the education reforms of the first two decades in Latin America (previous to the COVID-19 pandemic) and doing it from a shared perspective, this book offers a unique comparative framework.

In this first chapter, we introduce the context of the period under analysis and the reforms' historical roots and policy trajectories. Then we map the literature showing the lack of integral studies of this period (compared to the previous one of the 1990s). Based on the original research of the book chapters, we then present a summary of each of the six countries' educational reform agendas: Argentina, Brazil, Chile, Colombia, México and Peru. Finally, we present the predominant trends from a comparative perspective. This last part of the chapter functions as an analytical device to comprehend the synergies and divergences of the educational reforms in the period under study.

The Context: Crispy Democracies and Political Change

To introduce the analyzed period, we must focus on the political and economic context. The shifting democratic consolidation marks the Latin American political context during the period 2000–2020. In all the countries, the traces of the coups d'état and military dictatorships that planted state terrorism in the region started to fade away (Rouquié, 2011). For the first time, there have been widespread consolidated successive periods of democratic elections and even government changes that tested states' ability to obtain continuity in policy implementation. However, in many countries of the region, the democracies are still weak. They are threatened by concentrated powers and *soft coups* that live with a broad spectrum of institutionalized corruption, questioned governments' legitimacy and a persistent segmentation that favors the economy's most concentrated sectors (López, 2020; Robinson, 2020).

The political trajectory in the countries studied is disparate. In the 1990s, the neoliberal governments predominated with an economic openness to the global markets, privatization of public utilities and labor market deregulation. For instance, this was the case in Argentina, Peru and Colombia. The new century brought a wave of popular governments (such as Lula da Silva in Brazil or Néstor Kirchner in Argentina) that went along the trajectory of other more radicalized countries such as Uruguay, Ecuador, Bolivia or Venezuela. These countries moved towards the state's control of the economy and emphasized distribution policies (Ouviña & Thwaites Rey, 2018; Reid, 2007; Toer, 2012).

Chile had a long cycle of continuity with governments of the Concertación center-left coalition between 1990 and 2010. In 2010 Sebastián Piñera (center-right) interrupted the Concertación's victories. In 2014 Michele Bachelet (from the Concertación) reached the government again; she was then replaced by Piñera, in 2018. This alternation between two opposing political sectors tested the state apparatus's machinery, maybe the most institutionalized in the region, along with those of Uruguay and Costa Rica (OECD, 2020).

Even though Mexico had significant changes, they took place over more extended periods, given that its presidents are elected to a six-year term. For the first time, the PRI's historical tradition was interrupted by President Vicente Fox's election in 2000, succeeded by Felipe Calderón and Enrique Peña Nieto (PRI, once again). Beyond their deep-rooted differences, these governments followed a center-right political orientation up until the irruption of Manuel López Obrador in 2018, who ended the continuation of this political orientation.

In Peru, the changes were recurrent after the long period of Alberto Fujimori's government in the 1990s. Alejandro Toledo's (2001–2006) presidencies and Alan García (2006–2011) had a more pro-market orientation. Ollanta Humala's presidency (2011–2016) adopted a more state-interventionist vision. Lastly, Pedro Pablo Kuczynski, who resigned from the presidency amid accusations of corruption, and his successor, Martín Vizcarra, both shared pro-market visions, too.

Argentina and Brazil saw their long cycles of continuity of center-left governments interrupted by very different political movements. In Argentina, Mauricio Macri won the 2015 elections. He brought a center-right managerial character to the country's government, but his power construction's political weakness prevented him from winning again in 2019. In Brazil, a succession of politically biased investigations led to the impeachment of President Dilma Rousseff. Lula da Silva was not allowed to participate in the 2018 elections due to judicial accusations. Under these circumstances, Jair Bolsonaro, the far-right candidate, won the election. This process shows the combination of a form of corruption deeply rooted in the state apparatus with a new form of soft coups d'état via the judiciary.

When looking at the period, a stage of growing political upheaval can be seen, with countries becoming increasingly ideologically polarized and with government changes that marked abrupt stages of transition in weak democratic contexts (especially in the case of Brazil and Peru). The accumulated tension of these processes is a manifestation of the ideological and symbolic dimension that policies had. The ideological load has become more powerful, unstable and subcutaneous, forming bubbles of adhesion or rejection loaded with a deep inheritance of social dissatisfaction that lends itself to the ups and downs of the leaders of the day. This process sank the democratic architecture of societies into the well of antagonisms, the radicalization of ideas and polarization as a replacement for the *polis*, that is, the space for diverse ideas to improve power (Rosanvallon, 2020).

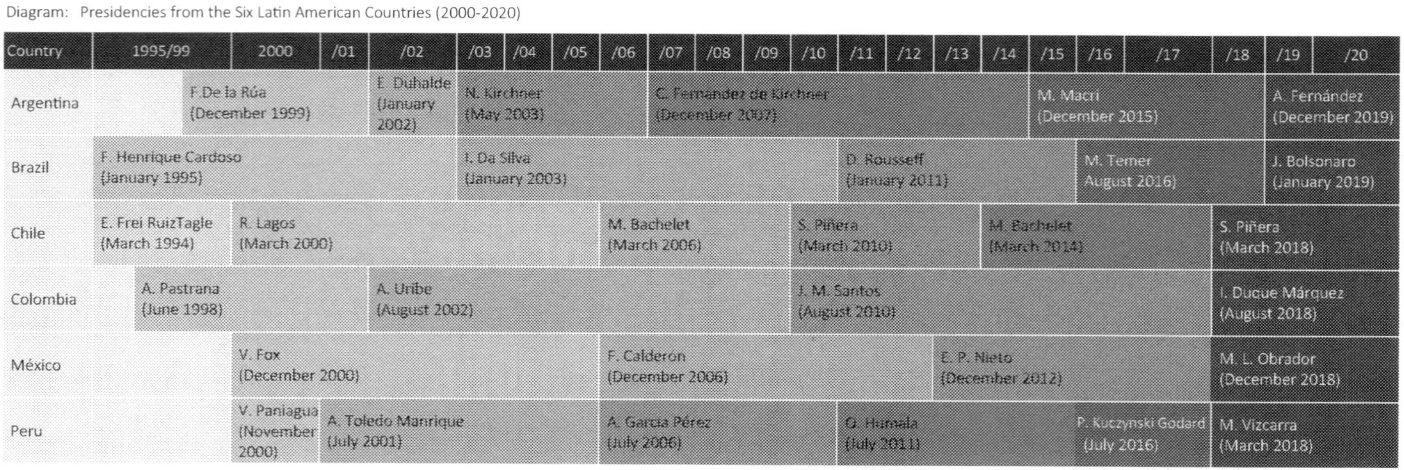

Diagram: Presidencies from the Six Latin American Countries (2000-2020)

Country	1995/99	2000	/01	/02	/03	/04	/05	/06	/07	/08	/09	/10	/11	/12	/13	/14	/15	/16	/17	/18	/19	/20
Argentina		F. De la Rúa (December 1999)		E. Duhalde (January 2002)	N. Kirchner (May 2003)				C. Fernández de Kirchner (December 2007)								M. Macri (December 2015)				A. Fernández (December 2019)	
Brazil	F. Henrique Cardoso (January 1995)				I. Da Silva (January 2003)								D. Rousseff (January 2011)					M. Temer (August 2016)		J. Bolsonaro (January 2019)		
Chile	E. Frei RuizTagle (March 1994)	R. Lagos (March 2000)						M. Bachelet (March 2006)				S. Piñera (March 2010)				M. Bachelet (March 2014)				S. Piñera (March 2018)		
Colombia	A. Pastrana (June 1998)			A. Uribe (August 2002)								J. M. Santos (August 2010)								I. Duque Márquez (August 2018)		
México		V. Fox (December 2000)						F. Calderón (December 2006)						E. P. Nieto (December 2012)						M. L. Obrador (December 2018)		
Peru		V. Paniagua (November 2000)	A. Toledo Manrique (July 2001)					A. García Pérez (July 2006)					O. Humala (July 2011)					P. Kuczynski Godard (July 2016)		M. Vizcarra (March 2018)		

Figure 1.1 Presidential terms of the six Latin American countries, 2000–2020
Source: Adapted from Rivas (2015)

The Golden Age of Economic Growth Meets its Limits

The new century marked the awakening of a stage of economic and social improvement in Latin America. The region went through a remarkable process of economic growth that favored the reduction of poverty levels. For instance, since the end of the Argentine economic crisis in 2003, the decrease in poverty and indigence ran parallel to the region's economic growth. Between 2002 and 2014, a total of 66 million people overcame poverty in Latin America, a reduction from 45% to 27% of the total population. At the same time, extreme poverty fell from 12% to 7%.

The process of economic growth was centered in a period of the raw material export boom, and it significantly affected the countries of South America. This was combined with a growing political awareness to reduce poverty, generate greater social inclusion and create more employment opportunities. However, this economic and social cycle of growth was weaker in the mid-2010s. Considering the region as a whole, poverty went up again since 2015, but with different trends depending on the countries. It increased between 2015 and 2018, especially in Brazil and Venezuela, and then Argentina (ECLAC, 2019).

Most of the remaining countries followed a cycle of weak economic growth – compared to the beginning of the century – but continued growing until the COVID-19 pandemic in 2020.

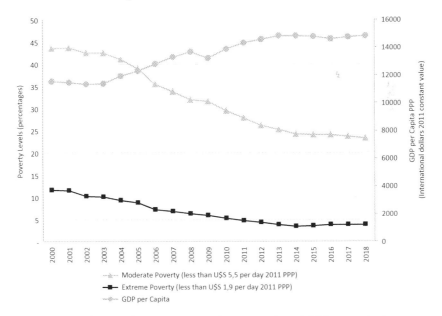

Figure 1.2 Moderate and extreme poverty (percentages), and GDP per capita (constant in 2011 international dollars). Latin America and the Caribbean 2000–2018
Note: GDP: gross domestic product; PPP: purchasing power parity
Source: CIAESA, Universidad de San Andrés and Quántitas, based on World Bank and LAC Equity Lab

This long economic cycle has an unresolved correlate in the levels of public investment allocated by governments. The global trend of the regional economy and the public spending share show two specially marked cycles. Between 2003 and 2014, the region's GDP grew by 88%, and public spending expanded from 27% of GDP to 34% in the six countries analyzed in this book. After this auspicious decade, the economy's pace slowed down; simultaneously, the increase in public spending was stopped, and was even reduced between 2014 and 2018, reaching 31% of GDP.

In recent years, the expansion of the state's role in most of the region's countries has met the limits of a growing fiscal deficit. This translated into policies to adjust public spending that affected the satisfaction of basic social rights in most of Latin America (Abramo et al., 2019). For other authors, even the growth achieved was based on bad development since, having focused on the export of primary goods, it oriented the economy towards extractive activities with little added value and future ecological risks (Svampa, 2017; Tortosa, 2011).

The indicators in Table 1.1 provide some coordinates on the socioeconomic context of the countries. Argentina shows evidence of being the second-largest economy of the group after Chile in GDP per capita. In the period assessed, it has reached growth levels below the average of the countries. It shows marked trends in reducing poverty and income inequalities in the population on a larger scale than the average of the countries analyzed in this study. This is related to the context of the deep crisis that the country went through at the beginning of the 21st century since it had reached remarkably high peaks of poverty. Economic recovery reversed this crisis. However, this improvement trajectory has turned into the stagnation of social and economic indicators during the last decade.

Brazil is one of the economies with the least resources in terms of GDP per capita. However, it is necessary to consider that it is the country with the largest population, with very marked inequalities. It is also one of the countries with least-reduced levels of poverty. As can be seen in the Gini coefficient, all the countries managed to reduce inequalities. However, vast differences persist in Brazil, making it the country with the most unequal distribution of income.

Chile shows exceptionally high growth rates for its economy in the period, being well above the regional average. Although the indicators are not directly comparable, the poverty indicators are lower than those of the rest of the region. Furthermore, they have been reduced in the period. In contrast, Chile continues to be a country with widespread social inequalities. Colombia shows a small per capita GDP value compared to the rest, but it registers growth rates higher than the average of the countries in the region. It has notably reduced extreme poverty levels, although it has high inequality levels, even above the average for the region.

Mexico is the third most important economy of the group in terms of GDP per capita, and, at the same time, it shows growth rates lower than the average for the countries in the region. The country markedly reduced the levels of

Table 1.1 Summary of economic and social indicators of selected countries. Circa 2017 and circa variation 2000–2017

	GDP per Capita adjusted by PPP*		Extreme Poverty**		Moderate Poverty**		Gini Coefficient***	
	(Ordinary international dollars, variation expressed in percentages)		(% of individuals below extreme poverty level)		(% of individuals below moderate poverty level)		(Coefficient value)	
	Circa 2017	Variation Circa 2000–Circa 2017	Circa 2017	Variation Circa 2000–Circa 2017	Circa 2017	Variation Circa 2000–Circa 2017	Circa 2017	Variation Circa 2000–Circa 2017
Argentina	20,830.1	74.4%	6.7	-14.4	32.0	-26.2	40.6	-9.2
Brazil	15,406.6	68.8%	7.4	-7.8	26.5	-8.6	53.3	-5.7
Chile	24,675.5	117.9%	2.3	-3.3	8.6	-11.6	46.6	-6.2
Colombia	14,392.2	118.6%	7.2	-10.5	27.0	-22.7	49.7	-9.0
Mexico	19,948.5	58.6%	7.4	-16.7	41.9	-11.7	43.4	-8.0
Peru	13,517.7	161.4%	3.8	-11.2	3.8	-27.7	43.3	-13.0
Average	18,128.4	91.7%	5.8	-10.7	23.3	-18.1	46.2	-8.5

*Data "circa 2000" correspond to the year 2000 for Argentina, Brazil, Chile, Colombia, Mexico and Peru. Data "circa 2017" correspond to 2017 for Argentina, Chile, Colombia, Mexico and Peru; 2016 for Brazil

**Data "circa 2000" correspond to the year 2000 for Chile, Peru, Mexico and Argentina; 2001 for Brazil and 2002 for Colombia. Data "circa 2017" correspond to the year 2018 for Argentina, Mexico and Colombia; 2017 for Chile and 2016 for Peru. Data for Argentina correspond only to urban areas

***Data "circa 2000" correspond to the year 2000 for Argentina, Brazil, Colombia and Peru; 2001 for Chile and Mexico. Data "circa 2017" correspond to the year 2017 for Argentina, Brazil, Chile, Colombia and Peru; 2016 for Mexico

Source: CIAESA, Universidad de San Andrés and Quántitas, based on GDP adjusted by PPP: WEO-IMF. Extreme and Moderate Poverty: SEDLAC, Official Poverty Rates 2000; except Mexico (CONEVAL). Poverty circa 2017 is based on official data: Brazil: IPEADATA (2014); Instituto Brasileño de Geografía y Estadística (IBGE); Chile: CASEN; Colombia: DANE; Mexico: CONEVAL (2014); Peru: INEI; Uruguay: INE. In the case of Argentina, poverty levels have been taken from secondary sources: Tornarolli (2018) Series Comparables de Indigencia y Pobreza. Índice de Gini: SEDLAC-Banco Mundial

extreme poverty at a higher rate than the rest. Although the poverty indicator is not strictly comparable, the magnitude of poverty in 2017 was high. It also reduced the inequality of income distribution at a rate like that of the rest of the region's countries. It is positioned in a favorable situation, above the average.

Peru is the smallest economy of the group in terms of GDP per capita. However, it grew steadily and at a higher rate than the rest of the countries included in this study. It is also one of the most salient cases in poverty reduction: in 2000, it started with percentages close to 50% of the population below the poverty line, and by 2016 this went down to 20.7%. Furthermore, despite still being one of the unequal countries, income distribution improved sharply.

Persistent Social Debts

Latin America is characterized by being an unequal region in the world. One of the classic measures to reflect this situation is the Gini coefficient, which measures income inequality according to population strata. In the period studied, economic growth favored the decrease in inequality, going from 0.53 to 0.47 between 2002 and 2017 (ECLAC, 2019).

These classic measurements have recently been revised in light of new methodologies. In a study by ECLAC (2019), the Gini coefficient's correction was analyzed considering the percentage of income that the wealthiest 1% of the population concentrated, which was not well depicted by previous measurements. Thus, it was found that inequalities are even more comprehensive and that in the period of remarkable economic growth, only a minimal reduction of the Gini coefficient was achieved (ECLAC, 2019, p. 25).

Structural inequalities have different correlates of political debts. Some perspectives emphasize the need to review the tax schemes of most countries in the region. A characteristic feature of Latin America is the limited capacity of the state to collect progressive taxes. However, the history of inequalities in Latin America cannot be limited to the fiscal perspective. The redistribution factors express an asymmetry of power consolidated from economic concentration schemes and labor exploitation schemes. As Pérez Sáinz (2016) explains, wealth concentration was based on the appropriation of labor markets, land, capital and knowledge. The tax systems' structural inequity also reflects the historical assymetries in the distribution matrix of the region. This more profound vision of inequalities in the region allows us to see the connection between justice domains: those born in affluent households will have more opportunities to obtain income, justice, health, security and education. Inequalities do not refer only to income but to the conditions of classes and social strata (Therborn, 2013).

Furthermore, in Latin America, social inequalities leaned towards certain historically oppressed groups, particularly women, indigenous people and the Afro-Latin American populations. In recent years, social justice struggles have included increasing movements seeking to acknowledge the diversity of identities and cultures that inhabit the region (Yashar, 2005). Building citizenship that is more open to the different marginalized populations is also part of a revision of the educational project that, in many countries of the region, implied a hegemonic cultural consolidation and ruled out the diversity of cultures that inhabit our countries (Puiggrós, 1991).

Interesting Times: Two Decades of Education Reform

In the first two decades of the 21st century, the education policy map has been an elusive research and analysis object in Latin America. The 1990s had captured the spotlight, as the reforms followed relatively convergent parameters called the Washington Consensus, with mostly neoliberal-oriented governments. More comprehensive studies reviewed the 1990s from different, more or less critical perspectives (Gajardo, 1999; Grindle, 2004; Martínez Boom, 2004; Martinic & Pardo, 2001; Reimers, 2001; Rivero, 2000).

Changes in governments framed the new century and political trends closer to the recovery of the state's role in a context of economic growth. However, the 2000s brought about a paradoxical time, more intense reforms and political contradictions. Linear ideological readings became limited or infertile in the face of a context in which governments of the left (such as those of Ecuador) or the center-left (such as those of Brazil or Chile) applied policies of accountability, competition, the publication of results and economic incentives to regulate the education systems' productivity.

Before this study, we attempted to map education policies and their results in seven Latin American countries between 2000 and 2015 (Rivas, 2015). We analyzed the trends in education policy in Argentina, Brazil, Chile, Colombia, Mexico, Peru and Uruguay. With the PISA and UNESCO tests for Latin America, we were able to study the evolution of the indicators of education systems and their results in quality assessments. This allowed us to develop the first map of these countries' policies and educational outcomes, analyzing the complexity of the policies' impact from a systemic perspective. Other studies went further and comparatively analyzed policies and pedagogical practices in the classroom from more sociohistorical (Carnoy, 2007) or technocratic (Bruns & Luque, 2014) perspectives. The field of educational research in Latin America presents few comparative studies that have looked into the relationships between education governance, pedagogical practices and the curriculum (Acosta & Ruiz, 2018; Beech, 2002).

In the last 20 years, the analysis of education policies had some relevant productions that allowed the appraisal of different education problems in Latin American (Cabrol & Székely, 2012; Ornelas, 2019, 2020; Schwartzman, 2015; Schwartzman & Cox, 2009; Tenti, 2004). Other studies sought to map the results of impact evaluations in Latin America and build proposals from that perspective (Vegas & Petrow, 2008). At the crossroads between the learning outcomes of the tests and the curricular analysis, there were the Latin

American Laboratory Studies for the Evaluation of Educational Quality of UNESCO, with works more focused on education policies (LLECE-UNESCO, 2013).

Juan Carlos Tedesco's (2012) work allowed lines of historical continuity to the region's challenges for the new century. The author's work defined a series of educational challenges that are still in force: the priority of preschool education, teaching policies, new curricular axes based on scientific literacy, citizenship education, training in digital skills and the challenge of subjectivity policies, as he called the challenge of involving actors in the educational change agendas.

Picking up the dialogue with these previous studies, here is a brief overview of the education policy trends in the six countries studied: Argentina, Brazil, Chile, Colombia, Mexico and Peru. Then the convergences and divergences in the different domains of education policy are analyzed and synthesized as an introduction to the book's chapters.

Argentina: From "Spray and Pray" to "Reform without Spray"

In Chapter 2, Sánchez and Rivas describe the educational policy agenda in Argentina during the period 2000–2020. The authors explain that following the devastating social, political and economic crisis in 2001, Argentina experienced economic growth under Néstor Kirchner's government between 2003 and 2007, followed by a period of stagnation in the two presidencies of Cristina Fernández. Education policy during this period can be divided into two stages. In the early years, Minister Daniel Filmus led a strategy to recover public education and leave the 1990s' education reform behind. This was a time of new laws that offered a comprehensive education framework. The National Education Law passed in 2006 as a centerpiece on, among others, education financing, technical education and sexual education (Beech, 2019; Terigi, 2016). Besides, Argentina's education budget increased from 4.2% to 6% of its GDP between 2004 and 2013 (Rivas & Dborkin, 2018). This growth enabled several programs to support the provinces: interventions that sought to expand social and educational rights, with different receptivity and appropriation.

This was also a period of policies aimed at redistribution and recognition of rights of disadvantaged groups. However, there were no significant reforms; there was no explicit theory of change to explain how education would improve. At the political level, the government's closeness to teacher unions favored a *conservative tie*. Thus, the risk of passing reforms that could face union resistance was not taken. This was, in sum, a time of "*spray and pray*": spraying the system with resources through a rise in educational investment and praying changes in teaching practices would happen since no mechanisms were devised that could effectively promote these changes.

Teaching policies were a priority during this period (Mezzadra & Veleda, 2014). The creation of the National Institute of Teacher Training could be seen as a step towards consolidating a national policy in a field with significant disparity among provinces, which are in charge of more than 1,300 tertiary teacher training institutions that make up a system whose governance is still weak. Teachers' professional careers, ruled by regulations drafted during the 1950s and dependent on each provincial administration, have not been subject to reforms. Discussions about increasing teacher salaries appear center stage with a growth of almost 70% (in real terms) between 2003 and 2007, but after that came a period of stagnation and disparity among provinces.

At the curricular level, no significant reforms have been promoted during the period 2003–2015. The Priority Learning Nuclei (NAP) were defined, which synthesized the curricular frameworks already in place (Coria, 2013; Feeney & Feldman, 2016). Other programs had to do with purchasing educational material such as textbooks and materials in other formats (among them, digital resources, whose production was led by the Educ.ar portal). Lastly, there has also been the intention of expanding cultural horizons by distributing literary texts to school libraries. This was complemented by creating a public educational television station, Encuentro, which produces and buys high-quality audiovisual material.

The legal foundations set during this first stage did not translate into more profound changes nor a long-term vision as the Minister of Education Juan Carlos Tedesco proposed in 2008. Instead, a way marked by agreements without reforms was chosen. Instead, education policy became more ideologized, and party politics became strained, with a growing gap between the government and the opposition. This led to the replacement of Tedesco, a scholar, by Alberto Sileoni, someone closer to the ruling party's core. During Sileoni's office (2008–2015), *Conectar Igualdad*, the nationwide initiative concerning the deployment of one computer per student, was launched (Tedesco & Steinberg, 2015; Zukerfeld & Benítez Larghi, 2015). The program managed to expand social rights at a time when technological equipment was vital. However, it was still part of the "*spray and pray*" model, in which there was no clear idea of how learning improvements would be steered.

The appearance of a new policy of in-service teacher training in schools, the creation of direct lines of work with the provinces and the financing of projects to renovate secondary schools were other initiatives during this period. These efforts helped keep a National Ministry of Education with leadership, resources and political alignment.

At the end of 2015, the elections marked a profound change in the political course. Mauricio Macri took office with a message of education reform, with the idea of carrying out an "education revolution" being held publicly by the Minister of Education, Esteban Bullrich. However, the Ministry did not have the resources, political wealth or knowledge of the previous education system. This view offered in the speeches was thus adventurous and unrealistic. It proposed modifying the teaching training programs, but there was no apparent ground to discuss and implement such intentions.

In particular, the new government installed a firmer policy for evaluating educational quality. Although there were evaluations in place, the Macri

Administration included new annual and census evaluations for the primary level. A process of reform for the secondary education level was also initiated. National programs saw their resources languish since more funds were transferred to the provinces, which choose their priorities more freely.

These policies took place in the context of public spending reduction to lower the fiscal deficit. The education budget suffered cuts during this period (Claus & Sánchez, 2019). The ambitious vision of the educational revolution rapidly shipwrecked in a "reform without water": ambitious discourses for change were not backed by sufficient investment and political capital. During the last two years of the Macri Administration, affected by a deep economic decline, the spirit of reform was rapidly weakened.

Brazil: Ambidextrous Policies for an Unbounding System

In Chapter 3, Recch, Soares Lopes and Hoogerbrugge assess the complexity of the Brazilian educational system. The author highlights the coexistence of thousands of subnational (municipal and state) educational systems enjoying a high level of autonomy. Reech argues that the Brazilian education system's history was marked by exclusion and inequality, with an immense and unmanageable federal system that began to settle late for the region's parameters.

In the last years of the 20th century, progress was made to reinforce the state's role in consolidating a federal education system (Abrucio, 2010). In these years, the compulsory school age was increased, the education budget was increased and the *Lei de Diretrizes e Bases da Educação Nacional* (LDB) was enacted in 1996. This process was also characterized by decentralization in the states and municipalities, which will be analyzed later. Furthermore, Reech describes that a central education policy was the creation of the Fund for the Maintenance and Development of Basic Education and the Assessment of Education Professionals (FUNDEF) in 1996; subsequently, in 2006, the fund was renamed FUNDEB.

This financing mechanism created a redistribution circuit to favor the most impoverished territories. However, it also functioned as a regulatory mechanism since it encouraged schools to incorporate students into local education systems to receive more funds. The implementation of accountability systems and sophisticated financing mechanisms and educational guidelines were the central frameworks of education policy in Brazil. These policies implied more significant support from the federal government to states and municipalities (Segatto, 2015).

During the government of Fernando Henrique Cardoso (1995–2003), in addition to implementing the FUNDEF and approving the LDB, the National Quality Assessment System was created – concentrated in the National Institute of Educational Studies and Research (INEP) – the *Sistema de Avaliação da Educação Básica* (SAEB) and, in 1998, the *Exame Nacional do Ensino Médio* (ENEM) (Segatto, 2015). In this period, the central elements of the increase and decentralization of education financing led to a strengthening of monitoring and accountability.

The period of government of Lula da Silva (2003–2010) was intense in defining new lines of education policy. On the one hand, the education budget was increased through FUNDEB, incorporating more students into the system. Besides, the country's cultural diversity was recognized as never before in policies and the curriculum. Scholarships were created for access to university, and the Bolsa Familia Program favored the most marginalized families so that they could send their children to school. Many of these children attending school were the first generation to complete their basic education.

On the other hand, national mechanisms for curricular control were increased with the delineation of curricular guidelines, the increase in the number of years of schooling, and the expansion of textbooks' mass purchasing to send to schools. The historic *Programa Nacional do Livro Didático*, initially reformed in 1996, was extended to the final years of secondary education. This expansion reinforced its function as a device for the systemic regulation of education, with broad powers for municipalities and schools to choose the texts (Bagolin et al., 2013).

These systemic regulatory policies were reinforced with the expansion of the use of standardized quality tests. The IDEB (Basic Education Development Index) measures from 1–10 the result of each school (and each municipality and state) in a combination of indicators of the students' trajectory and the learning achievements measured by the SAEB fifth and ninth year of basic education. The IDEB was a critical accountability mechanism. The results of the evaluations were made public, and schools and their communities were able to know their learning results. The publication of these results made it possible to set goals.

Moreover, incentive systems were created, which meant that financing was pegged to test results. This merit pay system caused education to significantly pressure tests and generated a change in education's social representation. These two significant branches of policies, social protection and pressure for results placed Brazil as an international case study in what can be defined as an "ambidextrous" government, which combined leftist and rightist policies. Some studies highlighted the first dimension, focused on social participation and the redistribution of education in favor of the poorest (Gentili, 2013), and others focused on the second dimension, which had to do with incentives and competition to improve results (Bruns et al., 2012).

During Dilma Rousseff's (2011–2016) presidency, these policies were consolidated with the deepening of inclusion and expansion of cultural diversity rights. In parallel, compulsory schooling was extended from 4 to 17 years old. Despite these advances, concerns about the fiscal deficit also began to force social spending to be limited. A key policy at this stage was the *Pacto Nacional pela Alfabetização na Idade Certa* (PNAIC), which established teaching guidelines in the first years of primary level. The *Ensino Médio Inovador* (PRO EMI) program was launched to increase the secondary level's workload and curricular flexibility. The *Programa Nacional de Acesso ao Ensino Técnico e Emprego* (PRONATEC) expanded the offer of professional and technological education. However, the programs sought to provoke better results in the states and municipalities, but technical and political difficulties led to poor results (Almeida et al., 2016; Schwartzman, 2016; Segatto & Abrucio, 2016).

At the end of its first term, Dilma Rousseff's government approved the National Education Plan, which established the goal of reaching 10% of GDP in education investment by 2024. Many of these goals continued the previous plan, approved in 2001. This period was marked by constant changes in the Ministers of Education, which limited the enactment of policies.

After the president's impeachment, a controversial transition stage was inaugurated with Michel Temer (2016–2018). This government implemented a change in the Constitution to set public spending at inflation and, in this way, limit the possibilities of reaching the goal of 10% of GDP, something that some analysts considered imprudent in fiscal terms. Another controversial measure was the implementation of the *Reformado Ensino Médio* through a provisional measure. The discussion on the reformulation of the parameters stipulated for secondary education in Brazil had been part of the education policy agenda since 2007 (Júnior et al., 2018). It was challenging to pass the bill in the National Congress. However, implementing the reform without the National Congress's prior approval generated a great debate in the Brazilian education community. Among the main changes were an increase in teachers' workload and the relaxation of requirements to enter the teaching profession.

During Temer's presidency, the Common Curricular National Base was approved, a central goal for many years. It defines competencies, skills and learning for each stage of basic education that serves as the basis for reviewing teaching materials and standardized tests. In 2019, the arrival of Jair Bolsonaro to the presidency consolidated a conservative vision of education. The areas of defense of cultural diversity were eliminated among other programs, and there has been a marked instability that caused constant changes in the ministers of education.

Chile: The Eternal Reform in Search of the Classroom's Black Box

In Chapter 4, Bellei and Muñoz describe the central tenets of the formulation of Chile's educational policies. The authors argue that the case of Chile is exceptional in many ways. The country has experienced four decades of education reforms that have transformed the heart of the education system. Augusto Pinochet carried out what has been referred to as the "great experiment" (Bellei, 2015; Jofré, 1988; Prieto, 1983); this experiment implied the installation of a market-based educational system in Chile.

During this period, two parallel reforms changed everything. On the one hand, the financing system was modified, creating a mechanism of *subsidy on demand* (voucher type, although it was given to the owners of the schools directly and not to the families) that consisted of a monthly payment per capita from the state to education providers (called *supporters*) per the adequate attendance of students to their establishments. On the other hand, public education was decentralized, and it remained in the hands of the municipalities. Teachers lost their labor protection system and began to depend on each municipality, whose professional competencies for management were limited and dissimilar (Espínola, 1992).

After the dictatorship ended, the democratic governments that began in 1990 carried out a growing and ambitious education policy agenda. In some respects, this new agenda meant the continuity of the reforms and the institutional framework created in the 1980s; but it also implied changes and innovation. The market model was maintained, but the focus was on creating compensatory and systemic improvement actions promoted by the central state (Bellei & Vanni, 2015). In practice, this caused a double dynamic: market incentives and competition at the local level and centralized mechanisms of government, regulation and curricular intervention at the systemic level.

The municipalities were an uncertain link: increasingly indebted because students switched to private schools, underfunding public education, and lacking technical skills to regulate what happened in the classrooms. The democratic period had intense political conditioning that left the dictatorship installed (with Augusto Pinochet as a senator for life) but with a broad continuity of governments of the Concertación, a center-left political alliance.

In this context of 20 years in power (1990–2010), mechanisms that perfected and deepened the market logic were installed. The Education Quality Measurement System (SIMCE) was created as a standardized evaluation that publishes the school's results to favor families' informed decisions. *Shared financing* was promoted. This allowed the collection of fees from subsidized private schools. Later, the Preferential School Subsidy was installed, which raised the state subsidy for students with a lower socioeconomic level.

On a second axis, democratic governments were even more active and implemented an impressive battery of education policies grouped into four types (Cox, 2003; García-Huidobro, 1999). First, there was the implementation of "education improvement programs" located in the establishments (P-900, MECE-Básica, MECE-Rural, MECE-Media, Enlaces). These interventions aimed to improve the pedagogical processes and develop teachers' professional skills by introducing didactic innovations, various forms of collective teaching work and additional training activities for students. Second, improving the conditions for teaching-learning processes, making investments to improve infrastructure, providing didactic materials, school texts, computer labs and libraries, and expanding available school time by implementing the "full school day," privileging the most disadvantaged sectors. The third line of policies was a crucial curricular reform of kindergarten, basic and secondary education that involved updating study plans and programs and a massive teacher training process. The fourth axis consisted of transforming the professional teaching career: a process was started in which performance was evaluated, and incentives linked to schools' performance in SIMCE tests were created.

In the mid-2000s, the dynamics of the reforms were an unstoppable train. An established notion of "lack of results" drove further change, despite improved PISA scores and other assessments. An attempt was made to bring "reform to the classroom" by creating new curricular devices that directly regulated teaching practices, with textbooks purchased by the state and didactic sequences for teachers. The Critical Schools Program favored creating external consultancies to advise schools, establishing a new private education market in a profuse effort to modify learning outcomes at the micro-level. However, contradictions emerged with the student protests of the Penguin Revolution. Socio-educational segregation had grown in parallel with the privatization of the system, which generated an evident problem of inequality in educational opportunities. The creation of an Advisory Council in 2006 was the attempt to reach a broader consensus for the new stage of reforms.

In 2007 the "new architecture of Chilean public education" was set out, which led to the General Education Law of 2009 and the Quality Assurance System (Bellei & Vanni, 2015; Larroulet & Montt, 2010). In practice, the pressure model to improve results was deepened. Each school had to define the state-controlled strategies through standards and evaluations (Muñoz & Vanni, 2008; Raczynski et al., 2013). The arrival of the first substantial change of government in 2010, with a right-wing government, failed to establish its policies but rather accentuated competition mechanisms and pressure for higher results. The training of school governing bodies was chosen as the local improvement axis, and tests and rankings were intensified to increase competition among schools (Alarcón & Donoso, 2017).

In 2014, the presidency of Michelle Bachelet coincided with a broad social demand for changes. For the first time, the foundations of a commercialized education system were discussed (Navarro & Gysling, 2017). In the first place, the new government proposed to guarantee that all the resources that supporters received were destined to improve the quality of education, which meant ending profit in the school system. Second, the program was established as a priority to move towards a free system (without co-payment) and without selection in access. Third, the program proposed creating a new institutional framework – no longer municipal – for public education. Fourth, it prioritized formulating a "teaching career" that would improve teachers' conditions and capacities. Therefore, it was an ambitious bet: four transformations of high technical and political complexity for only four administration years. The new teaching career consolidated several stages of reforms (Mizala & Schneider, 2014) that increased trained teachers' demands. It created a new induction process to enter the system. It established a new professional development mechanism based on performance evaluations. It significantly improved salaries (an average 30% increase), and it increased non-school time.

As a whole, educational priorities have become a central issue on the public agenda. This has generated a double record. On the one hand, it was possible to consolidate a constant pressure for improvement over time translated into numerous policies. On the other hand, the ongoing reforms caused instability, and the education system had to adapt to abrupt changes and learn to coexist with intense external pressure.

Colombia: Curricular Freedom and Control through Evaluation

In Chapter 5, Baxter and León Cadavid describe the Colombian educational policies between 2000 and 2020. Colombia is a country of contrasts and contradictions. On the one hand, its modern history presents a long period of violence, substantial economic and social inequalities, and imaginaries, perspectives and dualities based on the figures of the drug trafficker, the guerrilla and the paramilitary (Melo, 2017). On the other hand, Colombian history has consolidated a democratic state, a relatively stable economy, a diverse culture and a population with a tremendous civil resistance capacity despite all its suffering (Cepeda, 2007).

In the period Baxter and León Cadavid studied, education has been a central chapter in the country's political life. The presidency of Álvaro Uribe, which began in 2002, had as the Minister of Education Cecilia María Vélez, a figure of decisive leadership and continuity, which led to the ordering of the education system. The National Development Plan proposed an "education revolution" to increase the education budget to expand access in excluded sectors. A government model based on broad curricular freedoms and a strong emphasis on results was consolidated. The SABER tests were implemented with school results and improvement plans with a broad responsibility assigned to the management teams.

The curricular history of Colombia was marked by the constitutional stamp, which guarantees the freedom of education and limits the state's role in matters of curricular design. This tradition brought together two opposing political views during the Uribe government. On the one hand, the battle between the unions and a good part of the academic education sector defended academic freedom and the construction of pedagogical movements from the bottom up (Peñuela & Rodríguez, 2006). On the other hand, the government's neoliberal vision promoted management by results, with freedom of individual paths to achieve the evaluations' goals. The curricular model, although not prescriptive, was oriented to the formation of competencies with standards. A National Work Training System was also established, articulating the education system's expansion in the powerful state agency, SENA.

The arrival of the government of Juan Manuel Santos meant continuing in the same direction with some changes. A line of projects focused on human rights and citizenship was launched in a country where education for peace was a crucial issue. Evaluations that assessed civic education, which was barely covered in the standardized regional evaluations, were developed in this process. Moreover, the Everyone to Learn program was promoted. This program focused on low-performing schools. Outstanding teachers from the education system were appointed to assist these schools in an intensive training plan that included textbook development. This was an exception since, in Colombia, textbooks only circulated in the private market. The low curricular regulation and the broad powers of freedom in the classrooms are part of this paradigm of non-intervention that predominates in this country. However, the SABER tests ended up being the great regulators of the curriculum.

With a vision too focused on results, President Santos continued the saga of educational epics and promised that Colombia would be "the most educated country," referring to his commitment to improving the PISA tests. Extended day policies were launched, as were outgoing plans in early childhood (such as De Cero a Siempre), scholarships in higher education (such as the Ser Pilo Paga Program) and an online learning platform, Colombia Aprende. ICFES, the institution in charge of quality evaluations, became more relevant; its wealth of technical knowledge, accumulated over time, allowed the consolidation of new, more comprehensive and innovative measurements for the region, such as the Synthetic Index of Educational Quality (ISCE).

The central chapter of this stage was creating a new teaching career with teachers' evaluation and promoting incentives based on the quality of learning. However, the merit-pay system left behind a fundamental piece: the external verification of each school's improvements. Given that the schools themselves administer the SABER 3, 5 and 9 tests, it is striking that the incentives were focused on these tests and not on the SABER 11 test, which is the only test administered by external agents. It is not by chance that these tests' results are vastly different, with an improving trend in tests that pay for results and stagnation in externally measured tests which have no incentives.

In 2018, after Uribe's eight years of government and Santos's eight, Iván Duque became President. Duque appointed María Victoria Angulo as Minister of Education, a person with extensive experience in the sector. During her first years, the agenda turned towards the definition of clear educational goals, which were proposed to favor more efficient management and focus on results.

Mexico: Centralization Features and Political Battles of Education

In Chapter 6, Olmeda and Sifuentes analyze the turbulent and complex progress of educational policies in Mexico. To understand the reality of education in Mexico, it is imperative to refer to the National Agreement for the Modernization of Basic Education of 1992 that set the basis for the system's decentralization and resulted in the transfer of about 100,000 federal schools to the states (Fierro et al., 2009). This stage showed two main features: the new teaching career (Latapí, 2004) and the propagation of standardized learning evaluations (Martínez, 2013).

The idea of standardization was complemented by the strong centralized curriculum regulation employing textbooks with a long tradition in Mexico. Since creating the National Commission of Free Textbooks (CONALITEG) in 1959, Mexico has used the same textbooks for all schools. The federal state produces the books used by students of the primary level public system (and it buys from the private market the secondary level ones) – about 180 million books are manufactured a year in this state powerhouse of pedagogical regulation. Out of these features, it can be seen that the Mexican education government model centralizes power and decentralizes administration (Di Gropello, 1999; Fierro et al., 2009; Latapí & Ulloa, 2000; Ornelas, 1998;

Zorrilla & Barba, 2008). All this adds to the vital role that the National Union of Education Workers (SNTE) has historically played as an agent of the education system's co-government.

The education policy of the first decades of the century ended up being ambitious despite all these constraints. During the first decade of the 21st century, the Integral Reform for Secondary Education (RIES) was passed, and a curricular change that adopted the centrality of competencies was approved. Centralization was also channeled through large compensating programs (such as Quality Schools), frustrated attempts to introduce technology in the classroom (the Encyclopedia program) and standardized evaluations.

In 2002 the National Institution of Education Assessment (INEE) was created. It combined two systems: EXCALE is the test that measures the systems with sample evaluations and ENLACE is the census evaluation that allows keeping track of each school's performance. The country has become the most significant regional laboratory of standard evaluations. About 14 million evaluations per year were carried out, and even the teachers received a bonus according to the advances of students' results (Ornelas, 2010). This model of assessment created turmoil in the tests. The tests' effects were so profound that desperate outlets were implemented to improve results (such as preventing low-performing students from taking the test). In 2014, Enrique Peña Nieto's administration stopped this process and opened a new stage of measurements with the PLANET assessment. Before finishing its administration, Felipe Calderón fostered the inclusion of medium and higher education in basic education. In February 2012, Congress voted for a reform to the Constitution that established such education stage as compulsory, increasing to 15 years of compulsory education in Mexico. Simultaneously, during 2007 and 2012, a whole reform process focused on teacher training was developed.

The change of administration in 2012 meant the arrival of a new stage in Mexican education policy. The INEE gained grounds as an entity of constitutional status, and the Professional Teaching Service Act was passed. These two initiatives marked a rupture of historical alliances with the teachers' union (Ornelas, 2018) when its leader was arrested due to corruption. The federal state centralized education's government even more. A new school census was organized to detect irregularities in the payment of teachers' salaries. An ambitious and controversial reform to the teaching career that included evaluating teachers in charge of INEE was launched (Martínez Rizo, 2013). This reform attracted the attention of the political education agenda. It was an intervention with both work control and a pedagogical feature purpose (Gil-Anton, 2018). Between 2015 and 2018, 1.2 million teachers were assessed in a process that raised tension and resistance (Granados, 2018).

In the second part of Peña Nieto's six-year period, the focus was on developing curricula activities. After a consultation process with the most relevant stakeholders of the education system, in March 2017, the new Education Model (NME), which continued with old trends, looked innovative. This alleged new model was used to articulate compulsory education to end memory-based education, reduce the number of contents, resume constructivism, leave aside the competencies approach, foster collaborative work and use technologies. It also added challenging elements, such as flexibility, curricular autonomy and socio-emotional skills. English was also established as a compulsory course (Díaz-Barriga, 2018).

Simultaneously, school reorganization was promoted to adapt to the new model with greater autonomy (Mejía, 2017). This was combined with developing programs for school infrastructure improvement, which boosted direct resources transfer for schools to cover maintenance and minor equipment needs. Lastly, during this period, the Full-Time School Program was extended; it was challenging to reach due to the high costs of extending school hours.

This series of reforms were abruptly interrupted when Andres Manuel Lopez Obrador took office in 2018. The political change was so profound that it required a new constitutional reform to dissolve the INEE and replace it with the Federal Center for Teaching Reevaluation. The Professional Teaching Service was replaced by the System for Teacher Training, which aimed to change the most controversial teaching assessment features. Since the new administration's arrival, the Secretary of Public Education (SEP) stopped applying the assessments that had already been scheduled. Instead, an agenda centered on the Federal Strategy of Inclusive Education was posed, which focuses on the new policy of scholarships and the approach of a more abstract change.

Peru: Uncertainty in Times of Political Changes

In Chapter 7, Balarin presents Peru's case, affirming that the country has seen a slow maturation process of educational policies from 2000–2020. Balarin argues that the Peruvian case is marked by the period's political swings, with a substantial level of instability in the first decade of the century, an intermediate stage of continuity, and strong leadership of the education policies agenda between 2011 and 2016. In 2001 the Decentralization Bases Bill was passed with a constitutional reform that redesigned the government's educational territory with 25 autonomous regional governments. The General Law of Education of 2003 fostered this decentralization process. Local governments' accreditation was complicated between regions and municipalities cracked by overlapping functions and limitations in technical capacities (IDEHPUCP, 2017). This led to a subsequent recentralization starting in 2011.

The period from 2000 to 2010 was a time of economic growth which made it possible to reduce poverty and increase the education budget (without increasing its share in total spending, which remains very low in this period). However, there was discontinuity and an expansion of corruption prevailing at the multiple government levels (Panfichi & Alvarado, 2011). This political instability was only partially compensated by the National Council of Education's articulation as a body of independent experts that outlined a long-term vision. Standardized learning assessments also became more widespread. In these years, the ambitious Huascarán Project was launched to provide technology and connectivity to schools, although it was not fully realized (Balarin, 2013). This period's particularly prominent policy was initiated by the Law for Intercultural Bilingual Education, backed up by international funds to revitalize an education sector with meager state support (Ames, 2015).

In this context, the main policy focus was defining a new teaching career (Cuenca, 2011), complemented by a series of specific interventions and the META program, which offered incentives for teachers with more attendance in the classroom. This policy became more relevant in the government of Alan García with the enactment of the Law of Public Teaching Career, which established teacher evaluation as the primary promotion mechanism. However, most teachers chose not to enter the new system that assessed their competencies through a very instrumental and standardized "minimal curriculum" (Guerrero, 2009).

In 2008 there was a milestone in the education policy agenda: creating the Strategic Learning Achievements Program (PELA), which promoted budget allocation based on results. Learning assessments became more relevant and were made compulsory for *all* of second grade of primary school (rather than tests being taken just by a sample of students).

During the Ollanta Humala government, which began in 2011, the Peruvian education policy acquired another status, with more significant leadership, coherence and articulation. The Minister of Education, Patricia Salas, added a new and more professional-oriented logic to the government of education. This logic was deepened with the more technocratic vision of the next minister, Jaime Saavedra. In 2012, the Law on Teaching Reform was passed, which established a single regime for all teachers, with meritocratic evaluations that define the positions and a progressive salary structure. A central aspect of this stage was creating a *curricular system* that guaranteed coherence and articulation between teaching regulation devices (Cueto & Tapia, 2017). The National Curricular Framework was reviewed, learning standards were elaborated, the purchase of textbooks by the state was established and the Learning Routes were incorporated as instruments that guided the classrooms' curricular arrival. This was complemented with the Good Teaching Performance Framework and the pedagogical support interventions for teaching practices (Balarin & Escudero, 2018).

During this period, Minister Saavedra's management focused on performance assessments, management information systems, and the introduction of incentive mechanisms to push for better results. Progress was also made in the design of new training evaluations of teacher performance. In 2015, within the Teacher Reform Law framework, the first evaluation of teacher appointment and hiring was conducted. Teacher salaries were differentiated according to the type of school. The purpose of this policy was to incentivize teachers to work in schools located in the rural, border or coca-growing areas and bilingual, single teacher or multigrade schools. As of 2014, the School Performance Incentive Bonus was implemented. This Bonus provides a monetary award to all teachers and elementary school principals whose students have achieved good educational results (Cuenca & Vargas Castro, 2018). The policies oriented to the improvement of learning focused on strengthening pedagogical support programs. Full school day programs were promoted, and a system of high-performance schools was added (COAR). Saavedra continued with Salas's review process in curricular matters, which was finalized with the National Curricular Design's approval in 2015.

A New Agenda: Trends of Education Policy in Latin America 2000–2020

What were the transformations in education governance in Latin America during the first two decades of the new century? What changed in the education policy agendas? What were the convergences and divergences between the countries and in the changes of governments and contexts? How are these policies inscribed in the historical experience of the education systems of each country?

This section proposes a comparative view of the education system's new governance practices in the six countries that we studied. To analyze trends, we propose a theoretical framework centered on the governance mechanisms of education systems. In this perspective, four large domains of education policy intervention allow capturing different forcing-games between the actors and putting into practice different policy instruments. The analysis proposes to follow the education policy networks in a genealogical perspective of the government of education, mapping the reciprocal relations between the countries' policies and the regional perspective (Gale, 2001; Pierson, 1993; Raab, 1994).

First Domain: The Material Supply of the System – A Time of Expansion and Redistribution

This first domain is defined as the first economic cycle. Supply policies depend on three central factors: public financing, the capacity to manage material resources, and the social orientation of the distribution of resources. In the period that we analyzed, these policies were profuse in the education systems of Latin America. The cycle of economic growth was combined, in most countries, with an increase of the education budget in its share of total public spending.

All the countries that we studied expanded educational investment in relative terms, with different periods and intensities. For example, Brazil achieved a broad and sustained increase in the education budget: from 4.7% to 6.2% of GDP between 2000 and 2015.

In Argentina, four periods are recognized: the first years, marked by the enormous drop in GDP; the intense recovery of educational investment during the 2003–2009 period, in which educational spending went from 3.5% to 5.5%; a period of less intense growth following this; and, finally, a decline in the last two years of the period.

Chile decreased resource allocation from 3.7% of GDP for education in 2000 to 3.0% in 2006. After this, there was a sustained increase to 5.4% by 2017. Its public investment in education was remarkably high concerning public spending, but so was its private funding since families invested many resources in financing education. The sum of both factors makes the total investment per student in Chile the highest in the region. Furthermore, the high dependence on private spending is a factor that generates significant inequities due to the pre-existing social inequality in families.

Colombia had a minor increase, going from investing 3.5% of GDP in education in 2000 to 4.5% in 2017. What is particular about this case is that investment growth cycles are limited to some specific years. Mexico also had a similar upward trajectory, going from 4.0% to 4.9% of GDP allocated to education between 2000 and 2017, with intermediate fluctuations and short growth cycles.

Finally, Peru is the case with the most prolonged delay in educational financing: it went from 3.2% in 2000 to 3.9% in 2017. What is particularly noteworthy is that after a period of unrivaled stability in the share of spending education in GDP – even with some years of decline – from 2011 onwards, the increase has been sustained and at a higher rate compared to the other countries: in six years it went from 2.7% to 3.9%.

Parallel to the increase in the education budget, rights were expanded in multiple dimensions of education. For instance, the number of compulsory education years increased from 10 to 13 years between 2000 and 2015 on average. Pre-primary and secondary education became compulsory in all the countries studied.

The enactment of renewed education laws gradually built new symbolic networks that recognized the region's cultural diversity. In a massive operation of reversing the histories of cultural concealment, denial or imposition in

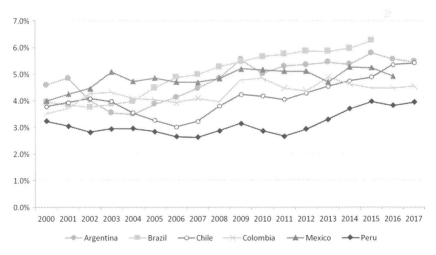

Figure 1.3 Evolution of expenditure in education compared to GDP. Selected countries, 2000–2017
Source: CIAESA, Universidad de San Andrés and Quántitas, based on UIS-UNESCO data

national educational paradigms, countries increasingly allowed marginalized communities to emerge. Brazil included Afro and Aboriginal history as mandatory content on its curriculum in 2008. Argentina promoted the recognition of the recent history of human rights violations. Similarly, Colombia expanded the teaching of citizenship education in response to the history of violence. Further, some countries were not included in this study, such as Bolivia and Ecuador, where intercultural bilingual education was more relevant in the policy agendas (Fajardo Salinas, 2011).

A central chapter in this policy field was expanding compensatory and socio-educational policies that began in the 1990s. The recognition of structural inequalities in the region was combined with more robust educational budgets. This translated into a social shift in education policies.

The bright appearance of conditioned transfers was essential to build a social bridge towards education by allocating resources to the most vulnerable sectors with the obligation to attend school (ECLAC, 2011). By 2011, transfers reached 120 million people in the region (20% of the total population), accounting for 0.4% of GDP (Cecchini, 2014).

At the same time, several education policies tried to alleviate social inequalities. There has been an increase in school meals, supplies, scholarships, infrastructure to create new learning spaces, the promotion of teaching positions for school support, tutoring and particular subjects (English, Computer Science, Physical and Artistic Education).

Another focus of the policies was the expansion of the human rights of marginalized populations through the recognition of social inequalities. There has been an effort to create different paths for the most disadvantaged students (UNICEF & UNGS, 2012). All countries studied created different alternatives that helped vulnerable sectors continue their educational trajectories. Dissimilar policies followed this path, from a consolidation of the historic Telesecundaria schools (distance schools) or the innovative tutoring networks in Mexico (Rincón-Gallardo, 2013) to the re-entry schools in Argentina (Terigi et al., 2013). Multiple programs sought to recognize that schools needed to change their homogeneous format to guarantee rights. The academic regimes' flexibility was central in this process, seeking alternatives to reduce drop-out rates.

The expansion of the education budget, combined with these policies, allowed more full-time or extended-day schools. All the countries analyzed advanced in this direction, although Chile was the only one that achieved the almost universalization of a scheme of eight hours a day of school hours.

A specific chapter in the expansion of education-related rights was the distribution of computers to students, which was massive in the cases of Argentina, Uruguay and Peru (Sunkel & Trucco, 2011). This made it possible to shorten the digital gap and create conditions to expand learning at home and in schools.

Finally, among many other chapters of the policies for recognizing rights, the actions developed for early childhood stand out. The growing international evidence of the positive impact that social and educational investment has at an early age was part of a new consensus to protect the most vulnerable in their age and social condition (Araujo et al., 2013; Berlinski & Schady, 2015; Heckman, 2008).

Second Domain: Teachers Policies – The Controversial Era of Reforming Teaching Careers

The second domain of education policy navigates between the technical and the political: it deals with the policies that regulate professional teaching careers. It is a broad chapter covering recruitment parameters, professional promotion rules, differences in wages, and working conditions, which are generally negotiated with the teacher unions. Teacher education and training are also part of this policy field, although they overlap with the following field, referring to pedagogical and curricular policies.

In the countries that we analyzed, this domain has been a focal point of crucial and crispy reforms. Teaching careers in many countries became the target of negotiations, tensions and resistance.

Initial teacher training was not the focus of the reforms in most countries. Peru, Chile and Colombia shifted all or a good part of their training at universities, closing tertiary institutions and creating mechanisms to raise qualifications required to study teaching (Cox et al., 2017). However, within the universities or tertiary (postsecondary) institutions, the six countries had low control of teacher education and tried to regulate it through external accreditation of its quality. Chile went further and developed a sophisticated system for attracting teaching candidates. The Vocation of Professor Program aimed to recruit candidates who scored high on university admission exams with a full-time scholarship (Paredes et al., 2012).

In periods of economic growth, teacher salaries improved in all the countries studied, but with significant variations and changing cycles. Chile stood out again on this point, with an overall increase of more than 200% in the period 1990–2009 (compared to an average increase of 70% in the rest of the labor market), achieving a salary base higher than the rest of the countries included in this study (Mizala & Ross Schneider, 2014). Salary improvements varied more in those countries where subnational governments have high autonomy to define salaries, as in Argentina and Brazil. In some cases, profound differences can be found in Argentina, where some provinces could pay a salary three times higher than others (Rivas & Dborkin, 2018).

In any case, the improvement in salary conditions was not enough to give prestige to most countries' teaching profession. Teaching conditions, overwhelmed by the social issues that teachers must address (especially in public schools), are part of a group of variables that explain the problem of teacher recruitment in the region (García & Vaillant, 2009). The most substantive reforms in this policy domain were those that changed the regulations of the teaching career by installing professional evaluation systems. Teacher unions showed their resistance on typical political battles regarding career regulations. Mexico, Chile, Peru and Colombia installed teacher evaluation devices and faced union resistance at vastly different times. From the pronounced confrontation with a part of the union sector in Mexico to the gradual political agreements in Chile, the array of disputes and agreements showed different paths between professionalization and teachers' persecution as nodal actors of the education system. Argentina and Brazil (except for some states with their reforms, such as Rio de Janeiro or São Paulo) maintained their previous systems as more credential models of vertical ascent in the teaching career (Cuenca, 2015).

A new narrative of educational change emerged in these years: *the virtuous circle of teaching*. This implied a significant state investment in salary improvement, while the quality levels of the training, recruitment and maintenance systems in teaching positions were also raised (Bruns & Luque, 2014; UNESCO, 2013). The reform paths were more sinuous than virtuous, given the negotiations' fragility and the political capacity to implement professionalization tools.

Third Domain: Pedagogical and Curricular Policies – Towards More Regulatory Curriculum Devices

The third domain relates to pedagogical and curricular policies, which permeate through channels that communicate the government of education with teaching practices. Channels are massive structures that communicate and distribute educational knowledge through schools and the central level of government. These channels (curricular reforms, teacher training, textbooks or national assessments, for example) are critical devices that allow the recontextualization and translation of legitimate knowledge into teachable practices (Bernstein, 1996).

In the period included in this study, this policy field was the center of multiple interventions that sought greater regulation of classroom practices. In the curricular channel, there was a transition from the vast curricular reforms of the 1990s that had an encyclopedic taste towards more pragmatic models of interventions based on standards, priority learning nuclei, scripted guides, learning routes and didactic sequences.

A second channel that gained vitality was the distribution of educational materials, mainly textbooks. Increased funding for education was combined with a stronger drive for learning outcomes. Textbooks had historically been a classic route to the curriculum to simplify its translation in practice. The countries with the longest tradition in policies for the provision of textbooks notably increased the doses of state distribution, either of books produced by the state as in Mexico, or purchased from the private sector such as Chile, Brazil, Peru and, to a lesser extent, Argentina. A complementary channel of pedagogical and curricular policies, still underdeveloped in the region, is the digital multiplication of educational resources through state platforms.

In the period analyzed, a focal channel that guided classroom practices was the dissemination of standardized assessments. In several countries that we studied, evaluations became a device for regulating education, moving from a softer technology (low-stakes) to having a more significant impact (high-stakes). This occurred in two formats: (1) with the publication of the results by schools (Brazil, Chile, Colombia, Peru and Mexico), which generated emulation and pressure through the externalization of achievements; (2) through economic incentives for schools and teachers who manage to improve in the tests (Mexico, Chile, Colombia, Peru and some states and municipalities of Brazil).

In some countries, this pressure began to generate a new regulatory mechanism, known as *teaching to the test*, which replaced the normative curricular regulation devices. Education became more visible, measurable, controllable and pressured from the outside (McGehee & Griffith, 2001; Verger et al., 2018). The exponential multiplication of standardized tests turned the region into a laboratory of educational externalization.

Fourth Domain: The Governance of the System – The Creation of the School Unit and Increasing Privatization

The last domain encompasses policy instruments focused on *systemic change* (McDonnell & Elmore, 1987) and refers to movements at government levels in education. A specific dimension that implied management changes in education systems was the increasing privatization of supply. Different authors have analyzed how increasing household resources allowed for paying for education (Elacqua et al., 2018) and how education policies contributed to this privatization process (Verger et al., 2018).

Peru went from having 15% of students in private schools at all levels in 2000 to 29% in 2016. It was a remarkable transformation: the transition occurred mainly in the initial and primary levels, where the proportion of students in private schools doubled in just a decade.

Chile also had a substantial influx of students, but in their case, the trend showed continuity since the 1980s, when the subsidy-on-demand system was established. Brazil had remarkable private education growth at the primary level, given that the proportion of students attending private schools doubled from 8% to 17% between 2000 and 2017. There was also a marked increase in secondary education. In Argentina, private education was concentrated in the initial and primary levels, while secondary education remained more stable.

The case of Mexico shows significant disparities in educational levels. However, as a whole, it continued to have the lowest proportion of students in private schools in the countries that we analyzed. The initial level transition was intense; it was also noted in primary that there was no increase in basic secondary. On the other hand, the proportion of students in state schools in the upper-middle increased. This shows the most significant disparity in the internal behavior of the levels in that country.

Finally, Colombia was the most notable exception, since not only was there no movement to private schools but quite the opposite: there was an increase in the proportion of enrollment in public schools in the initial level and the basic and superior secondary. This may have expressed the increase in coverage that the state managed to guarantee at these levels, something that also occurred in other countries, but which, at least in Colombia, does not seem to have had the counterweight of students who migrate to private education.

In parallel, education policies tended to strengthen the *school unit*, a new form of school autonomy. The more classical models of thinking about school autonomy as "devolution" assumed that the intense focus was to transfer responsibility for teachers' hiring and salary to school management (either in the hands of managers, associations or councils of parents). These models occupied a large part of the debate in the 1990s and advanced in some Central American countries (Rivas, 2001). However, in the analyzed stage, a softer form of school autonomy prevailed.

In the countries that we analyzed, the policies tended to form a triptych of interventions that shaped the school unit as an increasingly visible and differentiated entity of accountability and results management. The first focus was the creation of the school result through the census standardized assessments. In some cases, each school began to know its result by individual reports and, in others, by public diffusion of schools' rankings.

The second focal point was to offer more autonomy to develop projects with a specific budget managed by the school, as happened in Chile, Mexico,

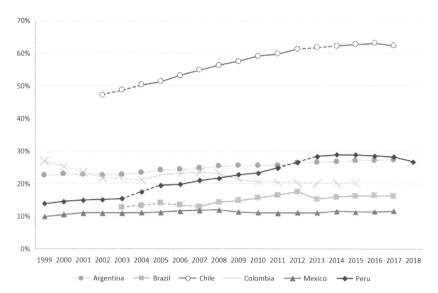

Figure 1.4 Evolution of the percentage of students in private schools per education level. Selected countries, 1999–2018
Source: CIAESA, Universidad de San Andrés and Quántitas, based on UIS-UNESCO

Argentina, Colombia and Brazil. This was accompanied by fostering the "institutional project" as a strategy that empowers and gives each school responsibility to pursue its path. In some countries, it was also sought that the secondary schools formed the school unit with teachers who concentrated their working hours in a single school and created a greater institutional identity.

The third crucial element involved giving greater relevance to the figure of school administrators. Historically relegated to a marginal place, managers became another stellar focus of reforms in the twenty-first century. Especially in Chile, and with more significant variation in the rest of the countries, it was sought to create competition, new functions, specific training and higher levels of authority to manage their schools autonomously (OREALC-UNESCO, 2014; Vaillant, 2011). Colombia, Chile, Mexico and Peru created or redefined managers' professional careers with new standards or frameworks of practices. In several countries, an attempt was made to professionalize managers' selection, especially in Chile, where there were 12 applicants for each position opened in 2014 (OREALC-UNESCO, 2014).

The Race to the Classroom: An Overview

In Latin America, education policy took two profound turns in the first two decades of the 21st century. The socio-educational shift made more significant efforts to reverse the profound social inequalities that characterize the region. A favorable economic context, the pressure to mobilize different social sectors, the more inclusive approach of many governments and the revision of certain educational paradigms of the past came together in a time of more comprehensive social protection for the most vulnerable.

The policies used actions, norms and resources to expand the right to education with a more significant state offer of entry-level places. In addition, there have been longer school hours in primary and an expansion of the secondary level. Conditional transfers were made to lower-income sectors. Even materials such as computers or textbooks were distributed to enable marginalized individuals to continue their studies. Policies were redefined, seeking not an ideal student profile but the multiple realities that young people in Latin America inhabit. Rural and intercultural bilingual education programs were created or deepened, although in directions that were not always sustained or sufficiently within budget. Among the countries studied, these efforts were especially prominent in Argentina and Brazil. Chile followed a similar path within its market regulation model, attempting to alleviate a mostly private educational segregated system.

However, these policies could not solve an overwhelming structural problem: the matrix of inequalities requires the consolidation of development models and inclusive and sustainable economic policies, which would be part of another analysis beyond the borders of education policy. However, the compensatory shift generated better conditions and changes in the beliefs of the education system actors, more focused on bridging social contexts with educational practices.

The second shift in education policies was introducing a new model of government based on the recentralization of the regulation of teaching practices. Following new international trends, several countries in the region promoted policy instruments that favored control, accountability and pressure on teachers and schools to achieve measurable and comparable learning outcomes (Verger et al., 2018).

The mix of political instruments of accountability, such as high-impact standard assessments, with regulatory instruments of curricular support, such as standards and textbooks, paved the way for a new *race to the classrooms*. As noted in previous research (Rivas & Sánchez, 2020), Chile and Mexico took the full turn; Brazil, Colombia and Peru also moved significantly towards this shift of regulatory governance. Argentina, instead, was the only exception among the countries with a less reformist perspective. Table 1.2 introduces the different national approaches based on four political instruments: regulation of the teaching career, curricular regulation, standard evaluations and accountability per school.

The shift of regulatory governance meant a change in the levels of intervention of education policy in several of the analyzed countries. Following the decentralization of education management in the 1990s, a recentralization process utilizing curricular control arose. A "command and control" approach prevailed in formulating curricular policies in the region (Valverde, 2014).

However, this shift comes along with a more complex context of the education system governance conditions. The process of a massive expansion of schooling was combined with the context of a crisis of the new democracies (Crozier et al., 1975; Sarason, 1990; Weiler, 1993). Consequently, a new paradigm of governance by results arose (Jessop, 1998; Wilkins & Olmedo, 2019). This new approach brought about a proliferation of government instruments and, along with them, several actors that mingled with the state.

The most technical role performed by many of these policies of curricular alignment could not be understood without the consolidation of specialized public agencies in some countries; whether for curricular design (such as The Unit of Curriculum and Assessment of Chile) in the development of textbooks (the CONALITEG from Mexico) or quality assessment (such as INEP in Brazil, SIMCE in Chile, the ICFES in Colombia or the INEE in Mexico). These agencies tried to create channels to centralize the control of overwhelmed education systems.

Another part of the recentralization process comes from specific leadership of ministers or presidents of those countries that wore the reformists' shirts and led significant changes in governing the education systems. These actors were political accelerators of reforms in the countries under study and several subnational cases.

The other side of these *key actors* was the political instability, a constant factor in the region. The turn to regulatory governance must not be understood as a linear journey to the classrooms. Many of its policies have raised resistance, tension, fear and confusion in teachers. Its technical quality has been

Table 1.2 Policy instruments related to the governance turn and the extent to which they were implemented in the studied countries

Policy Instrument	ARG	BRA	CHI	COL	MEX	PER
Teaching Career Regulation						
Career entrance regulations (merit-based limited access to teacher training vacancies, migration of teacher education to universities so as to reduce the number of teacher education outlets, etc.)	No	Partially (in some subnational states)	Yes (BSP)	Partially (BSP)	Yes (2005)	Yes (2006)
Differential pay based on training or merit-based criteria	No	No	Yes (2003)	Yes (2002)	Yes (2005)	Yes (2006)
Teacher performance evaluation	No	No	Yes (BSP)	Yes (2002)	Yes (BSP)	Yes (2006)
Curricular Regulation						
Increased regulatory strength of official curriculum (via standards, etc.)	Partially (2005–2011)	Partially (2009, 2012)	Yes (2013)	No	Yes (2006, 2009, 2011)	Yes (2009)
Creation and distribution of lesson guides and other prescribed material for teachers	No	Partially	Yes (2011)	No	Yes (BSP)	Yes (2008)
Massive textbook distribution policies	Partially	Yes (BSP, 2004)	Yes (BSP, 2011)	No	Yes (BSP, 2013)	Partially
Test-Based Regulation						
Standardized assessments with results published per school	No	Yes (2007)	Yes (BSP)	Yes (2001)	Yes (2006)	No
Results-based pay for schools or teachers	No	Partially (in some subnational states)	Yes (BSP, 2002)	Yes (2002)	Yes (2005)	Yes (2014)

Policy Instrument	ARG	BRA	CHI	COL	MEX	PER
Teaching Career Regulation						
Detailed reports with results per school	Partially	Yes	Yes (BSP)	Yes (2001)	Yes (2006)	Yes (2007)
Regulation Based on School Autonomy						
Higher school responsibility for resource allocation	Yes (2009)	Partially	Yes	Yes	Yes	No
Institutional projects to be elaborated by school	Yes (2009)	Partially	Yes	Yes	Yes (2001)	No
Principal training or recruitment policies	No	Partially (in some subnational states)	Yes (2003)	Partially	Partially	Partially (2013)
Overall result	No governance turn	Substantial governance turn	Full governance turn	Substantial governance turn	Full governance turn	Substantial governance turn

Notes: In brackets, the year when the policy instrument was created or expanded in each case is shown. BSP stands for "before the studied period" limited and crucial, at times, in the flaws of its implementation. Often, the discontinuation of governments has left the assemblies halfway, and, in most cases, it has gone back faster than forward. Significantly, the sudden changes in government have sown more discontinuity in an ever more politically unstable region. The *race to the classroom* of command and control, emphasizing centralized regulatory governance, is a blurred route, filled with political instability, lack of resources and distance from real-life classroom needs.

Our book presents these hypotheses from a comparative perspective in the six analyzed countries. The complexity of each context emerges to follow the double analytical path of what is particular and what is common to the region in these interesting times of intense educational reforms.

References

Abrucio, F.L. (2010). A dinâmica federativa da educação brasileira: diagnóstico e propostas de aperfeiçoamento. In R. Portela de Oliveira & W. Santana (Eds.), *Educação e federalismo no Brasil: combater as desigualdades, garantir a diversidade*. UNESCO

Acosta, F., & Ruiz, G. (2018). Revisiting comparative education in Latin America: traditions, uses, and perspectives. *Comparative Education*, 54(3), 1–15.

Alarcón Leiva, J., & Donoso Díaz, S. (2017). Hitos significativos de la política educacional del Gobierno de la Coalición por el Cambio (2010–2014). *Estudios Pedagógicos (Valdivia)*, 43(1), 371–388.

Almeida, R., Bresolin, A., Borges, B., Mendes, K., & Menezes-Filho, N. (2016). *Assessing the Impacts of Mais Educacao on Educational Outcomes: Evidence between 2007 and 2011*. The World Bank.

Ames, P. (2010). Hacer visible y mejorar la educación rural: una tarea pendiente. In Consorcio de Universidades (Ed.), *Metas del Perú al Bicentenario*. Asociación Peruana de Empresas.

Araujo, M.C., López-Boo, F., & Puyana, J.M. (2013). *Panorama sobre los servicios de desarrollo infantil en América Latina y el Caribe*. BID.

Bagolin Zambon, L., & Terrazzan, E.A. (2013). Políticas de material didático no Brasil: organização dos processos de escolha de livros didáticos em escolas públicas de educação básica. *Revista Brasileira de Estudos Pedagógicos*, 94(237), 585–602.

Balarin, M. (2013). *Las políticas TIC en los sistemas educativos de América Latina: el caso Perú*. UNICEF.

Beech, J. (2002). Latin American education: perceptions of linearities and the construction of discursive space. *Comparative Education*, 38(4), 415–427.

Beech, J. (2019). The long and winding road to inclusion: Educational policies in Argentina (2003–2015). In C. Ornelas (Ed.), *Politics of Education in Latin America: Reforms, Resistance and Persistence*. Brill-Sense Publishers.

Bellei, C. (2015). *El gran experimento: mercado y privatización de la educación chilena*. LOM Ediciones.

Bellei, C., & Vanni, X. (2015). Evolución de las políticas educacionales en Chile: 1980–2014. In C. Bellei (Ed.), *El gran experiment: mercado y privatización de la educación Chilena*. LOM Ediciones.

Berlinski, S., & Schady, N. (2015). *Los primeros años: el bienestar infantil y el papel de las políticas públicas*. Banco Interamericano de Desarrollo.

Bernstein, B. (1998). *Pedagogía, control simbólico e identidad*. Morata.
Bruns, B., & Luque, J. (2014). *Profesores excelentes: cómo mejorar el aprendizaje en América Latina y el Caribe*. BID.
Bruns, B., Evans, D., & Luque, J. (2012). *Achieving world-class education in Brazil. The next agenda*. World Bank.
Cabrol, M., & Székely, M. (Eds.) (2012). *Educación para la transformación*. Banco Interamericano de Desarrollo.
Carnoy, M. (2007). *Cuba's Academic Advantage*. Stanford University Press.
Cecchini, S. (2014). Educiación, programa de transferencias condicionadas y protección social en América Latina y el Caribe. In M. del C. Feijoó & M. Poggi (Eds.), *Educación y políticas sociales: sinergias para la inclusión*. IIPE-UNESCO.
Claus, A., & Sanchez, B. (2019). *El financiamiento educativo en la Argentina: balance y desaíos de cara al cambio de década*. CIPPEC.
Coria, A. (2013). Entre currículum y enseñanza: aristas de un proceso político-pedagógico en la construcción de la política curricular y de enseñanza en Argentina (2004–2007). In *Formación de Profesores, Currículum, Sujetos y Prácticas Educativas*. Universidad Nacional de Córdoba.
Cox, C. (2003). *Políticas educacionales en el cambio de siglo: la reforma del sistema escolar de Chile*. Editorial Universitaria.
Cox, C., Beca, C.E., & Cerri, M. (2017). The teaching profession in Latin America: change policies and the challenges of poverty and exclusion. In W.T. Pink & G.W. Noblit (Eds.), *Second International Handbook of Urban Education*. Springer International Publishing.
Crozier, M., Huntington, S., & Watanuki, J. (1975). *The Crisis of Democracy*. New York University Press.
Cuenca, R. (2011). *La carrera pública magisterial: una mirada atrás para avanzar*. Tarea.
Cuenca, R. (2015). *Las carreras docentes en América Latina: la acción meritocrática para el desarrollo profesional*. OREALC/UNESCO Santiago.
Cueto, S., & Tapia, J. (2017). *El apoyo de FORGE al desarrollo del Currículo Nacional de la Educación Básica del Perú*. GRADE; FORGE.
Di Gropello, E. (1999). Los modelos de descentralización educativa en América Latina. *Revista de La CEPAL*, 68, 158–170.
Díaz-Barriga, A. (2018). "El que mucho abarca…". *Revista Nexos*, 1 Octubre. Retrieved from www.nexos.com.mx/?p=39535.
ECLAC. (2011). *Social Panorama of Latin America*. Retrieved from http://repositorio.cepal.org/bitstream/handle/11362/1243/9/S1100928_en.pdf.
Elacqua, G., Iribarren, M., & Santos, H. (2018). *Private Schooling in Latin America: Trends and Public Policies – Education Division Social Sector*. Inter-American Development Bank.
Espínola, V. (1992). *Decentralization of the Educational System and the Introduction of Market Rules in the Regulation of Schooling: The Case of Chile*. CIDE.
Fajardo Salinas, D.M. (2011). Educación intercultural bilingüe en Latinoamérica: un breve estado de la cuestión. *Revista Liminar: Estudios Sociales y Humanísticos*, 9(2), 15–29.
Feeney, S., & Feldman, D. (2016). Regulaciones nacionales sobre el currículum: Argentina, las nuevas formas de gobierno e instrumentos curriculares. *Educação em Revista*, 32(2), 19–44.
Fierro, M., Tapia García, G., & Rojo, F. (2009). *Descentralizacion educativa en Mexico: un recuento analitico*. OECD.

Gajardo, M. (1999). *Reformas educativas en América Latina: balance de una década*. PREAL.

Gale, T. (2001). Critical policy sociology: historiography, archaeology and genealogy as methods of policy analysis. *Journal of Education Policy*, 16(5), 379–393.

García, C.M., & Vaillant, D. (2009). *Desarrollo profesional docente*. Narcea.

García-Huidobro, J.E. (Ed.) (1999). *La reforma educacional chilena*. Editorial Popular.

Gentili, P. (2013). *Política educacional, cidadania e conquistas democráticas*. Fundaçao Perseu Abramo.

Gil-Antón, M. (2018). La reforma educative: fracturas estructurales. *Revista Mexicana de Investigación Educativa*, 23(76), 303–321.

Granados Roldán, O., De la Mora, X.P., & Torres, E.O.B. (2018). *Fortalecimiento de Derechos, Ampliación de Libertades*, Vol. 1. Fondo de Cultura Economica.

Grindle, M. (2004). *Despite the Odds: The Contentious Politics of Education Reform*. Princeton University Press.

Guerrero, L. (2009). Política docente: balance del período. In R. Cuenca (Ed.), *La Educación en los Tiempos del Apra*. Foro Educativo.

Heckman, J. (2008). *Schools, Skills and Synapses. Discussion Paper No. 3515*. IZA.

IDEHPUCP. (2017). *Entrevista a Eduardo Ballón: "La descentralización estaba condenada al fracaso."* Peru, April 25.

Jessop, B. (1998). The narrative of enterprise and the enterprise of narrative: place marketing and the entrepreneurial city. In T. Hall and P. Hubbard, *The Entrepreneurial City: Geographies of Politics, Regime and Representation*. John Wiley.

Jofré, G. (1988). *El sistema de subvenciones en educación: la experiencia chilena (No. 99)*. Centro de Estudios Públicos.

Júnior, D.P.N., Da Silva Herculano, L., Pinto, I.C., Da Costa, L.M., De Azevedo, M.S., Miura, P.K., & De Souza, V.A.R. (2018). A reforma do ensino médio: histórico, desdobramentos e reflexões. *Perspectiva Sociológica: A Revista de Professores de Sociologia*, 1(21), 81–96.

Larroulet, C., & Montt, P. (2010). *Políticas educativas de largo plazo y acuerdo amplio en educación: el caso chileno*. Serie Working Papers 38. Universidad del Desarrollo, School of Business and Economics.

Latapí, P. (2004). La política educativa del estado Mexicano desde 1992. *Revista Electrónica de Investigación Educativa*, 6(2), 1–16.

Latapí, P., & Ulloa, M. (2000). *El financiamiento de la educación básica en el marco del federalismo*. Fondo de Cultura Económica.

LLECE-UNESCO. (2013). *Análisis del clima escolar: ¿Poderoso factor que explica el aprendizaje en América Latina y el Caribe?* OREALC-UNESCO Santiago.

López, M. (2020). State segmentation and democratic survival in Latin America. *American Behavioral Scientist*, 64(9), 1242–1270.

Martínez Boom, A. (2004). *De la escuela expansiva a la escuela competitiva: dos modos de modernización en América Latina*. Anthropos, Convenio Andrés Bello.

Martínez Rizo, F. (2013). El futuro de la evaluación educativa. *Sinéctica*, 40, 1–11.

Martinic, S., & Pardo, M. (2001). *Economía política de las reformas educativas en América Latina*. PREAL & CIDE.

McDonnel, L.M., & Elmore, R.F. (1987). *Alternative Policy Instrument*. Center for Policy Research in Education, The Rand Corp.

McGehee, J.J., & Griffith, L.K. (2001). Large-scale assessments combined with curriculum alignment: agents of change. *Theory into Practice*, 40(2), 137–144.

Mejía-Botero, F. (2017). *Cuatro años de desencuentros: recuento y reflexión sobre la reforma educativa*. ITESO.
Melo, J.O. (2017). *Historia mínima de Colombia*. El Colegio de Mexico AC.
Mezzadra, F., & Veleda, C. (2014). *Apostar a la docencia: Desafíos y posibilidades para la política educativa argentina*. CIPPEC, Embajada de Finlandia y UNICEF.
Mizala, A., & Ross Schneider, B. (2014). Negotiating education reform: Teacher evaluations and incentives in Chile (1990–2010). *Governance: An International Journal of Policy, Administration, and Institutions*, 27(1), 87–109.
Muñoz, G., & Vanni, X. (2008). Rol del estado y de los agentes externos en el mejoramiento de las escuelas: análisis en torno a la experiencia chilena. *REICE: Revista Electrónica Iberoamericana sobre Calidad, Eficacia y Cambio en Educación*. Retrieved from https://revistas.uam.es/reice/article/view/5430.
Navarro, L., & Gysling, J. (2017). Educación general en el gobierno de Michelle Bachelet: avances y rezagos. In P. Díaz-Romero, A. Rodríguez & A. Varas (Eds.), *Bachelet II: El diícil camino hacia un Estado Democrático Social de Derechos*. BPE.
OECD. (2020). *Panorama de las Administraciones Públicas América Latina y el Caribe 2020*. OECD Publishing.
OREALC-UNESCO. (2014). *El liderazgo directivo: un estado del arte en base a ocho sistemas escolares de América Latina y el Caribe*. OREALC-UNESCO.
Ornelas, C. (1998). La descentralización de los servicios de educación y salud en México. In E. Di Gropello & R. Cominetti (Eds.), *La descentralización de la educación y la salud en América Latina*. CEPAL.
Ornelas, C. (2010). *Política, poder y pupitres. Críticas al nuevo federalismo educativo*. Siglo XXI.
Ornelas, C. (2018). *La contienda por la educación: globalización, neocorporativismo y democracia*. Fondo de Cultura Económica.
Ornelas, C. (2019). *Politics of Education in Latin America: Reforms, Resistance and Persistence*. Brill-Sense Publishers.
Ouviña, H., & Thwaites Rey, M.C. (2018). *Estados en disputa: auge y fractura del ciclo de impugnación al neoliberalismo en América Latina*. El Colectivo.
Panfichi, A., & Alvarado, M. (2011). *Corrupción y gobernabilidad*. CIES; PUCP.
Paredes, R., Irarrázaval, I., Murray, M., Gutierrez, G., Bogolasky, F., & Contreras, C. (2012). *Evaluación de los primeros años de Implementación del Programa de Subvención Escolar Preferencial de la Subsecretaría de Educación*. Centro de Políticas Públicas Pontificia Universidad Católica de Chile.
Peñuela Contreras, D.M., & Rodríguez Murcia, V.M. (2006). Movimiento pedagógico: otras formas de resistencia educativa. *Folios*, 23, 3–14.
Pérez Sáinz, J.P. (2016). *Una historia de la desigualdad en América Latina: La barbarie de los mercados desde el siglo XIX hasta hoy*. Siglo Veintiuno Editores.
Pierson, P. (1993). When effect becomes cause: policy feedback and political change. *World Politics*, 45(4), 595–628.
Prieto Bafalluy, A. (1983). *La modernización educacional*. Ediciones Universidad Católica de Chile.
Puiggrós, A. (1991). *América Latina: crisis y prospectiva de la educación*. Aique.
Raab, C. (1994). Theorising the governance of education. *British Journal of Educational Studies*, 42(1), 6–22.
Raczynski, D., Wieinstein, J., & Pascual, J. (2013). Subvención escolar preferenial (SEP) en Chile: un intento por equilibrar la macro y micro política escolar. *Revista*

Iberoamericana Sobre Calidad, Eficacia Y Cambio En Educación, 11(2). Retrieved from https://revistas.uam.es/reice/article/view/2902.
Reid, M. (2007). *Forgotten Continent: The Battle for Latin America's Soul.* Yale University Press.
Reimers, F.M. (2001). *Unequal Schools, Unequal Chances: The Challenges to Equal Opportunity in the Americas.* Latin American Studies 5. Harvard University Press.
Rincon-Gallardo, S. (2013). La tutoría para el aprendizaje independiente como práctica y principio rector del cambio educativo en escuelas públicas mexicanas. *Revista DIDAC*, 61, 58–64.
Rivas, A. (2001). *Familia, libertad y pobreza: Un nuevo híbrido escolar. La experiencia de las escuelas autónomas de Nicaragua.* IIPE-UNESCO.
Rivas, A. (2015). *América Latina después de PISA: lecciones aprendidas sobre la educación en siete países.* CIPPEC, Natura e Instituto Natura.
Rivas, A., & Dborkin, D. (2018). ¿Qué cambió en el financiamiento educativo en Argentina? In *Documento de Trabajo N° 162.* CIPPEC.
Rivas, A., & Sánchez, B. (2020). Race to the classroom: the governance turn in Latin American education. The emerging era of accountability, control and prescribed curriculum. *Compare. A Journal of Comparative and International Education.* doi:10.1080/03057925.2020.1756745.
Rivero, J. (2000). *Educación y exclusión en América Latina: reformas en tiempos de globalización.* Miño y Dávila.
Robinson, W.I. (2020). Don't cry for me, Latin America. *Human Geography*, 13(1), 91–94.
Rosanvallon, P. (2020). *El siglo del populismo: historia, teoría, crítica.* Manantial.
Rouquié, A. (2011). *A la sombra de las dictaduras: la democracia en América Latina.* Fondo de Cultura Económica.
Sarason, S. (1990). *The Predictable Failure of Educational Reform.* Jossey-Bass.
Schwartzman, S. (2015). *Education in South America.* Bloomsbury Academic.
Schwartzman, S. (2016). *Educação média profissional no Brasil: situação e caminhos.* Fundación Santillana.
Schwartzman, S., & Cox, C. (2009). *Políticas educativas y cohesión social en América Latina.* Uqbar Editores.
Segatto, C.I. (2015). *O papel dos governos estaduais nas políticas municipais de Educação: uma análise dos modelos de cooperação intergovernamental.* Doctoral Thesis, Fundação Getulio Vargas.
Segatto, C., & Abrucio, F. (2016). A cooperação em uma federação heterogênea: o regime de colaboração na educação em seis estados brasileiros. *Revista Brasileira de Educação*, 21(65), 411–429.
Sunkel, G., & Trucco, D. (2012). *Las tecnologías digitales frente a los desafíos de una educación inclusiva en América Latina: algunos casos de buenas prácticas.* CEPAL.
Tedesco, J.C. (2012). *Educación y justicia social en América Latina.* Fondo de Cultura Económica.
Tedesco, J.C., & Steinberg, C. (2015). Avanzar en las políticas de integración de TIC en la educación. In J.C. Tedesco (Ed.), *La educación argentina hoy: la urgencia del largo plazo.* Siglo XXI.
Tenti Fanfani, E. (2004). *Gobernabilidad de los Sistemas Educativos en América Latina.* UNESCO.
Terigi, F. (2016). *Políticas públicas en Educación tras doce años de gobierno de Néstor Kirchner y Cristina Fernández.* Friedrich Ebert Stiftung.

Terigi, F., Briscioli, B., Scavino, C., Morrone, A., & Toscano, A.G. (2013). La educación secundaria obligatoria en la Argentina: entre la expansión del modelo tradicional y las alternativas de baja escala. *Revista del IICE*, 33, 27–46.

Therborn, G. (2013). *The Killing Fields of Inequality*. Polity Press.

Toer, M. (2012). *La emancipación de América Latina*. Editorial Continente.

UNESCO. (2013). Antecedentes y criterios para la elaboración de políticas docentes en América Latina y el Caribe. In OREALC/UNESCO (Eds.), *Proyecto Estratégico Regional sobre Docentes "Profesores para una Educación para Todos"*. OREALC/UNESCO.

UNICEF & Universidad Nacional de General Sarmiento. (2012). *Oportunidades para aprender: sistematización de programas en Argentina, Brasil, Chile, Colombia y México*. UNICEF, Universidad Nacional de General Sarmiento.

Vaillant, D. (2011). Improving and supporting principals' leadership in Latin America. In T.J. MacBeath (Ed.), *International Handbook of Leadership for Learning*. Springer International.

Valverde, G. (2009). Estándares y evaluación. In S. Schwartzmann & C. Cox (Eds.), *Políticas educativas y cohesión social en América Latina*. Uqbar Editores.

Vegas, E., & Petrow, J. (2008). *Raising Student Learning in Latin America: The Challenge for the 21st Century*. Banco Mundial.

Verger, A., Parcerisa, L., & Fontdevila, C. (2018). The growth and spread of large-scale assessments and test-based accountabilities: a political sociology of global education reforms. *Educational Review*, 71(1), 5–30.

Weiler, H. (1993). Control versus legitimation: the politics of ambivalence. In J. Hannaway & M. Carnoy (Eds.), *Decentralization and School Improvement: Can We Fulfill the Promise?*Jossey-Bass.

Wilkins, A., & Olmedo, A. (2019). *Education Governance and Social Theory: Interdisciplinary Approaches to Research*. Bloomsbury.

Yashar, D.J. (2005). *Contesting Citizenship in Latin America: The Rise of Indigenous Movements and the Postliberal Challenge*. Cambridge University Press.

Zorrilla, M., & Barba, B. (2008). Reforma educativa en México: Descentralización y nuevos actores. *Sinéctica, Revista Electrónica de Educación*, 30, 1–30.

Zukerfeld, M., & Benítez Larghi, S. (2015). *Flujos de conocimientos, tecnologías digitales y actores sociales en la educación secundaria: un análisis socio-técnico de las capas del Programa Conectar Igualdad*. Universidad Maimónides & Universidad Nacional de La Plata.

2 From "Spray and Pray" to "Reform without Spray"
The Two Stages of Education Policy in Argentina

Belén Sánchez and Axel Rivas

Introduction

At the beginning of the 2003–2019 period, Argentina was leaving behind a deep political, economic and social crisis. The first years of the new century had been marked by institutional instability, rising unemployment, social unrest, street protests and a substantial currency devaluation. This was part of the era of neoliberal policies, whose origin dates to the mid-1970s, which left behind unprecedented indicators regarding inequality and poverty (Kessler, 2016).

In May 2003, Néstor Kirchner, candidate of the Frente para la Victoria (FPV, in Spanish), became President, putting an end to a period of strong political instability, whose most eloquent indicator is, perhaps, the succession of five presidents in less than two years. Kirchner was succeeded in 2007 by his wife, then-senator Cristina Fernández de Kirchner, who remained in power until December 2015. In a regional scenario marked by the breakdown of the neoliberal consensus, the Frente para la Victoria (FPV) administration reversed several of the privatizations of public goods that had taken place in the 1990s, distanced itself from multilateral credit organizations and implemented policies that extended rights to a part of society. For instance, it expanded the scope of the pension system, legalized same-sex marriage and created a universal policy of conditional cash transfers for families living in poverty: Universal Child Allowance (Asignación Universal por Hijo, AUH).

At the economic level, a period of reactivation began towards the end of 2002, with practically uninterrupted GDP growth between 2003 and 2011 (except for 2009, the year following the 2008 international financial crisis). This trend can be attributed, to a large extent, to a substitutive productive model that sought to revitalize a sector of the national industry and to the profitability of primary exports, favored by the devaluation of the local currency and the high level of international prices (Svampa, 2007). Between 2012 and 2018, a scenario of economic stagnation can be distinguished, marked by the interannual alternation of growth (in odd years) and decrease (in even years) of GDP, the intensification of the inflationary process and the increase in the fiscal deficit (Rivas & Dborkin, 2018).

The presidencies of the Frente para la Victoria (2003–2015) were periods of state expansion. The economic recovery and active state policies that were strongest between 2003 and 2007 came along with improvements in social indicators. The country experienced a significant poverty reduction – which went from 54.3% in 2002 to 26.9% in 2006, leading to job creation, an increase in remuneration and other non-labor income such as pensions and transfers (Cruces et al., 2017). The inequality index, the Gini coefficient, went from 53.8 in 2002 to 41 in 2013 (World Bank, 2020). The evolution of social indicators kept pace with the economic trajectory: the most significant progress took place between 2003 and 2007, continued at a slower pace between 2008 and 2011, and there was a tendency to stagnation from 2012 onwards. It took about a decade for the country to recover from the poverty peaks reached during the 2001 crisis: in the second half of the 2000s, there was a recovery in poverty rates, reaching its minimum in 2011, when it equaled the 1993 statistics (Gasparini et al., 2019).

At the same time, it was a period of deterioration of the institutions in several ways. Between 2007 and 2015, the National government interfered with the statistics that the National Institute of Statistics and Census (INDEC, in Spanish) published; consequently, inflation rates and poverty measurement were systematically underestimated. The publication of these indexes was even interrupted. In the same way, it was a period of intense concentration of power in the Executive Branch, in the presidential figure; this period was also marked by open confrontations with the Judicial Power and the mass media. The period's achievements were overshadowed in the subsequent period when necessary legal actions were taken against the main profiles of the Kirchner administration for corruption cases.

The change of political direction in the national government, which took place at the end of 2015 with the inauguration of President Mauricio Macri, marked a new macroeconomic course and significant changes in terms of federalism. Regarding the former, external indebtedness was the privileged strategy for deficit reduction. A period of public spending contraction was opened, with the corresponding reduction in national and provincial education budgets (Claus & Sanchez, 2019). Regarding the latter, in 2007, the national government and the provincial governors celebrated a fiscal agreement that increased the mass resources that were distributed to the districts, responding to a historical claim and thus contributing to restoring the provincial public accounts.

The exchange rate and currency turbulences that affected the country in 2018 resulted in new inflationary waves that the macroeconomic policy could not contain. They had a negative impact on poverty and inequality indicators. The government resorted to an agreement with the International Monetary Fund (IMF) to stabilize public accounts. A new episode of macroeconomic volatility took place in August 2019, which compromised the country's chances of complying with the IMF agreement. Thus, Argentina ended the 2010s with a 68% devaluation of its currency in little more than a year, annual inflation of over 50%, and an economic contraction of 2.5% of GDP in 2018 and 2.2% in 2019 (World Bank, 2020).

Five ministers were in charge of the national Ministry of Education during the entire period studied in this chapter: Daniel Filmus was the Minister during Kirchner administration, Juan Carlos Tedesco took office with the inauguration of Cristina Fernández de Kirchner and was substituted in 2009 by Alberto Sileoni, who would leave by the end of the presidency and would become the minister with the longest tenure since the creation of the Ministry in 1854 (Rodríguez, 2017). Macri's inaugural Minister of Education was Esteban Bullrich, the previous holder of the same portfolio during his tenure as Mayor of the City of Buenos Aires. Bullrich was substituted, in mid-2017, by Alejandro Finocchiaro, who remained in office until the end of Macri's administration. Peronist Alberto Fernández succeeded Macri as President at the end of 2019 and appointed Nicolás Trotta as Minister of Education, who was still in office at the time of writing. This latter administration is not a subject of analysis of this study.

The national education policy agenda of the period can be subdivided into three major stages, which coincide with presidential terms rather than ministerial periods. The first period runs from 2003 to 2007, and it is marked by the overcoming of the effects of the crisis on the education system, the increase in investments and the passing of national laws. Between 2008 and 2015, a second stage was marked by the implementation of compulsory education, outlined in the National Education Law, and by programs of great scope and visibility, such as *Conectar Igualdad* in a context of economic stagnation. In the recent period, between 2016 and 2019, educational assessment and innovation were emphasized in reducing public spending. The following sections deal with each of the periods thoroughly.

2003–2007: The Distributive Stage and the Great Laws

When the 2001 economic crisis broke out, Argentina underwent a complex process of implementing a far-reaching educational reform. In the early 1990s, basic and post-secondary educational institutions had been transferred to the provinces, the academic structure of educational levels had been modified, new curricular guidelines (the Common Basic Contents, CBC, in Spanish) had been defined for the whole system, a federal system for the assessment of educational quality had been created and a new Higher Education Law had been passed.

These modifications were incorporated to very different extents among the provinces, which resulted in a disarticulated education system whose situation was aggravated by the impact of the crisis on the social conditions of students and teachers' salaries. Thus, in 2003, the educational scenario combined long-standing unresolved problems – inequality, the inadequate configuration of the teaching position, the educational backwardness of the adult population, and the selectivity of higher education – with those more directly associated with the educational reform of the 1990s, such as institutional disarticulation, the despecialization of technical training and the delays in the national validation of diplomas (Terigi, 2016).

The educational agenda of the Kirchner administration was aimed at overcoming the crisis (Beech, 2019). Following presidential action that expressed from the outset the political will to restore the normal functioning of the education system.[1] The Law of Guarantee of Teacher Salaries and 180 School Days (No. 25,864) was passed in 2003, and the National Fund for Teacher Incentives (No. 25,919) was passed in 2004. Both were aimed at re-establishing basic conditions for the teaching and teacher payment, which had been compromised in some provinces due to the economic crisis.

The legislation was the privileged instrument of educational policies during the 2003–2007 period, not only as an urgent response to emergencies. It was the time of the *great laws*. In 2005 the Technical and Vocational Education Law (No. 26,058) and the Education Financing Law (No. 26,075) were passed, and the following year the Comprehensive Sex Education Law (No. 26,150) and the National Education Law (LEN, No. 26,206) were passed. All of them were discursively devised in opposition to the reforms of the previous decade (Ruiz, 2009).

The Education Financing Law boosted a significant increase in resources for the sector, establishing that, by 2010, Argentina should reach an investment of 6% of its GDP in Education, Science and Technology, and establishing provincial and national responsibilities to achieve the necessary increase. In the context of a very favorable macroeconomic evolution, the budget in Education, Science and Technology went from representing 4.2% of GDP in 2005 to 6% in 2013[2] (Rivas & Dborkin, 2018). This growth correlated with the recovery in teacher salary, which grew 69.3% in real terms from 2003 to 2007 (Rivas & Dborkin, 2018). Both increases resulted from the growth of both national and provincial investment, although only the provinces increased the share of the education sector in their budgets (Vera, 2015).

The approval of the Education Financing Law meant a new swing in the pendulum of educational federalism (Rivas, 2009). The administrative decentralization of education remained unchanged, but mechanisms were defined that gave the national state a more significant role in coordinating policies and the compensation of inequalities. The law created a national negotiating body to define the minimum teacher salary, established the mechanism of bilateral agreements to agree on transfers to the provinces and to promote educational planning processes at the subnational level, and created the National Teacher Salary Compensation Fund, through which the national government supports provinces with difficulties in paying the national minimum salaries. However, the distribution of this fund could have had more significant compensatory effects on inequalities between provinces (Bezem et al., 2012).

The more significant funding available led to a stage marked by a greater distribution of human and material resources. In addition to the recomposition of teachers' salaries throughout the country, the state "sprayed" the system with new schools, teaching positions, scholarships, textbooks and other didactic materials. Between 2003 and 2008, 790 schools were built, and between 2003 and 2015, 92 million books and literary collections were distributed to schools across the country (National Ministry of Education, 2015). It was also a period in which the government and teacher unions were on good terms. Looking back at this period, many analysts wonder if the opportunity was not lost to discuss the teaching career, which today retains the features of the "first generation" careers (Cuenca, 2015): vertical, credentialist and bureaucratic. Organized based on regulations enacted in 1958, even today, the Argentine teaching career responds to a logic far from the reality of a complex education system in expansion, whose regulations are oriented to the full guarantee of the right to education (Perazza, 2015).

The enactment of the National Education Law (LEN, in Spanish), a central component of the legal framework approved at this stage, implied some changes and not a few continuities concerning its predecessor: The Federal Education Law. To a large extent, it was a symbolic act that formalized the widespread rejection of the educational reform of the 1990s in the educational field (Feldfeber & Gluz, 2011). Approved after a consultation process of disputed scope (Ruiz, 2009), the LEN introduced some definitions that guided the educational policies of the following years: it extended compulsory schooling to the whole secondary level; it redefined the academic structure of educational levels, returning to the scheme of primary and secondary levels and leaving to the jurisdictions the definition of the location of the seventh year of schooling; it established that the resolutions of the Federal Council of Education would be mandatory; and it defined the creation of the National Institute for Teacher Training (INFoD, in Spanish), the governing body of the national policy for the training of teachers and professors.

The new century of educational policies also had a curricular chapter for the country. In 2004, the Federal Council of Culture and Education agreed on the need to identify the Nuclei of Priority Learning (NAP), knowledge levels that would form "a common and equivalent basis of learning for all children and young people" (Res. CFCyE (Federal Council of Culture and Education) No. 214/04), based on the diagnosis of a fragmented system with unequal quality circuits. These documents, elaborated and approved between 2004 and 2011, did not repeal the CBC; they were organized following the main points proposed therein. However, they were construed as an expression of a policy focused on teaching (not on the curriculum or assessment) and knowledge (and not on competencies) (Coria, 2013), discursively constructed in opposition to the reform of the previous decade. Indeed, the CBC "disappeared" as references in official documents, textbooks, teacher training programs and daily teaching practice.

Another component of the policies aimed at restoring the *waterline* – in the words of the official discourse – after the crisis at the beginning of the century was the Integral Program for Educational Equality (PIIE, in Spanish), which replaced the Social Education Plan of the 1990s in the sense that it dealt with educational policies aimed at the most vulnerable sectors. Aimed at primary schools serving the most vulnerable children, the PIIE sought to strengthen teaching conditions through pedagogical support, financial support, distribution of teaching resources, computer equipment and funds for the refunctionalization of infrastructure. The program also sought to mark a distance from the previous decade: it discursively moved away from the search for *equity*, which was replaced by *equality*, in a movement that sought to leave behind the compensatory paradigm and replace it with the socio-educational one. Despite this, an analysis of its intervention mechanisms (such as the program organization modality with a specific team, and its rituals and practices, giving it a specific identity as "PIIE schools") allows identifying strong continuities with the similar programs of the 1990s (Feldfeber & Gluz, 2011; Veleda et al., 2011).

This was a period of reordering of the system with a strong anchoring in the legislative branch of the policy and a marked discursive imprint built in opposition to the educational policies of the previous period. This did not happen without ambiguities: many of the definitions embodied in the laws had meager correlates in practice, partly due to the absence of planning processes that organized actions in intergovernmental coordination, implementation deadlines, and financial resources (Terigi, 2016).

2008–2015: Computers, Stagnation and Concentration of Power

With Juan Carlos Tedesco at the head of the Education Ministry of the Fernández de Kirchner administration, in 2009 the Federal Council of Education approved the National Compulsory Education Plan (Res. CFE No. 79/09), a three-year measure that organized the actions of the national and provincial governments aimed at complying with the provisions of the LEN for compulsory education. In July of the same year, Tedesco left his position to head the new Unit for Strategic Planning and Assessment of Argentine Education (UPEA), which reported directly to the Nation's Presidency.

This renewed attention to educational planning was not sufficient. The unit focused on designing the bases for a Ten-Year Education Plan that was later abandoned, which dissipated the hopes that the creation of the UPEA had generated. In 2012, after the end of the three-year plan, national planning was renewed – this time with a five-year plan, which also included teacher training (Res. CFE No. 188/12), but neither the budget nor the expected results actions were defined. Nor was enough work done to strengthen the quality and opportunity of statistical information for educational planning: the national nominal educational information system is still a pending matter for Argentina, despite the drive that in 2012 was made with a ministerial resolution.[3]

The policies of the period dealt with the implementation of the National Education Law, which introduced compulsory secondary education as the main challenge. Educational inclusion was consolidated as an omnipresent discursive mandate in the sector policies (Beech, 2019), which prioritized the secondary level, where the highest exclusion indicators were concentrated (Terigi, 2016). Based on the stipulations of the National Compulsory Education Plan approved in 2009, that same year the Federal Education Council endorsed the policy of Institutional Improvement Plans, which financed technical profiles in provincial ministries and transferred financial resources directly to schools to cover institutional teaching hours and operating expenses for actions to comply with compulsory schooling (Perazza, 2012). In most cases, these resources were translated into tutoring and other similar interventions that sought to underpin the student's trajectories but did not significantly alter the school format (Dirié et al., 2015). They also defined new organizational guidelines for secondary school education to reverse the original selective tradition of the level, which were slightly translated into concrete low-scale policies by some provinces (Terigi et al., 2013).

Secondary schools were also the main target of *Conectar Igualdad*, the most critical educational policy regarding budget and public visibility of the period. Launched in 2010, the program delivered a netbook to every student and every teacher in secondary schools and state-run teacher training institutes. Financed with funds from the national social security agency, *Conectar Igualdad* delivered more than 5,000,000 computers between 2010 and 2015, in an effort that, in retrospect, was more recognized for its effectiveness in the distribution of devices than for its pedagogical impact (Tedesco & Steinberg, 2015; Zukerfeld & Benítez Larghi, 2015).

The distribution of devices converged with the boost given to the production of digital audiovisual content. In 2004, the Educ.ar portal was relaunched, and with it, the production of digital content to support the teaching of basic knowledge. In addition, in 2007 and 2010, respectively, the television channels Encuentro and Pakapaka were created. Both of them brought audiovisual proposals of high cultural value, both of their creation and imported, and gave the content a federal imprint that had been absent from the public television offered before.

At the same time, alternative secondary schooling proposals were developed for young people and adults who had been excluded from secondary school or had not been able to access it. The FinES Plan (Plan for the Completion of Primary and Secondary Education for Youth and Adults – known as FinES, in Spanish), created in 2008, was the most far-reaching policy in this sense, with its variants FinES I, for those who had not been able to pass all the subjects from the last year, but had completed the entire course; and FinES II, which offered young people and adults the possibility of completing the entire secondary school course and even primary school course. FinES has been questioned for its pedagogical quality and the substandard working conditions of its teachers. It is not clear to what extent it is justified given regular adult education programs (Beech, 2019). However, it has contributed to the democratization of access to the secondary school degree. A study by Scasso (2018) shows that, at least until 2010, the educational offer for young people and adults (including FinES) has been central to the process of expanding opportunities for secondary level completion that took place in recent decades.

Beyond the active participation of the national government through policies for the secondary level, different authors agree in pointing out that these were actions of low pedagogical impact, oriented to specific groups or designed as short-range alternative paths (Scasso, 2018; Terigi et al., 2013). The

Improvement Plans symbolize some of this: resources were transferred to schools that were mainly used to develop tutorials to support students who had fallen behind, spaces that were parallel to regular classes; thus, their effects were incremental rather than transformational. The organizational model of the secondary school, to a large extent a producer of exclusionary logics, remained practically unchanged, whereas the basic enabling conditions such as teaching hours and physical spaces for teaching practice or the rigidity of academic regimes were not modified (Gorostiaga, 2012; Terigi et al., 2013).

The extension of the school day, stipulated by the Education Financing and National Education Laws, stands out among the most important policies for the primary level. The first steps were taken in some provinces, and, in 2011, a national policy was launched that financed equipment, infrastructure, provincial technical teams and the creation of school funds. In addition, booklets with pedagogical guidelines and training courses for supervisors, managers and teachers were developed (Veleda, 2013). However, progress was meager in terms of coverage. In 2015, the extended school day covered 13.6% of the enrollment at the primary level, falling short of the 30% target set by the Education Financing Law. In contrast, in 2012, it was defined that the first two years of the primary level would form a pedagogical unit. This measure eliminated school repetition in the first grade throughout the country, associated with the different rates of acquisition of initial literacy.

The preschool level was also included in the national educational agenda, although comparatively less than other levels. The major milestone occurred in 2015 with the approval of Law No. 27,045, which declared compulsory schooling for four-year-old children.

Other significant national policies were the socio-educational programs to support school attendance through scholarships and other contributions; generating bridging spaces with the school; improving ties between the school, the family and the community; and democratizing access to cultural and sports experiences. Dependent on the National Directorate of Socio-educational Policies (which in 2009 replaced the Directorate of Compensatory Policies), some of these programs were the Children Activity Centers (CAI, in Spanish) and Youth Activity Centers (CAJ, in Spanish), the contributions for student mobility or the National Program of Youth Orchestras and Choirs.

Conditional cash transfers on school attendance, favored by the re-statization of pension funds in 2007, were another novelty of the period, following a regional trend (Rivas, 2015). In 2009 Argentina universalized the coverage of family allowances through the Universal Child Allowance (AUH, in Spanish), aimed at low-income families unemployed or employed in the informal market, which made the transfer of a monthly amount per child conditional on school attendance and compliance with health conditions. A study published in 2017 showed that the AUH had positive effects on poverty reduction and increased access to secondary education, particularly among males between 15 and 17 years old (UNICEF et al., 2017). In 2014, a presidential decree launched the Program to Support Argentine Students (PROGRESAR), which is also financed with social security funds and grants a monthly monetary benefit to low-income young people between 18 and 24 years of age conditional on their attendance at higher or secondary education institutions.

The three programs, AUH, PROGRESAR and *Conectar Igualdad* (the latter also financed by social security funds), expressed a new paradigm of universal social policies with strong educational components to expand opportunities for the most vulnerable. These were highly visible policies with high budgetary demand that, to some extent, were possible in a context of a strong concentration of financial and political power in the hands of the national government.

In terms of teacher policies, the most remarkable advances were in protecting salaries against inflation – whose marked growth trend stopped after 2008 – and teacher training. The National Institute for Teacher Training, created in 2007, led the processes of drafting regulations that were agreed upon in the Federal Council of Education and provided the training system with an organizational structure while strengthening the provincial offices of higher education. A federal registry of institutions and teacher training programs was also created. The system's functions were defined, and frameworks were agreed upon to define organizational, academic and competitive appointment examination regulations. Initial teacher training was also extended to four years, and a process of curriculum revision for all levels of education was carried out. In terms of strengthening student trajectories, economic incentives were granted to entrants, some scholarships were given, and student participation mechanisms were encouraged (National Institute of Teacher Training, 2015). Despite these advances and the creation of a computer system for the planning of the supply, the period ended with fundamental challenges in terms of planning and organization of the training supply: 1,200 institutions of uneven pedagogical quality and institutional strength reveals a scenario of persistent over-dimensioning and atomization at the end of this stage (Mezzadra & Veleda, 2014).

Another significant advance was recorded towards the end of the period regarding teacher continuous professional development. In 2014, the national state took part in this type of training offer, previously almost exclusively provincial, union or private (Coria & Mezzadra, 2013; Diker & Serra, 2008). For this purpose, it launched the National Continuous Learning Program *Nuestra Escuela* (Our School, in Spanish), which offered universal and free in-service training to all teachers in the education system and specific virtual courses for managers, supervisors, teachers and other school-related profiles.

Kirchner's educational administration ended with a significant set of advances and not a few pending challenges. The increase in educational investment and the recomposition and growth of teacher salaries, brought about by a scenario of economic growth during a good part of the period, is worth highlighting (Rivas & Dborkin, 2018); the expansion of the initial level, significant in age 4 (Steinberg & Scasso, 2019; Veleda et al., 2015); the hierarchization of teacher training (Mezzadra & Veleda, 2014; National Institute of Teacher

Training, 2015); the massive incorporation of new technologies into the school environment; the construction of school buildings; the profuse production of digital educational content; as well as the expansion and consolidation of a conception anchored in education as a right, educational inclusion as an imperative and the role of the state as its guarantor (Terigi, 2016).

These achievements were possible thanks to a significant allocation of resources to the sector. Educational policy was recentralized due to national resources, plans and programs throughout the country. This leads us to think that there was a lack of strategies to strengthen the effects of these efforts, focusing on their results based on mechanisms that would lead to improvement. In this sense, the government policy was closer to the "spray and pray" model (Rivas, 2015), as resources were allocated without sufficient measures to supervise the impact on teaching and learning practices, expecting them to have an impact. Argentina had a substantial increase in educational investment, but the regulation, governance and monitoring of the system were weak.

At the end of the period, the teaching career was once again among the pending accounts. This also meant a lost opportunity to generate mechanisms in order to strengthen the teacher's performance. Even though the National Education Law sets forth that the teaching career must include at least one option for classroom work and another option for school management, no changes were made during the period other than partial modifications in some provinces. The last term of office of Fernández de Kirchner was characterized by a cooling of ties with the national teacher union associations, marked by the salary stagnation that took place at the same time as the more generalized macroeconomic stagnation.

Among other pending challenges, it should be noted that the goal (outlined in the Education Financing Law for 2010) of expanding the extended school day at the primary level to 30% of the most vulnerable students could not be achieved. Also, the significant gaps in access, trajectories, learning and graduation at the secondary level still reveal a mandate of inclusion stronger in discourse than in its real impact (Beech, 2019). There was scarce progress in institutionalizing long-term educational policy planning processes, the definition of budgetary allocations and jurisdictional responsibilities (Terigi, 2016).

2016–2019: Assessment, Innovation and Financial Restrictions

The signing of the Purmamarca Declaration by all members of the Federal Council of Education (provincial and national education ministers), announcing the promise of an "educational revolution" that would take place 200 years after the Declaration of Independence, was the inaugural milestone of the educational management of the Mauricio Macri administration. Shortly after that, the same body agreed on a new five-year plan for education: the National Strategic Plan 2016–2021 "Argentina Enseña y Aprende" (Argentina Teaches and Learns).

Once again, it was about statements of goals that did not specify expected results or define the budget allocation and sectoral documents with little significance outside the scope of the educational sphere. The latter was intended to be overcome by revitalizing the ten-year plan bases devised by Tedesco in 2010, employing a "Master Plan" project for Argentine education to be dealt with by the National Congress. This attempt failed in 2017 when Minister Bullrich left his position to take office as a national senator.

One of the main features of the 2016–2019 period was the decentralization of the education policy. The transfer of funds to the provinces to execute national programs decreased significantly after the Fiscal Consensus of 2017. The resources co-participated to the provinces increased, as, therefore, did their autonomy to define the allocation of the funds. At the same time, the dynamics of transfer and accountability were modified towards a model that emphasized transparency and budgetary planning. Instead of transferring funds for each of the national programs, now each province should prepare an annual plan for the implementation of resources, which would only be transferred once the accountability for the previous transfer had been carried out. This caused delays and reductions in transfers, whose total volume decreased significantly in the context of the generalized adjustment of public accounts (Claus & Sanchez, 2019). In line with this, in 2017, the national instance of the negotiations of salaries at the national level was discontinued, leaving the definition of teacher salaries in the hands of the provinces. The national government maintained its participation in the co-financing of teacher salaries, but its weak role in compensating the historical interprovincial inequalities was diminished (Rivas & Dborkin, 2018). In the same sense, the national directorates of educational levels (initial, primary, secondary) and their modalities were eliminated, so the drafting of specific policies depended on more autonomous processes of the provinces as the federal meetings by level and modality were discontinued or reduced in frequency.

A novelty in this period in terms of the relationship with the provinces was creating a School of Government of Educational Policy in response to a claim shared by several analysts regarding the need to strengthen the capacities of the technical teams of the provincial ministries. Thus, the national government took on training provincial technical teams in a move that coincided with the decentralizing approach. To date, there have been no assessments of the School of Government's experience that can provide evidence of its effects and/or its acceptance by the provinces, except for the trajectories on teacher training led by the INFoD, on which primarily high assessments are reported (National Institute of Teacher Training, 2019).

The *educational innovation* was at the center of the official discourse throughout the period, following the inaugural public promises of an *educational revolution*. A new Secretariat controlled the central pedagogical and curricular policies for Educational Innovation and Quality. Its importance would increase in comparison with that of the Secretariat of Educational Management. Their functions were partially dissolved by eliminating the national directorates of levels (for instance, primary education, secondary education) and modalities (rural education, special education, among others).

Under the national policy *Aprender Conectados* (To Learn Connected), Digital Education competencies were defined, and the Nuclei of Priority Learning in programming and robotics were developed. The *Conectar Igualdad* Program, on the other hand, underwent a significant reconfiguration: it was transferred to the scope of the national Ministry of Education, and the equipment distribution model was altered. The one-to-one model (one computer per student) was left behind. It was substituted by distributing mobile digital classrooms and programming and robotics laboratories in kindergarten, primary and secondary levels.

The PROGRESAR program was also reconfigured in 2018. It was transferred to the scope of the National Ministry of Education, and the conditions required to access and hold the scholarship were modified, leading towards a more meritocratic model that no longer required class attendance but also a performance threshold. At the same time, the amounts were increased according to a scheme of paying more to those who were more advanced in their studies and those pursuing careers considered strategic for national development. The program also took over the *Compromiso Docente* scholarship scheme, specific for teacher training, and was created in the INFoD in 2017. They have a similar logic, although academic performance grows in importance as an allocation criterion due to the selection exam, whose results are considered to grant scholarships along with social vulnerability and teaching commitment. They also grant monthly allowances equivalent to between 40% and 70% of the teacher salary (higher in careers whose graduates are more in demand). A certain threshold of academic performance is required to sustain them.

The pedagogical-curricular policy of the period was structured around the teaching of six basic skills defined in a new *National Framework for the Integration of Learning*, which was added to the national curricular guidelines already formed by the NAPs. From the INFoD, continuity was given to the Our School program (now the National Program for Situated Training). It was reoriented, emphasizing specific didactic training to teach two prioritized skills: communication and problem-solving. Between 2016 and 2019, the program reached 900,000 teachers and school authorities per year, being the largest policy regarding teacher training (National Institute of Teacher Training, 2019). Towards the end of the period, an external assessment identified high levels of policy coverage in the education system, that there was some consistency between the national guidelines and those adopted by each of the provinces, and that there was satisfaction on the part of teachers receiving the guidelines (OEI, 2019).

Other changes in teacher training during the period can be identified in the approval of a national framework on professional teaching skills; the creation of guidelines and the development of a specific training program for school authorities and supervisors; the creation of training programs for professionals who do not hold a teaching degree; the training of teacher trainers and jurisdictional technical teams; and the reconfiguration of the virtual teacher professional development programs from the model of comprehensive postgraduate courses towards a format of short virtual courses, aimed at specific challenges of teaching practice. Special emphasis was put on planning processes that would meet the demand for teachers in the different territories and the oversizing and fragmentation of institutions, but necessary agreements to carry out these processes were only reached in a few provinces (National Institute of Teacher Training, 2019). In this respect, the INFoD developed an active agenda of policies to solve critical issues of the training system with an orientation strongly marked by the concern for improving teaching at compulsory levels.

The Aprender test was the most visible educational policy of the national government during this period. The area of educational quality assessment was promoted to the rank of Secretariat within the ministerial structure. Since 2016, an annual census test of the fundamental curricular areas at the primary and secondary levels has been performed by this area.[4] This scheme, which faced defiance in its initial implementation and succeeded the previous National Assessment Operations, which had been carried out every three years, presented some comparability problems, and their publication times were not in line with the monitoring needs of the education system. The results of Aprender are published one semester after the implementation of each operation, employing national and jurisdictional reports that, in addition, deal with the results in terms of inequality around context variables. Results reports are also collated for each school. Although the National Education Law protects the identity of schools when it comes to making results known, the President's speech has urged Congress on several occasions to allow this, which at the time of writing had not taken place. Following this thrust given to assessment, in 2017, an exploratory scheme for evaluating teacher training called Enseñar (To Teach, in Spanish) was implemented for diagnostic purposes (Zacarias, 2018).

The results of Aprender were taken as a basis for the outlining of the program Escuelas Faro, a pedagogical support program, which focused on the 3,000 primary and secondary schools with the most significant difficulties. Similar to the previous PIIE program in many ways, Faro assists these schools in the design of improvement projects and, to this end, encourages the preparation of institutional diagnoses, allocates specific instances of additional situated training, displays territorial support networks, and provides didactic resources and funds for minor repairs.

The tests were also the starting point for a national program to improve mathematics teaching. After unsatisfactory results throughout the country, the national Ministry issued a diagnosis – even replicated in the presidential speech – about the need for a change in the teaching of the subject that would bring it closer to "real life." Foreign teams were called to develop a new curricular framework for teaching the area, translated into *Learning Progression Indicators*.

Both documents were added to the variety of national curricular instruments; it was not clear whether these documents complemented or supplemented each other. On that basis, materials for continuous teacher training and didactic resources for classroom work were developed and distributed in the provinces, complemented with teacher training sessions channeled through the National Program of Situated Training.

Other outstanding policies can be recognized in specific initiatives for educational levels. At the preschool level, shortly after having taken office, the President announced an ambitious program for the construction of 3,000 school buildings. Shortly, the goal was reduced to the construction of 10,000 classrooms[5] due to problems with land management. This reduced goal could not be achieved either due to operational difficulties or cuts in funding for the sector.

The focus on the secondary school level was renewed in 2017 when the Federal Council of Education agreed on the *Federal Secondary School Education 2030* policy. The national government relaunched the Institutional Improvement Plans, which were intended to finance interdisciplinary school projects. The jurisdictions were urged to present a plan for transforming their educational proposal, recovering many of the agreements celebrated in 2009: concentration of teaching work, curricular integration and the flexibility of promotion regimes, among others. In response, some provinces developed new initiatives, and others presented developments in the plans they had already been working on; many others did not progress in redesigning their educational proposals. In all cases, these are very recent advances. However, they are promising as they seek to transform the regular secondary school model, surpassing the tendency to create alternative models oriented to re-entry or completion, which is typical of the policies of the previous decade (Steinberg et al., 2019).

In terms of education policy, the Macri administration had a timid closing of administration, tinged by the bitter taste of the failure of significant initiatives (such as the construction of 3,000 kindergartens) due to the adjustment of public spending. The reformist approach to educational policies did not prevail due to a lack of political strength and resources. The national funding allocated to the education sector fell significantly in the last years (Claus & Sanchez, 2019). In this sense, as opposed to the metaphor chosen to assess the educational management of the previous stage, this government came closer to a formula of "reforming without spraying" by directing its efforts and speeches towards the reform of the education system without giving sufficient thrust – in part restricted by an adverse macroeconomic context – to the necessary supporting policies that would transfer resources and mitigate inter-provincial inequalities.

Among the positive results of the administration, it is worth highlighting a robust educational assessment system, which seems to have been assimilated by the schools and which achieved the consolidation of a process of assessment and feedback of results within the suitable timeframe and with the necessary level of disintegration for the decision-making processes of educational policy. Another achievement of the period was the continuity and consolidation of a national teacher training program situated in the school, which led to the construction of didactic and institutional agreements of universal scope.

On the negative side, we can point out the still pending issue of reviewing the teaching career and, to such effect, the reduction of educational investment and the decline in the national education portfolio's role in compensating provincial inequalities through salary compensation and transfers. This is a worrying issue as it results in the provinces having very disparate policy agendas in strategic planning and budget, strengthening the historical inequalities gap among them.

Final Remarks

Overall, Argentina's pathway in education policy over the last 15 years (summarized in Figure 2.1, below) shows both over- and under-estimation of the power of material resources to steer policy changes towards guaranteeing quality education for all. "*Spraying*" the system with resources without

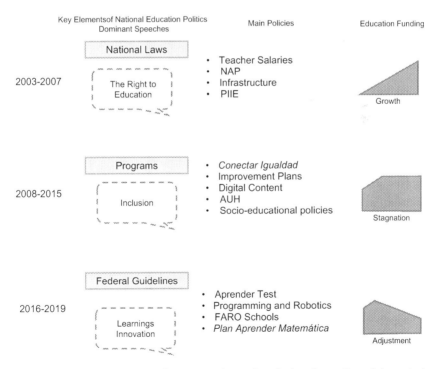

Figure 2.1 Graphic summary of the national agendas of education policy of the period 2003–2019
Source: Own preparation

planning and monitoring mechanisms and making long-needed changes in teaching careers feels like a lost opportunity in favorable contexts. Furthermore, the innovative and reformist wave that came in 2016 lacked the resources needed to transcend the sphere of discourse, in what can be seen as the reverse of the "spray and pray" scenario: praying for seeds of change to grow without spraying them with the basic resources they need to do so.

In the period, Argentina did not go through the *regulatory governance turn* as other Latin American countries did via the combination of four policy instruments to get governance closer to the regulation of classroom practices. It did not implement teaching career regulation nor use textbook policy to prescribe teaching practice. It did not take the path of test-based regulation through publishing test results per school (Rivas & Sanchez, 2020). The reasons for avoiding these pathways can be found in a position closer to teacher unions by the Kirchner governments until 2015 and the lack of political strength to push such changes forward (or even to place them in the political agenda) by the Macri administration that followed.

However, the country could not develop an alternative set of policy instruments that could work together towards improving teaching and learning with equity. Instead, a set of loosely coupled interventions with disparate strength to reach school practices make up the national education policy scenario – one that is not complete if the federal dimension is not considered: 24 subnational states with disparate available resources and technical skills comprise the Argentine territory and make education policy even more complex.

Thus, at the turn of the decade, Argentina faces the challenge of building a systemic education policy strategy based on solid planning mechanisms, considering budgetary needs and federal complexity. Particularly, secondary education still faces significant challenges, with high exclusion rates showing the need to transform its selective matrix. Though many provinces are working towards it, national support will be critical to strengthening the weakest jurisdictions. Also, mechanisms to ensure public funds for the education sector need to be revised and strengthened to protect the education systems from economic volatility. Most importantly, the frequent changes of direction in educational policies show the need to institutionalize mechanisms for building policies that transcend the temporal limits of governments and are sustained despite macroeconomic ups and downs. It is necessary to promote concerted planning instances involving provincial governments, teacher unions and other key stakeholders and guarantee the necessary funds. In this sense, developing a ten-year plan for education constitutes a postponed goal that would be essential to address in the coming years. The "spray and pray" and *pray without spray* approaches could undoubtedly be overturned by a strategy involving *strategic planning* as part of the formula.

Notes

1 Two days after taking power, Néstor Kirchner traveled to Paraná (Entre Ríos province) to solve the teachers' protest with immediate financial aid.

2 At the time of implementing the Education Financing Law, the GDP calculation based on 1993 was in force. Taking this GDP as a basis, the 6% investment target was met in 2010 (see Bezem et al., 2014).
3 Ministerial Resolution No. 1041 of 2012 approved the Comprehensive Education Information System (SINIDE, in Spanish), and Res. No. 215/14 of the Federal Council of Education endorsed its implementation. The system is currently used by very few provinces, while others either lack nominal information systems or have developed their own (Observatory "Argentinos por la Educación," 2018).
4 In 2016, all students in sixth grade of primary school level and fifth/sixth year of secondary school level were assessed in the subjects Mathematics, Spanish Language, Biology and Social Sciences, as were samples of students in third grade of primary school level and second/third year of secondary school level. In 2017, the subjects Biology and Social Sciences were assessed for census purposes in sixth grade of primary school level, and Spanish Language and Mathematics in fifth/sixth year of secondary school level. In 2018, only the last year of the primary school level was evaluated in Spanish Language and Mathematics for census purposes. In 2019, all students in the last year of secondary school were assessed in the same areas.
5 Classrooms for preschool or pre-primary education are called "salas" in Argentina.

References

Beech, J. (2019). The long and winding road to inclusion: educational policies in Argentina (2003–2015). In C. Ornelas (Ed.), *Politics of Education in Latin America: Reforms, Resistance and Persistence*. Brill-Sense Publishers.

Bezem, P., Mezzadra, F., & Rivas, A. (2012). *Informe final de Monitoreo de la Ley de Financiamiento Educativo*. Informe de Monitoreo y Evaluación. CIPPEC.

Bezem, P., Mezzadra, F., & Rivas, A. (2014). ¿Se cumplió la Ley de Financiamiento Educativo? In CIPPEC (Ed.), *Documento de Políticas Públicas/Análisis N° 135*. CIPPEC.

Claus, A., & Sanchez, B. (2019). *El financiamiento educativo en la Argentina: balance y desafíos de cara al cambio de década*. Discussion paper. CIPPEC.

Coria, A. (2013). Entre currículum y enseñanza: aristas de un proceso político-pedagógico en la construcción de la política curricular y de enseñanza en Argentina (2004–2007). In E. Miranda & B.N. Paciullu (Eds.), *Formación de Profesores, Currículum, Sujetos y Prácticas Educativas*. Universidad Nacional de Córdoba.

Coria, J., & Mezzadra, F. (2013). *La formación docente continua en las provincias: un análisis comparado de las políticas y regulaciones provinciales*. Discussion paper. CIPPEC.

Cruces, G., Fields, G., Jaume, D., & Viollaz, M. (2017). *Growth, Employment, and Poverty in Latin America*. Oxford University Press.

Cuenca, R. (2015). *Las carreras docentes en América Latina: la acción meritocrática para el desarrollo profesional*. OREALC/UNESCO Santiago.

Diker, G., & Serra, J.C. (2008). *La cuestión docente. Argentina: las políticas de capacitación docente*. Fundación Laboratorio de Políticas Públicas.

Dirié, C., Fernández, B., Landau, M., D'Andrea, A.M., Torres, D., Barbuyani, C., & Vila Torres, P. (2015). *Las tutorías en la educación secundaria en el marco del plan de mejora institucional*. Red Federal de Investigación Educativa, Ministerio de Educación de la Nación.

Feldfeber, M., & Gluz, N. (2011). Las políticas educativas en Argentina: herencias de los '90, contradicciones y tendencias de "nuevo signo." *Educação & Sociedade*, 32 (11), 339–356.

Gasparini, L., Tornarolli, L., & Gluzmann, P. (2019). *El desafío de la pobreza en Argentina*. CEDLAS, CIPPEC, PNUD.

Gorostiaga, J.M. (2012). Las políticas para el nivel secundario en Argentina ¿Hacia una educación más igualitaria? *Revista Uruguaya de Ciencia Política*, 21(1), 141–159.

Kessler, G. (2016). *La sociedad argentina hoy: radiografía de una nueva estructura*. Siglo XXI.

Mezzadra, F., & Veleda, C. (2014). *Apostar a la docencia: desafíos y posibilidades para la política educativa argentina*. CIPPEC, Finland Embassy and UNICEF.

Ministry of Education of the Nation. (2015). *La política educativa nacional 2003–2015: inclusión y mejores aprendizajes para la igualdad educativa*. Ministry of Education of the Nation.

National Institute of Teacher Training. (2015). *Memoria de gestión Instituto Nacional de Formación Docente 2007–2015*. Ministerio de Educación de la Nación.

National Institute of Teacher Training. (2019). *Management Annual Report of National Institute of Teacher Training 2016–2019*. Renovar la enseñanza, garantizar aprendizajes. Ministerio de Educación de la Nación.

Observatorio Argentinos por la Educación. (2018). *Los sistemas de información educativa en Argentina*. Observatorio Argentinos por la Educación.

OEI. (2019). *Evaluación de diseño, implementación y resultados de las políticas de formación docente situada del INFD*. OEI.

Perazza, R. (2012). *Acerca de la obligatoriedad en la escuela secundaria argentina: análisis de la política nacional*. E. Duro (Ed.). UNICEF Argentina.

Perazza, R. (2015). *La norma laboral docente en Argentina: entre la historia y los retos futuros*. Master's Thesis, Buenos Aires: FLACSO Academic Headquarters Argentina.

Rivas, A. (2009). *Lo uno y lo múltiple: esferas de justicia del federalismo educativo*. Academia Nacional de Educación.

Rivas, A. (2015). *América Latina después de PISA*. CIPPEC..

Rivas, A., & Dborkin, D. (2018). *¿Qué cambió en el financiamiento educativo en Argentina?* Discussion Paper No. 162. CIPPEC.

Rivas, A., & Sanchez, B. (2020). Race to the classroom: the governance turn in Latin American education. The emerging era of accountability, control, and prescribed curriculum. *Compare: A Journal of Comparative and International Education*. doi:10.1080/03057925.2020.1756745.

Rodríguez, L.G. (2017). "Cambiemos": la política educativa del macrismo. *Questión*, 1 (53), 89–108.

Ruiz, G. (2009). La nueva reforma educativa argentina según sus bases legales. *Revista de Educación*, 348, 283–307.

Scasso, M. (2018). ¿Cuántos jóvenes terminan la educación secundaria en la Argentina? Cómo monitorear las metas de universalización de la educación secundaria. *Propuesta Educativa*, 1(49), 32–47.

Steinberg, C., & Scasso, M. (2019). El acceso a la educación inicial en Argentina. In C. Steinberg & A. Cardini (Eds.), *Serie mapa de la educación inicial en Argentina*. UNICEF-CIPPEC.

Steinberg, C., Tiramonti, G., & Ziegler, S. (2019). *Políticas provinciales para transformar la escuela secundaria en la Argentina: avances de una agenda clave para los adolescentes en el siglo XXI*. UNICEF-FLACSO.

Svampa, M. (2007). Las fronteras del Gobierno de Kirchner: entre la consolidación de lo viejo y las aspiraciones de lo nuevo. *Cuadernos del Cendes*, 65, 39–61.

Tedesco, J.C., & Steinberg, C. (2015). Avanzar en las políticas de integración de TIC en la educación. In J.C. Tedesco (Ed.), *La educación argentina hoy: la urgencia del largo plazo*. Siglo XXI.

Terigi, F. (2016). *Políticas públicas en educación tras doce años de gobierno de Néstor Kirchner y Cristina Fernández*. Friederich Ebert Stiftung.

Terigi, F., Briscioli, B., Scavino, C., Morrone, A., & Toscano, A.G. (2013). La educación secundaria obligatoria en la Argentina: entre la expansión del modelo tradicional y las alternativas de baja escala. *Revista del IICE*, 33. doi:10.34096/riice.n33.1099.

UNICEF, CEDLAS & FCE/UBA. (2017). *Análisis y propuestas de mejora para ampliar la Asignación Universal por Hijo*. UNICEF, CEDLAS & FCE/UBA.

Veleda, C. (2013). *Nuevos tiempos para la educación primaria: lecciones sobre la extensión de la jornada escolar*. CIPPEC, UNICEF.

Veleda, C., Rivas, A., & Mezzadra, F. (2011). *La construcción de la justicia educativa*. CIPPEC, UNICEF y Embajada de Finlandia.

Veleda, C., Mezzadra, F., & Rivas, A. (2015). *10 propuestas para mejorar la educación en la Argentina*. Documento de Trabajo No. 134. CIPPEC.

Vera, A. (2015). Hacia una mayor institucionalidad en el financiamiento educativo de la educación argentina. In J.C. Tedesco (Ed.), *La educación argentina hoy: la urgencia del largo plazo*. Siglo XXI.

World Bank. (2020). *Argentina: panorama general*. Retrieved from www.bancomundial.org/es/country/argentina/overview.

Zacarias, I.G. (2018). La evaluación de la formación docente inicial en Argentina: la experiencia innovadora del dispositivo enseñar. *Revista Iberoamericana de Educación*, 77(1), 141–152.

Zukerfeld, M., & Benítez Larghi, S. (2015). *Flujos de conocimientos, tecnologías digitales y actores sociales en la educación secundaria: un análisis socio-técnico de las capas del Programa Conectar Igualdad*. Universidad Maimónides y Universidad Nacional de La Plata.

3 From Structural Reforms to Controversial Changes

The Education Policy Landscape in Brazil

Filipe Recch, Vinícius Baptista Soares Lopes and Lucas Hoogerbrugge

Introduction

Since the enactment of the 1988 Federal Constitution (CF-1988), Brazil has made great strides in education. This progress has been made mainly in terms of access to basic education,[1] but also in reducing the age-grade/year distortion and improving learning results, particularly in elementary education, focusing on the early years. While learning in the last years of elementary and secondary school also shows signs of improvement, it is still far below desired levels. For example, only two-thirds of youth under 19 complete secondary education,[2] an educational stage that is considered especially problematic in Brazil (Krawczyk, 2009). Those who do finish often do so with low academic outcomes, as evidenced by the standardized exams students take at the end of high school.

In order to better understand the current moment in Brazilian education, it is crucial to consider the Brazilian social context and the historical development of national and subnational education systems in the country – a history that is heavily marked by inequality and exclusion, with relevant educational reforms being implemented almost exclusively in the last century and predominantly only after the enactment of CF-1988 (Abrucio, 2010).

To that end, this chapter aims to describe the historical development of education policies in Brazil, focusing mainly on federal government initiatives that have, in one way or another, a national influence on basic education. This contextualization is a necessary step in understanding the broader backdrop of educational services against which Brazilian states and municipalities operate, which, in turn, helps in facilitating a complete understanding of the subnational success stories that comprise the backbone of the research presented in this chapter (Rivas et al., 2020).

Taking up the project outlined above, the present chapter delineates the broad contours of Brazilian education policy. The chapter focuses on the period since the enactment of the 1988 Federal Constitution (CF-1988), and more specifically on the period since the administration of President Fernando Henrique Cardoso (1995–2002), when national education policies acquired a more systematic structure, until 2020 when the COVID-19 pandemic had a significant impact on the provision of education all over the world.

DOI: 10.4324/9781003225782-3

From the Empire to the Fall of the Military Dictatorship: The Elite, National Developmentalism and Social Inequality

Marked inequalities among the most diverse social classes of the Brazilian population date back to at least the Portuguese Empire. Under the Empire, an educational model was conceptualized and implemented that privileged the country's economic elite, which was the only group permitted to pursue higher education (Moacyr, 1936). This model fomented and strengthened an elitist social mindset, which contributed to creating an advocacy coalition that held the privilege of higher education over other levels of education until at least 1988, when the universalization of education began to be implemented in the country.

The educational model established during the Empire was also responsible for the subsequent proliferation of overlapping educational networks, as more than one entity within the federation could offer the same educational level. However, as Abrucio (2010) affirms, this overlap in itself is not the principal problem. Instead, it is imperative to consider the lack of inter-entity coordination and cooperation toward common objectives. In combination with the elitist mindset that prevailed until at least 1988, this absence of coordination helped deepen socioeconomic inequalities and regional inequalities between the various federal entities.

As to subsequent periods, as far as the First Republic (1889–1930) is concerned, no significant change to the political or social status quo that had predominated since the Empire is worth highlighting as having altered Brazil's socioeconomic reality. The Vargas Era (1930–1945) saw the emergence of national developmentalism, which consolidated a pattern of development in Brazil by favoring economic policies over social ones. Such a model did not include any effective proposal to change the national social foundations. Instead, it reinforced the elitist educational mindset, focusing on preparing a small population for qualified access to the labor market. During the 20th century, these practices allowed Brazil to become one of the most industrialized nations on the planet, with one of the highest gross domestic products (GDP), despite the country's increasingly high economic and social inequality levels.

The Vargas Era was followed by the Democratic Interregnum (1946–1964), a period that did not significantly modify Brazil's educational model. On the contrary, the cooperative federalism that emerged along with re-democratization served more to reduce the federal government's interventions in individual states than it did to increase intergovernmental collaboration, focusing on improving and expanding educational coverage. Consequently, inequality among both federal entities and social classes has increased dramatically since the 1960s, as several scholars have shown in researching the relationship between socioeconomic inequality and education in Brazil (Fishlow, 1972; Langoni, 1973).

Under the military dictatorship (1964–1985) that followed the Democratic Interregnum, decision-making power was re-centralized in the hands of the federal government, with education policy decisions being taken in a "technocratic-authoritarian" style (Abrucio, 2010). One of the main initiatives implemented during the military regime was the reorganization of basic education to have eight years. However, the military regime generally followed the predominant trend of privileging higher education to the detriment of other educational levels. In that regard, the regime focused on expanding the number of available spots at universities, encouraging the creation of private higher education courses and establishing a national graduate study system.

Further, the authoritarianism of the military period proved to be effective in politically controlling the states and municipalities, which could do little to improve the quality of education in their respective territories. The national developmentalist project pushed full steam ahead, favoring economic development at the expense of social development and further cementing the country's socioeconomic inequalities even while the national economy experienced its highest growth rates.

The 1988 Federal Constitution and Education Rights: From Municipalities' Autonomy to Federal Recentralization

With the decline of the military dictatorship and under the motto of re-democratization, the desire to decentralize educational management has grown stronger, spurring wide-ranging debates about how to reorganize educational systems. This period was marked by a widespread desire for "deconcentration," above all as a way of fighting with the authoritarianism of the national executive in force during the military dictatorship. Social policies, including those concerning education, were no exception.

Efforts to formalize education rights in the 1988 Constitution were reflected in the decentralization of educational provision, wherein municipalities were made responsible for providing a significant portion of educational services. However, to do so, the states and municipalities needed to have the necessary resources to manage the educational networks under their responsibility. Article 212 of the 1988 Constitution represents a breakthrough in that regard by determining the financial amounts that each entity must allocate to education based on its revenues. In other words, the 1988 Constitution was concerned with delineating decentralized responsibilities regarding the educational provision and the means of financing such policies.

It should be noted that the Constitution was not intended to correct the duplication of networks providing the same levels of education that had existed since the Empire. For instance, the states and municipalities were designated partners in implementing elementary education. However, municipalities were tasked with managing pre-K education, while the states were tasked with overseeing primary and secondary education. The federal government[3] was in turn tasked with coordinating higher education, which the states could also offer. To encourage coordination and cooperation among the various entities, it was decided that the federal government should regulate the educational offering through binding measures that would apply to all states and municipalities. Further, the federal government was also responsible for redistributive and supplementary policies "in order to guarantee equal educational opportunities and a minimum standard of educational quality through technical and financial assistance to the states, the Federal District, and the municipalities" (Brasil, 1988, article 211).

The 1988 Constitution represents a considerable advance in education policies, especially in the form of the universalization of offerings and the deconstruction of the elitist mindset that relegated all educational levels outside of higher education to the background. However, the absence of federal coordination mechanisms meant that at least between 1988 and 1995 – a period in Brazil's history commonly referred to as "self-governed municipalism" – federal entities did not necessarily cooperate to achieve common objectives. In other words, in the early years of the newly created post-1988 democracy, there were no clear incentives to encourage cooperation among government entities, mainly due to the absence of mechanisms capable of coordinating educational offerings.

In response to such problems in the early post-1988 Constitution years, the federal government, and the federal executive in particular, under the prerogatives at its disposal as outlined in the Constitution (Arretche, 2013; Borges, 2013; Limongi, 2008), recognized that it was necessary to put an end to certain disputes among federal entities that did not contribute to the implementation of public policies. These public policies included those about organizing education in a more coordinated and cooperative manner.

To put it another way, within the framework of the constitutional prerogatives at its disposal, the federal government has managed to recover the leading role in creating and implementing policies in post-democratization Brazil. However, to do this, it was necessary to re-establish conditions like a certain (re)centralization of the federation so that the federal government might exercise its federative coordination function and promote cooperation among the federated entities (Abrucio, 2005; Almeida, 2005, 2007; Arretche, 2002, 2012).

In this context, and acknowledging the need to establish mechanisms capable of more efficiently regulating the provision of educational services, President Itamar Franco (1992–1994) and his Minister of Education, Murilo Hingel, gathered different sectors of the educational field to discuss proposals related to the creation of a regulatory framework capable of guiding the country's public education policies in the future.

Several third-sector academic institutions that represent education professionals (e.g. the *Confederação Nacional dos Trabalhadores em Educação* (CNTE)) or state and municipal education secretaries (e.g. the *Conselho Nacional de Secretários de Educação* (Consed) and the *União Nacional dos Dirigentes Municipais de Educação* (Undime)), as well as the advocacy and epistemic communities, participated in this process. This process can be considered the starting point of what, years later in 1996, during Fernando

Henrique Cardoso's first term in office (1995–1998), became the *Fundo de Manutenção e Desenvolvimento do Ensino Fundamental e de Valorização do Magistério* (FUNDEF) and the *Lei de Diretrizes e Bases da Educação Nacional*.

To sum up, with the enactment of the 1988 Federal Constitution, social policies in Brazil began to be primarily provided by subnational entities, and the education sector was no exception in this regard. Thus, municipalities and states became direct executors of educational policies, particularly in primary and secondary education. The federal government, for its part, took over the broader functions of organization and regulation of the country's general education programs in all their levels, stages and modalities. Under this new model, each of the 26 states, the Federal District (*Distrito Federal*, DF), and the 5,570 municipalities currently offer some level of basic education.

It is worth pointing out that each state and municipality in the country has a highly varied size, fiscal structure, institutional structure and path dependency, implying different capacities to provide educational services. There is also a territorial overlapping of municipalities and states, which creates the possibility that the same territory might offer similar educational services through more than one educational network.

Therefore, in order to present the principal education policies implemented from President Fernando Henrique Cardoso's 1995 inauguration to the present, we consider it analytically useful to subdivide these initiatives into two large groups: first, policies of broader scope that persist through several governmental administrations; and second, a group of more specific policies that are restricted to specific administrations and that tend to obtain more limited results. FUNDEF/FUNDEB[4] is exemplary of the first group, as initiated during Cardoso's first term in office, reformulated during the first Lula government (2003–2006), and made permanent in 2020, during the current (Bolsonaro) government, which assumed power in 2019. One initiative in the second group is the National Program for Access to Technical Education and Employment (PRONATEC), implemented during the Dilma Rousseff administration with the main objective of expanding educational offerings and access to professional and technological training courses, meaning that the federal government should support the states in this offering, especially from the technical and financial point of view.

The First Period of Structural Reforms: 1995–2002

In the education sector, the Cardoso governments (1995–1998 and 1999–2002) were characterized mainly by a restructuring of Brazil's public education programs. The CF-1988 started a new era in terms of standardization of social policies, which resulted in a burgeoning need to regulate the offering of several of these policies, including education, which needed, among other things, a more comprehensive definition of financing mechanisms and the decentralization of the educational offering. In addition, it was necessary to institutionalize a financing structure capable of satisfying the provision of educational services by the states and municipalities.

It was in this context that, eight years after the enactment of the CF-1988, the new National Education Guidelines and Framework Law of 1996[5] (LDB by its Portuguese initials) gained importance. This law comprehensively regulates the specific responsibilities of each federal entity concerning the provision of public education in the country. The document establishes a collaboration system between the federal government, the states, the Federal District and the municipalities as a fundamental principle of the organization's provision of public education services in Brazil. Regarding basic education, which includes early education (daycare and preschool – 0 to 6 years old), elementary education (first to ninth grade – 6 to 14 years old), and secondary education (tenth to twelfth grade – 15 to 17 years old),[6] the LDB establishes that the federal government must coordinate national education policy as well as directly organizing, maintaining and developing its educational system, especially for higher education. Apart from maintaining their respective educational systems, the states and the Federal District are also in charge of defining, along with the municipalities, the collaboration for the provision of elementary education, which both subnational levels of government will provide. In addition, the states and the Federal District are also primarily responsible for providing secondary education. Finally, the municipalities are mainly responsible for providing initial and elementary education.[7]

Even though the federal government is the central entity responsible for regulating primary education in Brazil, it provides almost no direct offering for basic education. Instead, the states and municipalities share responsibility for providing elementary education. Nowadays, most of the enrollment in elementary education is under the responsibility of municipal governments due to the decentralization process this stage of education has passed through since the 1990s.

It is essential to point out that the figures resulting from the INEP school census show significant variation among states and municipalities in the provision of elementary education. In Ceará, for instance, more than 90% of elementary education enrollment is in municipal networks. On the other hand, in Minas Gerais, two-thirds of the enrollments in the last years of elementary education (sixth to ninth grade) are in the state-run system. The reverse is true for the first years of elementary education in Minas Gerais, in which two-thirds of enrollment is in the municipal networks.

Brazil's states and municipalities present a heterogeneous political-institutional scenario, with a large part that is very administratively fragile (Abrúcio et al., 2018), contributing to diverse quality standards in the provision of educational services around the country. There was no policy to reduce inequalities in the capacities of subnational entities that went hand in hand with decentralizing enrollment to states and municipalities (Segatto & Abrúcio, 2016).

Moreover, the decentralization of primary and elementary education offerings was very intense. This was partly due to the constitutional mandate itself, but also due to the existence of recently created financial incentives, which promoted the expansion of resources for the states and municipalities, especially from the implementation of the *Fundo de Manutenção e Desenvolvimento do Ensino Fundamental e de Valorização do Magistério* (FUNDEF), in 1996, and its subsequent updating, through the *Fundo de Manutenção e Desenvolvimento da Educação Básica e de Valorização dos Profissionais da Educação* (FUNDEB), in 2006. However, due to the lack of reliable mechanisms to articulate the federative pact in education, the decentralization stimulated by financial mechanisms took place in an uncoordinated fashion. Added to each educational network's historical trajectories and conditions, this resulted in a heterogeneous panorama concerning enrollment levels between states and municipalities, in elementary education and the state capacities of the federative entities.

In practice, this meant that, through complementary and redistributive programs, the Cardoso administration defined more objective criteria for allocating resources among the federation's various entities, encouraging the states and municipalities to achieve their objectives. FUNDEF established that many state and municipal resources allocated to education should be redistributed according to the total number of enrollments in each educational network. As a result, municipalities have assumed more and more responsibilities in providing educational services, especially in elementary education. FUNDEF also established that the federal government should financially supplement those states that cannot reach a certain level of investment per student per year. The first results produced by FUNDEF and the other instruments used by the federal government to re-balance the federal education pact show that these initiatives were successful in ensuring the deepening of the municipalization of elementary education and increasing educational coverage overall.

Another relevant event during the Cardoso administration was the development of the national educational evaluation system, concentrated in the *Instituto Nacional de Estudos e Pesquisas Educacionais Anísio Teixeira* (INEP). During this period, the *Sistema de Avaliação da Educação Básica* (SAEB) was strengthened and the *Exame Nacional do Ensino Médio* (ENEM) was created in 1998. The indicators and the systematic supervision of educational data carried out by INEP would serve as the basis for creating, after a few years, the Basic Education Development Index (IDEB). From the point of view of large-scale evaluations, the IDEB centers the quality of Brazilian educational systems in the debate, at all levels of the federation, "not only... teaching and management processes, but mainly... students' learning and school trajectory" (Soares & Xavier, 2013, p. 904).

By setting performance targets for all schools and all educational networks, IDEB focuses on the centrality of educational evaluation, though this indicator is also subject to criticism (Soares & Xavier, 2013). Nevertheless, it is vital to recognize a gap between the definition of these objectives by the federal government and the implementation of educational policy. In Brazil, both states and municipalities have autonomy in creating and implementing education policies within their networks. In some subnational cases, standardized assessments were used to create incentive mechanisms to improve learning. However, this was not carried out systematically and was not even encouraged by the Ministry of Education.

As such, we can consider FUNDEF, the 1996 National Education Guidelines and Framework Law, and SAEB as the most critical milestones in the country's education policy. They show more significant and consolidated support from the federal government for subnational entities, especially during and after the Cardoso administrations, having been continued and/or perfected during the administrations of Luiz Inácio Lula da Silva (Segatto, 2015).

Another nationwide initiative, also developed during Cardoso's first administration (1995–1998), is the 1995 Direct Money in School Program (Programa Dinheiro Direto na Escola, PDDE). Generally speaking, the PDDE transfers financial resources directly to schools. Though the program has changed since its creation, the basic mechanism has been maintained. The program is currently divided into three axes: PDDE Integral, PDDE Structure and PDDE Quality.

On the one hand, the PDDE is considered by some critics to be a program that harms the autonomous self-governance of states and municipalities, seeing as the federal government transfers financial resources directly to schools, thereby overriding state and municipal governments. On the other hand, the program is considered very innovative. It allows schools to directly manage the allocated resources, making their allocation more flexible and making it possible for their application to be more relevant to local demands. Currently, states and municipalities with greater technical capacity replicate programs such as the PDDE in their administrations.

In enrollment expansion, which occurred mainly due to the compulsory elementary education outlined in the CF-1988, the greater participation of municipalities in the provision of basic education was not homogeneous among the federated entities nor linear over the years. Due to different political and historical circumstances, states and municipalities have organized themselves differently and have chosen to follow, more or less intentionally, different paths in providing educational services.

For instance, in some states, such as Ceará and Maranhão, the initial years of elementary education are offered almost entirely by the municipalities. In contrast, other states, such as Roraima, Paraná and Amapá, have chosen to operate this stage mainly through the state system. A third case, which has been a reality for most states in the country, is a co-participation in the offering of enrollment in elementary education.

Understanding this diversity in the enrollment offerings in each state is key to understanding the Brazilian educational system. In addition, the high rates of municipalization require that municipalities have a higher capacity to manage their educational networks.

Considered a reformist period in which legislation, evaluation systems and financing were restructured, the Cardoso administration was echoed in subsequent administrations. However, many of its initiatives were maintained and/or improved during the Lula administration, as outlined in the next section of this chapter.

The New Era of Structural Reforms: 2003–2010

Luiz Inácio Lula da Silva's administrations were characterized by valuing diversity and inclusion in the educational sector (Moehlecke, 2009; Rebelo, 2016). However, it is not necessarily possible to specify substantive differences between the policies implemented during Fernando Henrique Cardoso's administrations and Lula's (Oliveira, 2009).

Recognizing the successes of FUNDEF and other education policy coordination mechanisms, the Lula administrations not only continued with the initiatives implemented during the Cardoso years but also substantially expanded them, especially with the creation of the *Fundo de Manutenção e Desenvolvimento da Educação Básica e de Valorização dos Profissionais da Educação* (FUNDEB), which extended FUNDEF to early childhood and secondary education. Further, the Lula administration continued to improve the criteria for perfecting the allocation of resources among the federation's various entities and using indicators to measure student performance. The success achieved by these funding models has turned FUNDEB – and, before that, FUNDEF – into the primary funding mechanism for public education in Brazil. Although FUNDEB comprises state accounting funds and most of the resources come from the states and municipalities, the federal government must supplement the resources in states where the minimum amount per student is not reached. The program thereby plays a vital role in reducing inequality in education financing.

In 2003, the LDB was modified to incorporate the compulsory teaching of Afro-Brazilian history and culture in elementary and middle school regarding inclusion and diversity policies. Within the Ministry of Education (MEC), the *Secretaria de Educação Continuada, Alfabetização e Diversidade* (SECADI) was created in 2004 to encourage the articulation of policies aimed at diversity in education.

Later, in 2006, Law No. 11.274 was enacted, amending the LDB by extending elementary education from eight to nine years, with compulsory enrollment starting at age six. This was a first step in expanding compulsory education, a process that was later further consolidated through Emenda Constitucional (Constitutional Amendment) No. 59 (EC No. 59) in 2009, which established compulsory schooling for all children from 4 to 5 years old, as well as compulsory education up to 17 years old, an initiative that was to be implemented by 2016. Thus, the ages for which enrollment in basic education was compulsory – previously 6 to 14 years old – were extended to include all ages from 4 to 17. In other words, EC No. 59 expanded the scope of public authorities' obligation in the provision of essential education services, especially in early childhood education and secondary education.

By way of EC No. 59, the need for the federal government, the states, the Federal District and the municipalities to define forms of collaboration in the organization of their educational systems was also included in the Magna Carta. In theory, this mechanism would help the national coordination of education. In practice, however, the initiative has thus far not been duly regulated. This lack of regulation contributes to a certain disarticulation of actions between the different levels of government and the continuation of various educational inequities, either in terms of the level of an offer or, primarily, in terms of the quality of educational services provided by the states and municipalities.

Recognizing the need to foster cooperation among all federated entities for the proper provision of educational services, the *Plano de Desenvolvimento da Educação* (PDE) was created in 2007 as a mechanism to create an integrated plan among municipalities, states and the federal government. The actions of the PDE are materialized in the *Plano de Ações Articuladas* (PAR), which encourages the federated entities to carry out a situational diagnosis and, based on the reality uncovered, to plan an education policy in a more focused and assertive way, aimed at obtaining financial resources from the Ministry of Education. However, due to the lack of provisions to regulate the instances of agreement and an effective governance structure among the different levels of government, the federal executive branch has adopted financial incentives as the primary strategy to obtain the cooperation of the other levels.

In addition to technical difficulties and federative coordination, education financing continued to challenge the government. Therefore, in 2006, FUNDEF was reformulated as FUNDEB, establishing new rules to reallocate educational resources. Furthermore, in line with the enactment of EC No. 59, FUNDEB also includes elementary and high school education.

After the implementation of FUNDEF and FUNDEB, the equity of funding among the federative entities improved significantly. The inequality of investment per student between municipalities with varying resource levels went from 13,800% before FUNDEB to 570% after its implementation. Nevertheless, even with the increase in FUNDEF and FUNDEB participation, inequality is still considerable. The federal government's contribution to basic education has remained small compared to the contribution of states and municipalities, especially considering the Brazilian tax structure, which gives the federal government greater collection power and, therefore, greater fiscal capacity (UNDIME, 2016).

Finally, it is essential to mention the National Education Conference (CONAE), held at the end of President Lula's second administration in 2010. Out of which was born a proposal to institutionalize the National Education Plan (PNE by its Portuguese acronym). It was sent to the National Congress in December of that year and lasted until 2014, at the end of President Dilma Rousseff's first administration.[8]

Due to the success of the Lula administration – especially in economic and social policies – and Lula's considerably high approval rating at the end of his second administration, Lula's party (Partido dos Trabalhadores, or PT) was able to get its candidate elected despite fierce competition between the primary candidates for the presidency. As a result, his successor, Dilma Rouseff, would be the first woman to head Brazil's executive branch.

The Period of Instability: 2011–2016

The Dilma Rousseff administrations (2011–2016) continued developing inclusion and cultural diversity policies, primarily through the actions prepared, implemented and coordinated by SECADI, which took over control of the Special Education Office in 2011. Furthermore, along with the proposals arising from the 2010 CONAE mentioned above, the federal government created the *Secretaria de Articulação com os Sistemas de Ensino* (SASE) in 2011, whose main objective was to foster cooperation among the federative entities and coordinate proposals related to the institution of the National Education System. Unfortunately, this demand has not yet been met, although it is recognized in articles 23 and 211 of the CF-1988.

Two concrete policies concerning education implemented during Dilma Rouseff's administration deserve particular mention. First is the National Pact for Literacy at the Right Age (PNAIC by its acronym in Portuguese), which aimed to train and support educators focusing on literacy for children up to the age of 8. Second is the Innovative Program for Secondary Education (PROEMI by its acronym in Portuguese), which aimed to expand daily classroom hours and make the high school curriculum more flexible. These were in line with the high school reform proposal and the National Program for Access to Technical Education and Employment (PRONATEC by its acronym in Portuguese), which sought to expand vocational and technological education.

Finally, after her first administration, President Dilma Rousseff set the National Education Plan (NEP) (2014–2024) in motion, established by Law 13.005 of June 25, 2014, after a long process in the National Congress (2011–2014). According to Lopes (2021), the NEP

> can be considered the main initiative effectively aimed at transforming the Brazilian educational reality. It contemplates actions ranging from initial education to higher education, going through the three layers of government, levels, stages, and modalities of education, and includes actions aimed at both teachers and other education professionals and stipulating budgetary resources to finance all these initiatives. The current PNE also stipulates that all government levels, in collaboration, (re)elaborate their respective Educational Plans within one year from the enactment of the national law.
>
> (Lopes, 2021, p. 46)

President Dilma Rousseff's administration was characterized by political turbulence, as evidenced by the constant changes in the Ministry of Education, which had five ministers during this period. The leadership turnover in the sector probably made it difficult to expand and consolidate policies aimed at basic education, especially in Dilma's second term, when Brazil's political and economic crisis worsened. Although the policies sought to induce certain behaviors in subnational entities to improve results in primary education, a portion of them generated overlapping policies and poor results (Almeida et al., 2016; Schwartzman, 2016; Segatto & Abrúcio, 2016). In 2016, under the pressure of the political crisis and low economic growth (Bastos, 2017), Dilma was impeached and subsequently replaced by her vice president, Michel Temer.

The Period of Controversial Reforms: 2016–2020

The Temer administration (2016–2019) was characterized by adopting controversial education policies with profound repercussions on Brazil's educational system. For example, Constitutional Amendment No. 95 (EC 95) was approved in late 2016 and linked, for 20 years, the growth of public spending and investment to the Broad National Consumer Price Index (IPCA by its Portuguese acronym), the official index used by the government as a measure of inflation in the country.

Critics point out that this measure is in direct conflict with the goals outlined in the NEP (Amaral, 2017) and makes it difficult, for instance, to reach 10% of GDP invested in education by 2024. Others point out that the Amendment will allow balancing public accounts and, therefore, the sustainability of public policies.

Another controversial measure was the implementation of the High School Reform through a provisional measure (PM). The debate on the reformulation of the parameters the LDB had established for high school in Brazil had already been part of the educational policy agenda since at least 2007 (Júnior et al., 2018), and all attempts to pass a relevant bill in the National Congress had been unsuccessful. However, the ultimate implementation of the reform without the prior approval of the National Congress generated a great deal of debate in the Brazilian educational community. Among the main changes instituted by the High School Reform were an increased high school workload and the flexibilization of the high school curriculum to allow for the implementation of training itineraries – different from the curriculum model that the country had adopted until then.

Finally, the *Base Nacional Comum Curricular* (BNCC) was also approved during the Temer administration, initially only for elementary education (2016) but eventually also extending to secondary education (2018). The BNCC defines competencies, skills and learning outcomes for each stage of basic education, which serve as parameters for revising teaching materials, external evaluations and the initial and continual training of teaching professionals. Therefore, they are policies that likely have broad and profound effects on the organization of the Brazilian education policy.

In 2019, Jair Bolsonaro took over the presidency of Brazil and established a conservative turn in Brazilian politics. The educational policies adopted followed this conservative bent. For instance, the dissolution of SECADI diminished the visibility and importance of policies targeted at minorities. However, it is also important to point out that the Ministry of Education under Bolsonaro has been strongly marked by instability. In just two years, four ministers have been in charge.

In addition to a politically turbulent context, with a high turnover of ministers and management marked by ideological controversies, the MEC has also been criticized for its ineffectiveness and low-budget execution. During this period, the government has engaged in little dialogue and has distanced itself from supporting state and municipal educational networks. This situation was marked in Bolsonaro's first year in office when an External Monitoring Commission of the MEC was established within the Chamber of Deputies. It became even more marked with the outbreak of the Coronavirus pandemic in March 2020.

In the context of a weakening and increasingly apathetic Ministry of Education, the National Congress assumed leadership of reform programs. In 2020, FUNDEB became permanent, thus ceasing to appear in the CF-1988 as a transitory provision and expanding its redistributive capacity. In 2020, the federal government was responsible for supplementing 10% of the fund's value; as of 2021, this value is progressively increasing and is forecasted to reach 23% by 2026. FUNDEB, as we have tried to show throughout this chapter, is one of the country's milestones in the decentralization of basic educational offerings and, due to its solid redistributive bias, in standardizing the level of funding for education across states and municipalities.

Additionally, a set of incentive mechanisms to improve educational results were introduced into FUNDEB by Constitutional Amendment 108/2020, earmarking part of the federal government's contribution to go toward improving results (2.5%) and expanding the possibility for states to redirect part of their fiscal transfers to municipalities based on improved learning.

Finally, it is essential to point out that, at the time of writing, most of the country's educational networks have suspended face-to-face classes due to restrictions taken in reaction to the Coronavirus pandemic. Although several municipalities and states have found ways to mitigate the damage caused by school closures, many subnational entities have not been able to plan adequately. However, in the face of this, the federal government has not mobilized to support states and municipalities, instead claiming that decisions surrounding how to address the pandemic are the responsibility of governors and mayors. A collateral effect of this has been that the lack of consolidated data from the Ministry of Education about schools in the subnational entities prevents a more in-depth analysis of the present situation.

Conclusions

The Brazilian educational system has witnessed a series of achievements in educational indicators over the years. However, several of those indicators still fall short of what the educational legislation indicates and what would be desirable to guarantee the right to quality education. While access rates have steadily improved at all levels of schooling, learning rates have progressed differently at each stage, implying a still poor and very unequal outcome, especially when comparing between regions and when considering socioeconomic indicators.

In many cases, the unsatisfactory and unequal results of basic education in Brazil have a close relationship with the socioeconomic context of families (Alves & Soares, 2007; Soares & Collares, 2006), although they are also a direct consequence of the low quality of the education offered, especially in middle school. Furthermore, factors such as low learning achievement and high failure rates directly affect student motivation to stay in school and impair their schooling trajectory, especially in the last stage of basic education, with consequences for young people's chances of enjoying a better future.

In their paper on intra-state differences in Brazil, Carnoy et al. (2017), for instance, found that improvements in the performance of ninth-grade students vary considerably across the 27 units of the federation. However, among the states that have shown remarkable improvements, there are various socio-economic and demographic profiles, with diverse historical trajectories and educational policy choices leading to good indicators.

Although some elements are specific to each of these cases, several joint initiatives deserve to be studied and analyzed as critical elements that contributed decisively to the success of these educational networks in providing quality education. Elsewhere, we highlight the education policies implemented in the municipality of Sobral in Ceará and the policies implemented in the states of Ceará and Pernambuco (Rivas & Scasso, 2020). The most outstanding initiatives include actions from the first years of elementary school to middle school. Several successful experiences in the country should be investigated thoroughly so that specific options can be better understood. In addition, such successful examples can inspire and inform other educational networks, both at state and municipal levels.

In short, the history of basic education in Brazil is recent. The main advances were only really seen after the Federal Constitution of 1988 and, more precisely, after the National Education Guidelines and Framework Law (LDB) of 1996. The country has generally moved from a more centralized model that focused on the elites and had little scope to a more decentralized model that provides greater autonomy and greater scope (Abrucio, 2010).

Among the main factors contributing to explaining this increase in the population's schooling is the demographic transition resulting from the fall in birth rates between the 1960s and 1990s. Additional principal factors include the following, as by pointed out by Menezes-Filho & Kirschbaum (2015): (1) the decentralization of prerogatives related to the management of educational policies; (2) the decentralization of resources allocated to education; (3) the creation of the Fund for the Maintenance and Development of Basic Education and the Valorization of Teaching (FUNDEF) and, subsequently, the Fund for the Maintenance and Development of Basic Education and the Valorization of Education Professionals (FUNDEB), funds that transferred resources from wealthier municipalities with few students to poorer municipalities with many students; (4) the *Bolsa Escola* and later *Bolsa Família* programs; and finally (5) the Continuous Progress Policies, which were decisive in reducing drop-out and abandonment rates.

However, despite this developing scenario, and although access to fundamental and secondary education has improved considerably since the 1990s, there are still significant differences in completion rates and the quality of education offered, especially considering the striking socioeconomic disparities in Brazil (OECD, 2016).

Suppose that the elitist, authoritarian and national-developmentalist legacies are present in our contemporary democratic history. In that case, there should also be efforts to minimize the perverse consequences of such legacies, especially concerning the inequalities still so marked among Brazil's regions and the quality of education offered to our children and young people. Dos Reis & De Barros (1991) suggested that investing in education policies more focused on the less favored population is essential if we aim to have a society increasingly less based on positions of privilege. The 1988 Constitution started a new era in terms of social rights in Brazil, notwithstanding the educational challenges that remain tremendously notable.

Notes

1 In Brazil, basic education comprises 12 years of schooling. Elementary education comprises the years of basic education that range from 1 to 9 years.
2 IBGE Historical series and statistics (https://seriesestatisticas.ibge.gov.br/) and INEP (www.gov.br/inep/pt-br/areas-de-atuacao/avaliacao-e-exames-educacionais/saeb/resultados).
3 The political-administrative organization of the Federative Republic of Brazil comprises the federal government, the states, the federal district and the municipalities, which are self-governed under the terms of the 1988 Constitution.
4 Fundo para Manutenção e Desenvolvimento do Ensino Fundamental e Valorização do Magistério (FUNDEF) and Fundo de Manutenção e Desenvolvimento da Educação Básica e de Valorização dos Profissionais da Educação (FUNDEB).
5 National Education Guidelines and Framework Law; law number 9.394 passed on December 20, 1996.
6 These ages correspond to those considered ideal for attending a particular level/stage of education.
7 Articles 8 to 11 of the LDB set forth these functions of the federated entities.
8 Regarding the history of National Education Plans in Brazil, it is essential to highlight that during the administration of President Cardoso, the first National Education Plan was instituted and effectively became law in the country. However, as the presidency of the republic vetoed several of the provisions contained in that PNE, including the financing objective (Sena, 2014), the elaboration of the Plan was not accompanied by an effective implementation structure, so the document ended up being a "letter of intent" (Sena, 2014; Sguissardi, 2006; Valente & Romano, 2002).

References

Abrucio, F.L. (2005). A coordenação federativa no Brasil: a experiência do período FHC e os desafios do governo Lula. *Revista de Sociologia e Política, 24,* 41–67.
Abrucio, F.L. (2010). A dinâmica federativa da educação brasileira: diagnóstico e propostas de aperfeiçoamento. In *Educação e federalismo no Brasil: combater as desigualdades, garantir a diversidade.* UNESCO.

Abrucio, F.L., Seggatto, C.I., & Pereira, M.C.G. (2016). *Regime de Colaboração no Ceará: funcionamento, causas do sucesso e alternativas de disseminação do modelo*. Instituto Natura.
Almeida, M.H.T. (2005). Recentralizando a Federação? *Revista de Sociologia e Política*, 24, 29–40.
Almeida, M.H.T. (2007). O Estado no Brasil contemporâneo: um passeio pela história. *Melo CR, Sáez MA, organizadores. A democracia brasileira: balanço e perspectivas para o século*, 21, 17–34.
Alves, M.T.G., & Soares, J.F. (2007). As pesquisas sobre o efeito das escolas: contribuições metodológicas para a sociologia da educação. *Sociedade e Estado*, 22(2), 435–473.
Arretche, M. (2002). Relações federativas nas políticas sociais. *Educação & Sociedade*, 23(80), 25–48.
Arretche, M. (2004). Federalismo e políticas sociais no Brasil: problemas de coordenação e autonomia. *São Paulo em Perspectiva*, 18(2), 17–26.
Arretche, M. (2009). Continuidades e descontinuidades da federação brasileira: de como 1988 facilitou 1995. *Dados*, 52(2), 377–423.
Arretche, M. (2012). *Democracia, federalismo e centralização no Brasil*. SciELO-Editora FIOCRUZ.
Arretche, M. (2013). Quando instituições federativas fortalecem o governo central? *Novos Estudos CEBRAP*, 95, 39–57.
Borges, A. (2013). Eleições presidenciais, federalismo e política social. *Revista Brasileira de Ciências Sociais*, 28(81), 117–136.
Brasil, S.F. (1988). *Constituição da república federativa do Brasil*. Senado Federal, Centro Gráfico.
Carnoy, M., Marotta, L., Louzano, P., Khavenson, T., Guimarães, F.R.F., & Carnauba, F. (2017). Intranational comparative education: what state differences in student achievement can teach us about improving education—the case of Brazil. *Comparative Education Review*, 61(4), 726–759.
Dos Reis, J.G.A., & De Barros, R.P. (1991). Wage inequality and the distribution of education: a study of the evolution of regional differences in inequality in metropolitan Brazil. *Journal of Development Economics*, 36(1), 117–143.
Fishlow, A. (1972). Brazilian size distribution of income. *The American Economic Review*, 62(1/2), 391–402.
Hochman, G., & de Faria, C.A.P. (Eds.) (2013). *Federalismo e políticas públicas no Brasil*. SciELO-Editora FIOCRUZ.
Instituto Nacional de Estudos e Pesquisas Educacionais Anísio Teixeira (INEP). (2020). *Relatório do 3o ciclo de monitoramento das metas do Plano Nacional de Educação*. INEP.
Krawczyk, N. (2011). Reflexão sobre alguns desafios do ensino médio no Brasil hoje. *Cadernos de pesquisa*, 41(144), 752–769.
Langoni, C.G. (1973). *Distribuição de renda e desenvolvimento econômico no Brasil*. Expressão e Cultura.
Limogni, F. (2008). O poder executivo na Constituição de 1988. In R.G. Oiven, M. Ridenti & G.M. Brandão (Eds.), *A Constituição de 1988 na Vida Brasileira*. Aderaldo & Rothschild, Anpocs.
Lopes, V.B. (2021). *Financiamento e cooperação de políticas educacionais no Brasil: o processo de implementação do Plano Nacional de Educação entre 2015 e 2020*. Tese de Doutorado, Departamento de Ciência Política, UFMG – no prelo.

Menezes Filho, N., & Kirschbaum, C. (2015). Educação e desigualdade no Brasil. *Trajetórias das desigualdades: como o Brasil mudou nos últimos*, 50, 309–334.
Moehlecke, S. (2009). As políticas de diversidade na educação no governo Lula. *Cadernos de Pesquisa*, 39(137), 461–487.
Oliveira, D.A. (2009). As políticas educacionais no governo Lula: rupturas e permanências. *Revista Brasileira de Política e Administração da Educação-Periódico científico editado pela ANPAE*, 25(2), 197–209.
Palgrave Macmillan. (2016). Organisation for Economic Co-operation and Development (OECD). In *The Statesman's Yearbook: The Politics, Cultures, and Economies of the World 2017*. Palgrave Macmillan.
Rebelo, A.S. (2016). Política de inclusão escolar no Brasil (2003–2010). *Journal of Research in Special Educational Needs*, 16, 851–854.
Rivas, A. et al. (2020). *"Keys to education." Estudio comparado sobre la mejora de los sistemas educativos subnacionales en América Latina*. Fundación Santillana.
Segatto, C.I., & Abrucio, F.L. (2016). A cooperação em uma federação heterogênea: o regime de colaboração na educação em seis estados brasileiros. *Revista Brasileira de Educação*, 21(65), 411–429.
Sena, P. (2014). A história do PNE e os desafios da nova lei. *Plano Nacional de Educação*, 2024, 9–42.
Sguissardi, V. (2006). Preface. In C. Brandão (Ed.), *PNE passo a passo: Lei no 10.172/2001, discussão dos objetivos e metas do Plano Nacional de Educação*. Avercamp.
Soares, J.F., & Collares, A.C.M. (2006). Recursos familiares e o desempenho cognitivo dos alunos do ensino básico brasileiro. *Dados*, 49(3), 615–650.
Soares, J.F., & Xavier, F.P. (2013). Pressupostos educacionais e estatísticos do Ideb. *Educação & Sociedade*, 34(124), 903–923.
UNDIME (2016). *Orientações ao Dirigente Municipal de Educação: Fundamentos, Políticas e Práticas*. Fundação Santillana.
Valente, I., & Romano, R. (2002). PNE: Plano Nacional de Educação ou carta de intenção? *Educação & Sociedade*, 23(80), 96–107.

4 Educational Policies in Chile

Between the State, the Market and Accountability based on Academic Achievement Tests

Cristian Bellei and Gonzalo Muñoz

Historically, education in Chile had a slow and uneven development. Even though it was established in the Constitution of 1833 – "public education is a preferential awareness of the Government" – the educational impulse was weak. Only in the mid-19th century was it possible to speak of the beginning of the construction of an education system, with the founding of the Universidad de Chile and the Escuela Normal de Preceptores, both in 1842. Then, in 1860, the Law of Primary Instruction established the state's responsibility to provide free education to the population through public and municipal schools, recognizing, in addition – under the principle of freedom of education – the legitimacy of private schools, some of which it began to support financially at an early stage. Since that decade, the public education in Chile served the highest number of children. However, over the years, the percentage of the population attending public schools has consistently decreased, especially the upper and middle sectors of the cities (Bellei & Pérez, 2010; Núñez, 2015).

From this fragile institutional base, the national state began to expand its educational work, displacing both the municipalities, the Catholic Church and other private groups, which showed no great interest in the education of the masses and concentrated on the elites. Public senior high schools usually served lower income students, and private schools trained the upper and middle classes in urban areas, who then attended university or worked in administrative positions. Primary schools and trade schools provided literacy and mathematics and job training for the popular sectors and the working class, mainly in urban areas. In the countryside, illiteracy was the norm. Although growing in coverage, this institutionalized socio-educational segmentation scheme lasted until the twentieth century, when the educational reform of 1965 put an end to it (Bellei & Pérez, 2016).

The administration of this "Teaching State" – a concept that synthesizes the idea of a state that assumes the responsibility, steering role and, to a large extent, the provision of educational services – was increasingly centralized, bureaucratic and highly hierarchical (Núñez, 1984). Its institutional consolidation was achieved in the second decade of the 20th century with the Ministry of Education (Mineduc) creation in 1927, which concentrated the

DOI: 10.4324/9781003225782-4

school system's regulatory, curricular, supervisory, administrative and financial functions. The organization of the Mineduc at the central level decided on school administration, including the hiring of directors and teachers. This centralism was strengthened with quantitative growth until it became a technical, bureaucratic system challenging to manage. In addition, the enormous boost to democratize access to secondary education and to combat school drop-out in primary education, initiated in the 1965 reform and continued until the military coup of 1973, brought the public education system to its maximum historical expression (Núñez, 1984).

A defining feature of the historical development of Chilean education was that the state directly took over the provision of educational services, which were legally guaranteed to the population and provided free of charge as a right and an obligation. For the state, public education had an irreplaceable value within the republican, democratic and developmentalist projects, depending on the historical period in question (Bellei & Pérez, 2010). At an early stage, the state guaranteed freedom of education by recognizing private education and even promoting the education system's diverse nature by providing it with financing, although always within a scheme with an unequivocal hegemony of the public system. Thus, until the advent of the dictatorship in the last quarter of the 20th century, both financial resources and educational policies were fundamentally oriented towards expanding and consolidating public education.

As part of a broader economic, political and social reform process, the civil-military dictatorship (1973–1989) implemented an educational reform that substantially modified the two defining features that characterized Chilean educational development during most of the 19th and 20th centuries. Firstly, the supremacy of public education over private education and, secondly, the direct role of the national state in the provision of such public education. Ideologically, it was about replacing the *teaching state* with the idea of the *educational market*, inspired by economic neoliberalism.

Essentially, the neoliberal reform sought to introduce market dynamics to regulate the provision of education in Chile (Bellei, 2015; Jofré, 1988; Prieto, 1983). To this end, the financing system was modified, creating a *demand subsidy* procedure (a *voucher*, which was delivered to school owners directly and not to families) consisting of a monthly per capita payment from the state to educational providers (called *sustainers*). To receive the subsidies, students had to effectively attend the educational institutions. This subsidy was the same in amount and payment method for both public and private institutions, without distinguishing between for-profit and non-profit providers. In practice, this reform created the third sector of schools. Along with public (municipal) and private schools financed exclusively through fees charged to families (concentrated in the upper class), subsidized private education (i.e. private property with public financing) was institutionalized. The idea was that schools would compete for families' preferences expressed in the enrollment of their children. Having the subsidy as the only funding for schools, teachers, school principals and *sustainers* would feel the pressure of competition to maintain their jobs and sources of income, which would lead them to improve the educational service to satisfy families and ensure the viability of the school (Prieto, 1983).

To produce a dynamic educational market, the requirements for private providers to establish schools and access state funding were minimized (Jofré, 1988). The academic curriculum and teachers' labor laws were also made more flexible. A universal and mandatory learning achievement evaluation system was created (first called PER and then SIMCE). The results of the tests would be published in the form of school rankings so that families could compare the *quality* of the educational service offered by different schools. However, it did not become effective until the middle of the following decade. Technically, families could choose any educational institution (regardless of residence), although they were not obliged to accept their children even if they had vacancies. Moreover, schools (mainly private, but also some public) began to implement selection mechanisms during the admission process, making demands on families (e.g. parents married in the Church or baptized children), and applying academic requirements to students (e.g. using selection tests, or demanding a particular prior performance) (Contreras et al., 2010).

According to its promoters, the municipalization of public education distanced the Ministry of Education from education provision, thus facilitating local competition for enrollment. In addition, it allowed for more efficient management of resources by reducing the bureaucracy of educational administration, bringing it closer to the educational institutions, and governing the administration by rules different from those of the public system. (Nuñez, 1984; Prieto, 1983). Thus, personnel working conditions in the schools were regulated by the Labor Code. Due to this change, teachers lost the rights and benefits they had had as public servants, protected by an ad hoc labor statute. It also sought to reduce the power of the central state (an objective common to the rest of the reforms in the other fields mentioned above), breaking it up and thus limiting its influence in the educational field. Municipalization implied a severe change in the working and contractual conditions of teachers. Finally, most municipalities did not have the professional capacities to take charge of the complex educational administration, which weakened school management (Espíndola, 1992).

After the end of the dictatorship, the democratic governments that began in 1990 implemented a growing and ambitious agenda of educational policies. In some respects, this agenda was a continuation of the reforms and the institutional framework created in the 1980s, while in others, the new policies proposed change and innovation. Fundamentally, thorough institutional reforms were not favored, nor was there any attempt to reverse the structural changes of the previous decade. Instead, efforts were concentrated on improving the substantive processes of education, with a focus on equity.

Democratic governments tried to improve market dynamics and complement them with compensatory and systematic development actions promoted by the state (Bellei & Vanni, 2015). For example, in this first axis of policies, learning assessments increased, and their results were published to inform families when choosing schools. Besides, family fees were encouraged, promoting "shared financing" that allowed private providers (and municipalities only in high schools) to charge regulated fees without ceasing to receive the state subsidy. Moreover, to make the financing system more equitable and to increase competition for students from more impoverished families, the value of the state subsidy for students of lower socioeconomic status increased through the creation of the *"Subvención Escolar Preferencial"* (Preferential School Voucher). Generally, democratic governments adopted the principle of *equal treatment* for public and private, for-profit and non-profit providers. Although the share of public education in national enrollment continued to fall (mainly since the second half of the 1990s) to reach historic lows, turning Chile into one of the most privatized education systems in the world, to reverse this situation was never defined as an educational policy objective.

On a second axis, the democratic governments were even more active, implementing an impressive battery of educational policies that can be classified into three groups (Cox, 2003; García-Huidobro, 1999). First, by applying a wide variety of *educational improvement programs* located in the schools, which aimed to improve pedagogical processes and professionally develop teachers by introducing didactic innovations, various forms of collective teaching work and complementary training activities for students (e.g. P-900, MECE-Basic, MECE-Rural, MECE-High School, Enlaces – Links, in Spanish). Second, improving the teaching-learning processes, making significant investments in infrastructure, providing didactic materials, textbooks, computer laboratories, libraries and significantly expanding the available school time by implementing the *entire school day*. It is important to note that these two policy lines contained different equity devices, favoring schools that taught students of lower socioeconomic status, regardless of whether they were public or private schools. The third policy line was a major curricular reform of preschool, elementary school and secondary school education, which involved updating study plans and programs, together with a massive teacher training process.

According to its promoters, the combination of market dynamics that pressured schools and high schools to compete and be efficient (based on better material conditions and greater professional capacities, along with compensatory policies for the most disadvantaged sectors) would produce an improvement in educational quality and equity, being the main objectives of these policies. Within this framework, public education did not receive preferential treatment. Its share of enrollment continued to decline and obtain low learning results, which was also shared with subsidized private education. As a result of the migration of the upper and middle sectors to private schools, chronic underfunding and growing socioeconomic segregation appeared. Democratic governments implemented some measures to support municipalities, but all these policies had partial and short-lived effects (Bellei et al., 2018). In short, the educational policies inaugurated in 1990 failed to respond to the structural problems affecting public education, probably, because they did not place the institutional regulatory framework at the center of their concern. In this dimension, educational policies followed their course in an orientation traced many years before.

The Education System and Reform under Criticism (2000–2006)

During the 1990s, educational policies had a high level of public opinion and in the political sector. This does not mean that there were no critical sectors, but they did not have significant repercussions. In addition to the socio-political consensus that supported the reform during the 1990s, there was progress in schooling indicators and student learning results measured by the official SIMCE tests. However, this period ended abruptly with the turn of the millennium. In mid-2000, the results of the 1999 SIMCE test for fourth-grade students were released, which was the first national assessment of the reform. Compared to the 1996 fourth grade cohort, the results showed that the *reform* students achieved similar responses in both reading and mathematics. The majority did not surpass the performance level considered basic. This criticism worsened when Chile's results in the TIMSS 1999 test became public, which were later added to those of the PISA test. At the national and international level, both results would mark a vision that accompanied the country for almost the entire decade and, in a certain sense, up to the present: that student learning results are *stagnant*. [1]

The government that took office in 2000 tried to make public management more dynamic. Recognizing that education had been a political and budgetary priority in the previous decade, it adopted a message of impatience with the lack of results. Salaries, working conditions, and teaching-learning conditions in schools had been improved, so it was time to "take reform to the classroom" (Cox, 2003). In addition, the government increasingly expressed a sense of powerlessness because the state lacked adequate tools to *demand quality* from teachers and school owners; nor could it close schools with chronically poor performance. These ideas were expressed in educational policies that were more structured and focused than in the previous stage. For example, the Reading, Writing, and Mathematics program (LEM, in Spanish) was implemented. This program focused on achieving concrete progress in these curricular areas, with more explicit pedagogical materials and instructions than the improvement programs of the 1990s. Another emblematic program was the *Critical Schools* program. The Ministry of Education hired a group of academics and experts to advise schools with chronically low performance to raise their SIMCE scores within five years. This program would later be institutionalized by creating a large market of private consultants (financed with public resources). These consultants helped schools and high schools design and implement their improvement plans, thus assuming a role previously assigned to supervisors of the Ministry of Education.

In addition, there was an extensive agenda of new policies to expand coverage, especially in preschool and secondary school. For example, the latter was established as a universal right and became part of compulsory schooling in 2003, accompanied by the Liceo Para Todos program. The Liceo program combined pedagogical, psychosocial and student support to reduce drop-out and increase school achievement for socio-educationally disadvantaged young people.

The crisis of the early 2000s revealed the fragility of the national agreements previously reached. Both the right-wing and left-wing opposition demanded more significant institutional change, although in opposite directions: emphasizing market reform and restoring the centrality of the state, respectively. The *third way* seemed to have found its limits. Indeed, the country had accumulated sufficient knowledge and experience about modifying structural aspects of the school system's organization if it wanted to trigger more sustained and significant quality and equity improvement processes (OECD, 2004; World Bank, 2007). In this context, and just after a new government took office (2006–2010), a powerful movement of secondary students entered the scene: the *penguin revolution*. For the first time since the dictatorship, this student movement allowed the Chilean political arena to open to more structural questions about the changes required by the educational system, opening the door to a significant turn in the direction of Chilean educational policies.

The student movement made a broad critique of Chilean education, impacting public opinion and the recently inaugurated fourth democratic government. Along with short- and medium-term demands, the movement also identified institutional aspects as the cause of some of the most urgent educational problems. Among these problems they complained about the insufficient regulatory framework embodied in the Constitutional Organic Law on Education (LOCE, in Spanish) (enacted on the last day of the dictatorship), state funding to private for-profit providers, discrimination caused by co-payment, the relative abandonment of public education in charge of municipalities, among others (Bellei & Cabalin, 2013). To process these demands through open and plural dialogue, the government created a broad Presidential Advisory Council, with representation from various sectors of the educational field. The Council was entrusted with carrying out a diagnosis and proposing solutions for Chilean education. The diagnosis made in the Progress Report of September 2006, and the proposals contained in the Final Report of December of the same year, constitute a turning point in the public debate on educational policies in Chile after the return to democracy.

The Advisory Council's report contained a large number and a variety of recommendations, ranging from strengthening the right to free and quality education to reforming the institutional framework for the administration of public education and creating a new Professional Teaching Career. However, the consensus was not achieved within the council (Presidential Advisory Council, 2006). In other words, the *great agreement* of the Advisory Council was that Chilean education required a major institutional reform to advance regarding the objectives of educational quality and equity. Besides, the significant disagreement regarding educational policies and education in Chile was also shown in the report. Considering public education, the council established the need for an institutional restructuring of municipal educational administration.

Summarizing, the diagnostic report prepared by the Advisory Council (2006) identified a set of main critical points. The most salient issues were the high heterogeneity in the quality of the management of the services administered by the municipalities, the poor management of their human resources, the high dependence on the political cycle and will of the mayors, the confusion of roles with Mineduc, as well as other structural limitations of the municipality as an institution, which had a direct impact on the quality of educational administration. The Advisory Council also made progress in developing a proposal to overcome these limitations, mainly by creating more professional organizations specializing in educational management and greater autonomy in their decisions. The consensus reached in the Advisory Council on what the new public education administrator should be like was so crucial that it guided all the policy proposals on the subject made by the following three governments. However, the political priority given to this reform was so low that another decade still had to pass before seeing results, despite the accumulated evidence on the weaknesses of municipal education (Bellei et al., 2010, 2018; Marcel & Raczynski, 2009).

The Emergence of the Evaluating State: Standards-Based Educational Reform (2006–2014)

As already mentioned, the crisis of the early 2000s revealed a certain fragility of the national agreements previously reached, which led public opinion and the political world – with clear differences depending on the sector – to call for significant institutional changes. This was supported by international evidence and perspectives on Chilean education. At the beginning of the last decade, the country had accumulated sufficient knowledge and experience about modifying structural aspects of the school system's organization if it wanted to trigger more sustained and significant quality and equity improvement processes (OECD, 2004; World Bank, 2007). The truth is that the political field had not assumed such an orientation.

Once the work of the Presidential Advisory Council was completed in 2006, the government decided to draft a proposal for legislative changes for school education, which was called the *New Architecture of Chilean Education*. It proposed a new regulatory and institutional framework for the school system, which implied modifying several laws in force – above all, repealing the Constitutional Organic Law on Education (inherited from the military dictatorship) and substituting it with a new General Education Law. The opposition (Alianza por Chile, right-wing) reacted critically to these proposals, which led to an extended negotiation process with the government coalition (Concertación, center-left). The result was a political agreement, signed in November 2007, by the leaders of both coalitions that were subsequently operationalized in a proposed General Education Law, enacted in 2009, and in the creation of a Quality Assurance System, finally passed in 2011 (Bellei & Vanni, 2015; Larroulet & Montt, 2010). The shared diagnosis that both the quality and equity of Chilean education were in debt[2] was always at the basis of this agreement.

The legislation that was processed and approved after the political agreement consolidated a hybrid educational system (public and private provision financed by the state). However, it recognized, at the same time, that market dynamics alone were inefficient to affect the quality and equity of education positively. That is the reason why one of the main novelties of this new legal framework was the incorporation of new requirements for schools and providers – in order to offer education and receive public resources – along with the creation of a public institutional framework that could promote and ensure adequate compliance with these new rules.

Therefore, the General Education Law strengthened the attributions of the Ministry of Education, making it responsible for safeguarding educational quality. The Law also created two new institutions, the Quality Agency and the Superintendence of Education, which is charged with assessing and guiding the quality of education and supervising compliance with the regulations and the rights and duties of the participants in the education process. It also transformed the configuration and functioning of the National Education Council, an autonomous collegiate body whose mission is to approve substantive and long-term definitions for the school system (such as the curricular bases or the national assessment plan).

The agreement that gave rise to all these changes also included a consensus to pass the Preferential School Subsidy Law (SEP, in Spanish), created in 2008 to provide additional funding to students belonging to the 40% most socio-economically disadvantaged public and private schools. This policy – which has undergone significant extensions in amounts and scope in other recent laws – in addition to inaugurating the association between the provision of public resources and the demand for a higher quality of educational service, has to some extent strained and modified the logic in which school improvement is promoted in Chile, delivering greater importance and resources to schools so that they could define their strategies for change and improvement (Muñoz & Vanni, 2008; Raczynski & Muñoz, 2007; Raczynski et al., 2013).

The educational policy approach at the basis of these changes, the regulatory framework approved in 2009, established what in comparative literature is recognized as "standards-based reforms" (Hargreaves & Shirley, 2012). These reforms generated specific quality requirements (at school process and result level) for educational providers, which are evaluated periodically – with a strong focus on standardized learning tests – and whose non-compliance may result in a set of consequences for schools (including their closure).

This logic, which has also been conceptualized as the *Evaluating State* (Maroy, 2009; Martinic, 2010), began to coexist in Chile with other pre-existing elements, typical of the market dynamics in education (such as the subsidy per student, the competition between centers to access this funding and the possibility of obtaining economic gain from education). To summarize, because of the reforms originated in the social mobilizations of 2006, politically processed and with results in 2009, a market education system was maintained in substance, although with regulations that aimed, through incentives and penalties, to correct some of the shortcomings of this market and guarantee minimum levels of quality in the educational service (Bellei & Vanni, 2015; Parcerisa & Falabella, 2017).[3]

This process of adjustment of the educational system omitted – mainly because it was established by the previous political negotiation – a set of other relevant aspects that the Presidential Advisory Council, the student movement and specialized evidence had highlighted as necessary to deal with. For example, it did not put an end to profit-making in general education (although it was prohibited at the higher education level), it allowed the selection of students by the providers, it did not deal with the challenge of improving the training and development of teachers and school system authorities, and it did not include in the general design a structural reform of public education, which at that time was municipal. It is possible to affirm that the agenda of changes promoted, although sizable, was also unbalanced: more emphasis was put on the pressure on schools than on the generation of teaching and management abilities to respond to that pressure; on incentive mechanisms than on support mechanisms; on generating accountability and control devices than on creating a strong public education institutional framework.

The first government of a post-dictatorship right-wing coalition (2010–2014) was marked by enacting and implementing the law that created the Quality Assurance System and the new institutions of the Agency and Superintendence. Besides, it promoted the development of an accelerated and meaningful curricular change in basic education, through which some subjects were prioritized and contents were adjusted. It also made progress in the implementation of some programs aimed at improving learning results in limited groups of schools or high schools, among which the Shared Support Plan and the *Bicentennial High Schools* stood out in terms of communication; the creation of a scholarship system to encourage students with outstanding performance to access teaching careers ("Vocation as a Teacher" scholarship); the expansion of the powers and training opportunities for school principals through Law 20.501, which also created an improved selection system for these authorities in the case of the public system; and, above all, the intensification of standardized measurements at different levels and learning areas, which applied 40 SIMCE national assessments in three years, four times more than in the early 2000s, and whose symbolic use, as the primary reference of school quality through the creation of public rankings from the Mineduc, transformed the SIMCE instrument into a central axis of all educational policy discussion[4] (Alarcón & Donoso, 2017).

At the end of 2010, the government set a bill calling for *quality and equity* as a top priority. The bill made the teachers' statute more flexible and gave public school and high school principals more power. This bill was passed in a record time of two months by Parliament (Donoso et al., 2014).

Despite the multiple measures and efforts of various kinds, this period of educational management was characterized by the lack of a clear and unifying project that would allow educational actors to understand this set of policies (Berner & Bellei, 2011). The main characteristic of this period of government in education was the massive and sustained resurgence of the student movement. This movement broke out in 2011, although this time led by university students, which brought education, its challenges in Chile, and the need for additional institutional changes to those agreed upon by the main political coalitions after the Penguin Revolution back to the center of the national discussion (Bellei et al., 2014; UNICEF, 2014).

The Attempt to Overcome the Market Stirring the Chilean School System (2014–2018)

Following the sustained student movement, the need for educational reform became the focus of political discussion in the run-up to the 2013 presidential elections. This educational debate was marked not only by the pressure for change that the student protests had established but also because general education had entered a phase of stagnation in its learning levels – as reported by national and international standardized tests – which, in addition, was accompanied by a consolidation of its levels of inequity and segregation (OECD, 2017).

Another feature of the educational debate in this period was the analysis of different actors regarding the factors behind the central problems of the Chilean educational system; the involvement of multiple actors complicated the formulation of policies. Although national research allowed the identification of factors of different types, which had influenced the educational processes and results of the school system (Bellei et al., 2008; Cox, 2003; Martinic & Elacqua, 2010; Verdejo, 2013; Weinstein & Muñoz, 2009), it was at this point when the argument for an "educational market" and the generation of favorable conditions for privatization emerged more strongly. This weakened the public education sector in the country (Bellei, 2015; OECD, 2004; OECD, 2017; Verger et al., 2016). The promise of the school market had not been fulfilled. Its introduction brought negative consequences for the education system, such as the breakup and atomization of educational provision, the increase in socioeconomic segregation, the segmentation of the teacher labor market, and the emptying or *skimming* of municipal education in favor of the private subsystem with public funding (Treviño, 2018).

The Government Program of the New Majority, a new center-left coalition that governed between 2014 and 2018, processed this debate by developing a proposal that explicitly set the goal of guaranteeing the "right" to education and ending or significantly reducing its commercialization (Navarro & Gysling, 2017). The central axis was to propose a *paradigm shift*, which implied making education a *social right*, in which all children and young people have the opportunity to access and remain in it free of charge and without discrimination, and to eliminate market rules from the education system, which also implied strengthening public education (Bachelet Administration Program, 2014). This general educational policy proposal represented a substantive turn regarding the previous decades, generated strong resistance from the beginning (Navarro & Gysling, 2017) and put the educational debate at the center of the public agenda during the entire administration period.

Firstly, the government program proposed to guarantee that all the resources received by the fund holders would be destined to improve the quality of education, which implied putting an end to profit-making in the school system. Secondly, the program established a priority to move towards a free system (without co-payment) and without selection during the admission processes, which was expected to deal with the socioeconomic segregation of compulsory education. Thirdly, the program proposed creating a new institutional framework – no longer municipal – for public education. Finally, it prioritized the formulation of a "teaching career" that would make it possible to improve the conditions and skills of teachers. It was an ambitious initiative: four highly complex technical and political transformations in only four years of administration. Besides, the institutional framework of preschool education was modernized (including the scope of coverage at this level, the definition of a new regulatory framework, and the creation of a new institutional framework, led by an undersecretariat that leads the entire preschool education system and an intendancy specialized in the supervision of this level) and significant tax reform was carried out to finance the government program, especially in the educational field.[5]

The Bachelet administration began its education reform process by presenting, in June 2014, a bill called the *Inclusion Law* to modify three central aspects of the functioning of the Chilean education system: (1) end profit-making with public resources; (2) ensure the existence of a completely free school system (gradually eliminating families' co-payment, widely prevalent until that moment); and (3) end the practices of selection and discrimination that were also applied by a part of the Chilean school system. The law defined a gradual trajectory whereby publicly funded private schools would become non-profit institutions to achieve these objectives. This same subsystem would progressively become utterly free because of the progressive increase in the state subsidy. Also, a new online school admissions system that was centralized (to avoid discrimination) and based on families' school choice would be implemented. In cases of over-demand, places would be allocated randomly.

The Inclusion Law should be read as a response to student demands,[6] but also as a reaction to the accumulation of evidence on the adverse effects that profit, selection and co-payment had produced in the Chilean school system, including the poor results of for-profit institutions (Chumacero & Paredes, 2008; Contreras et al. 2011; Elacqua et al., 2011, 2012, 2014; Zubizarreta et al., 2014), the effect of co-payment on the education system segregation (Flores & Carrasco, 2013; Gallegos & Hernando, 2009; Roje, 2014; Valenzuela et al., 2013, 2014) and discrimination and the adverse effects of selection processes (Carrasco et al. 2014; García Huidobro & Corvalán, 2009; Villalobos & Valenzuela, 2012), in addition to not being shared by the educational policies of countries with better educational indicators (Muñoz & Weinstein, 2019).

This project had highly complex processing due to the magnitude of the projected changes and the resistance many actors involved put up to the ending of profit, selection and co-payment (Bellei, 2016). Despite this, in January 2015, and after an intense negotiation within the government coalition, as well as between the government and the right-wing opposition, the Inclusion Law (20.845) – which regulates the admission of students, eliminates shared financing and prohibits profit-making in educational institutions that receive state contributions – was enacted by the National Congress.

A second pillar of the educational reform was the creation of a new regulation for the teaching function. The need to consider creating a long-term policy that would improve conditions and provide a permanent development opportunity for the teaching profession was based on a high academic, political and social consensus. The evidence showed that the strengthening of the teaching profession, in terms of its preparation, career and recognition, was vital to improving the quality of education in Chile (Avalos & Bellei, 2019; Bellei et al., 2008; Cox, 2003; Manzi et al., 2011; Martinic & Elacqua, 2010; OECD, 2004; Weinstein et al., 2020), especially considering the accumulated international experience regarding this matter (Barber & Mourshed, 2008; Hargreaves & Fullan, 2014).

In January 2015, the government presented a bill that created a teacher professional development system and included initial teacher training to shape a lifelong career path. After complex processing, marked by a teachers' strike that lasted 52 days and a cross-cutting criticism of some bill components, a large majority passed the teaching career law in January 2016.

This reform, which involved in practice all teachers in the state-funded school system (public or private schools), introduces a set of measures: (1) increases the requirements for those who study pedagogy and their training institutions; (2) establishes "induction" as a formal and indispensable procedure for the entry of new teachers into the school system; (3) creates a professional development system based on performance levels (based on a new teacher assessment mechanism) and experience, associating incentives to progress in this trajectory; (4) significantly improves the basic salaries of classroom teachers (30% increase on average); and (5) increases non-teaching time (from 25% to 35% or 40%, depending on the level of vulnerability of the institution). In 2017, the implementation of this second pillar of educational reform began, which will come into effect in 2025.

The third institutional reform of this period was creating the New Public Education through Law 21040 of 2017. This reform put an end to the "municipalization" of public education implemented during the dictatorship through a gradual process that will extend until 2025. The law that creates the Public Education System establishes a set of "purposes" and an "object" for the new system, highlighting its orientation towards a quality education understood while establishing that the education provided by the public system must be secular, pluralistic, free, inclusive and tolerant, as well as respecting the particularity of the territories, levels and educational modalities.

In the previous market scheme, public education had no purpose but to be the educational provider for the territories and students that the private supply was not interested in. Institutionally, the new Public Education System is made up of the universe of public educational institutions, with their different levels and educational modalities, as well as 70 local education services to be created throughout the national territory and, finally, by a new Public Education Directorate, which in turn is directly related to the Ministry of Education. The law also creates new mechanisms of direct state financing for the national and local levels of the system, but not for schools, which will continue to be financed through vouchers.

The most significant modification of the new public education law is related to a change in the dependence of public preschools, schools and high schools, which implies that the direct responsibility for administering educational institutions must be assumed by a network of new institutions: The Local Public Education Services (SLE, in Spanish). Therefore, these services are now ultimately responsible for the provision of public education in the territory.

The purpose of this territorial reconfiguration is to accumulate, develop and institutionalize professional and technical capacities in each territory to guarantee that intermediate levels can drive the continuous improvement of educational units. The SLEs are public organizations specializing in educational management, functionally and territorially decentralized, with highly professionalized personnel, legal status and assets. The local services are headed by an executive director, who signs an educational management agreement with the National Directorate of Public Education for a six-year term and has a specialized professional team. The law also creates two consultative bodies: the local council, which brings together representatives of the educational community in the territory, and the local steering committee, which creates additional space for deliberation and dialogue between the executive director of the service and representatives of the mayors of the territory, parents and guardians, and the respective regional government.

The governance design of the public education system defines two means of accountability of local services: a model of accountability from *above*, through the agreement signed with the Public Education Directorate and the permanent assessment of the institutions of the Quality Assurance System (SAC, in Spanish), and another from *below*, through the management committee, the local council and the representatives of the educational community. In addition, the new public education system introduces changes that will directly affect the work of schools and high schools by strengthening the management function (giving additional roles to authorities, who establish a performance agreement with their SLE) and a new regulatory framework that favors the participation of school actors in the relevant decisions of each institution, particularly by granting more powers to School Councils, in matters of coexistence, and to the Teachers Councils, in technical-pedagogical matters.

As new public education providers, the main levels of the NEP are educational institutions and local education services. However, a significant change introduced by the law is that the system is coordinated by a Public Education Directorate, a national body in charge of supporting, strategically leading and coordinating the SLEs. In legal terms, it is a centralized public service of the Ministry of Education. The senior manager is assigned to the Senior Public Management System and holds a first hierarchical level in the state administration. The DEP must design a national strategy and draft educational management agreements with the executive directors of the SLEs. In the previous market design, the Ministry of Education did not have a specialized organization for managing the public education system since the principle of *equal treatment* of private and public providers prevailed.

Lastly, without being a matter of law,[7] other initiatives aimed at improving the quality of education were also promoted during this administration, which complemented the legislative effort. Some of the most critical measures in this area were: (1) the implementation of a four-year improvement cycle in all schools, based on a review and updating of institutional, educational projects (PEI, in Spanish) and educational improvement plans (PME, in Spanish); (2) the creation and implementation of school improvement networks throughout the country, a series of horizontal development instances in which principals and teachers participate; (3) the creation of associative centers for educational leadership, which collaborate with the Mineduc in an agenda of innovations and concrete support for school principals and the new public education system; and (4) the significant reduction of the SIMCE standardized tests, a measure based on the curricular narrowing that these tests are causing in school practice. Although the government failed to create a consistent and systemic agenda, partly due to the attention focused on the legislative agenda, the measures related to the SIMCE generated an essential debate on quality and measurement.[8]

Final Reflections: An Open Future

As we have argued (and as summarized in the table below), Chilean education has undergone significant institutional reforms in recent decades, accompanied by very intense educational policies and programs for educational improvement and change, all of which have resulted in a significantly transformed school system. From a historical situation characterized by the state as the leading provider of education and a private sector *cooperating with the educational function of the state* (as it was traditionally defined), since 1980, a highly privatized system governed by market dynamics has evolved, leading public education to a state of crisis and jibarization. Once democracy was reinstated in 1990, an attempt was made to reconcile this market-oriented system with an active role of the state, no longer as a provider but as an implementer of compensatory and school improvement policies. This scheme of *two parallel logics* of educational policy showed its exhaustion in the mid-2000s. A new role of the state, now as assessor and quality assurer, was *embedded in the functioning of the market*, trying to guide it towards purposes of the common good; in this case, mainly, greater educational efficiency measured by standardized tests.

In general terms, this is the institutional arrangement that remains to this day. However, since 2014, two changes have been implemented that, for the first time since 1980, have the open purpose of reversing, and no longer just *guiding*, some market dynamics and reinstating a leading role for the state as an educational provider, partially overcoming the logic of "equal treatment" to public and private providers. The Inclusion Law ends public funding to private for-profit schools and high schools (the fastest growing in the market scheme) and contains measures to reduce segregation resulting from the dynamics of deregulated market competition.

The New Public Education creates a system specialized in the management of public schools and provides them with specific economic and institutional resources, which give it some supremacy in the educational system. Indeed, central elements of the educational market continue to operate, such as financing via vouchers, free choice of schools by families, and competition among schools for enrollment (resources), which is encouraged by official academic performance assessment mechanisms. To what extent these initiatives will fulfill their purpose of *rebalancing* the Chilean educational system from its situation of extreme privatization is an open question that, in substantial part, will depend on the priority and capacities that government authorities place on the implementation of these complex and demanding reforms in the coming years.[9]

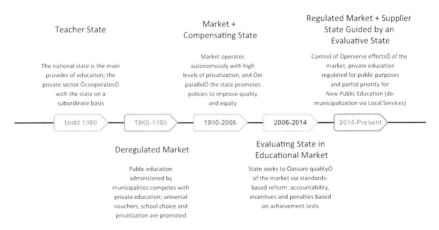

Figure 4.1 Evolution of institutional designs and educational policies in Chile
Source: Own research preparation

The trajectory of policies followed by Chile shows some partial achievements but also severe limitations. Although access to the educational system has expanded, the deregulated, privatized and socially segregated way in which this process occurred has shaped an inequitable and inefficient system (Bellei, 2015; Carrasco et al., 2019; Grau et al., 2018; Muñoz & Weinstein, 2019). Although the implementation of compensatory and systemic improvement policies increased the average performance of Chilean education (Bellei & Vanni, 2015; Cox, 2003), this improvement was small and short-lived, allowing the country to barely move from a meager achievement standard to a medium–low one, without continuing to advance towards higher levels of learning (OECD, 2019). Thus, although Chile seems to have consolidated a massive educational system that can provide most students with elementary learning, it has not been able to trigger largely sustained processes of improvement to develop more complex cognitive, social and interpersonal skills (Bellei & Morawietz, 2016; Carnoy et al., 2007; Mourshed et al., 2010).

These results place Chile in a critical dilemma for the coming years. On the one hand, whether to persevere on the path of *coexistence* or *hybridization* (Maroy, 2009) of these different types of educational policy models or frameworks (which we have described as *regulated market + provider state, guided by an evaluative state*). Or, on the other hand, to introduce new institutional reforms that modify this scheme, focusing energy and resources on policies such as strengthening public education, better working conditions and professional development for teachers and capacity building through peer support and collaboration, as suggested by evidence on systemic educational improvement (Hargreaves & Fullan, 2015).

Notes

1. In technical terms, this interpretation is debatable, given that the SIMCE test does not allow for robust longitudinal comparisons over long periods and that the PISA test has shown significant – although not systematic – advances in some of its measurements, not to mention that the school system has been subject to constant curricular reforms and adjustments and has experienced a significant increase in school retention.
2. This was expressly stated in the agreement signed by the representatives of both coalitions. However, it is essential to point out that it is in this same period when Chile begins to show some relevant progress in the TIMSS and PISA international comparative assessments (Bellei & Vanni, 2015).
3. In this way, the state would produce markets in public goods (school education) through competitive funding per student, along with the creation of "mechanisms" that assign a value to the school supply (scores, rankings, classifications of "educational quality"), thus building hierarchies, differentiations and a sense of competition, both for funding and for symbolic prestige (Parcerisa & Falabella, 2017).
4. The strong use of standardized measurements as mechanisms for the quality of the system and its school's assessment began during the 2000s. In the right-wing government, the number of applications increased dramatically (more than doubling in these years). The ministerial agenda gave to the use of standardized measurements a much higher priority. Most of the policies and programs during this period had a

SIMCE goal associated with them. Even the President of the Republic himself, in his campaign and government program, set the "improvement of SIMCE results by 10 points" as a general goal of his administration in education.
5 The reforms to the school system involved a significant financial effort by the Chilean State, which was carried out through a tax reform that allowed the government to collect – only for the educational area – resources close to 6 billion dollars, of which approximately two-thirds were granted to the changes in school education (Weinstein et al., 2018).
6 The main slogans and demands of the 2011 student movement (as well as its 2006 predecessor) were "end to profit" and "public, free and quality education" (UNICEF, 2014).
7 During this period, other laws of a more specific nature were also passed. However, they were relevant due to their effect on the entire school system, such as the law establishing the obligation for all educational institutions to have a Citizenship Education Plan or the postponement until 2027 of the implementations of the new curricular structure established in the General Education Law, which sets six years of primary education and six years of secondary education).
8 Despite this, the Bachelet administration decided not to modify any of the pillars of the Quality Assurance System, which, as mentioned above, consolidates an educational logic based on standards, incentives, and consequences for educational actors, which is not consistent with a comprehensive notion of educational quality and may collide with the principle of understanding education as a right (Navarro & Gysling, 2017).
9 At the time of writing, the administration of Sebastián Piñera (2018–2021) was entering its last year in office. Although, initially, the authorities tried to modify some of the components of the reforms of the previous period (such as, for example, replenishing academic selection in secondary education), the National Congress's rejection of these proposals and the crisis policy in which the government was involved during a vital part of the period – marked by a strong outbreak of social protest in October 2019 – resulted in an educational policy of continuity and implementation of the laws passed in the previous period and of emergency management (associated with the COVID-19 pandemic), without changes in the institutional design of the educational system or its most relevant policies.

References

Alarcón Leiva, J., & Donoso Díaz, S. (2017). Hitos significativos de la política educacional del gobierno de la coalición por el cambio (2010–2014). *Estudios Pedagógicos (Valdivia)*, 43(1), 371–388.

Ávalos, B., & Bellei, C. (2019). Recent education reforms in Chile: how much of a departure from market and new public management systems? In C. Ornelas (ed.), *Politics of Education in Latin America: Reforms, Resistance and Persistence*. Sense-Brill Publishers.

Barber, M., & Mourshed, M. (2008). *Cómo hicieron los sistemas educativos con mejor desempeño del mundo para alcanzar sus objetivos, documento núm. 41*. Programa de Promoción de la Reforma Educativa en América Latina.

Bellei, C. (2015). *El gran experimento: mercado y privatización de la educación chilena*. LOM Ediciones.

Bellei, C. (2016). Dificultades y resistencias de una reforma para des-mercantilizar la educación. *RASE: Revista de la Asociación de Sociología de la Educación*, 9(2), 232–247.

Bellei, C., & Cabalin, C. (2013). Chilean student movements: sustained struggle to transform a market-oriented educational system. *Current Issues in Comparative Education*, 15(2), 108–123.

Bellei, C., & Pérez (2010). Conocer más para vivir mejor. Educación y conocimiento en Chile en la perspectiva del Bicentenario. In R. Lagos Escobar (Ed.), *Cien años de luces y sombras*. Editorial Taurus.

Bellei, C., & Perez, C. (2016). Democratizar y tecnificar la educación: la reforma educacional de Eduardo Frei Montalva. In C. Huneeus & J. Couso (Eds.), *Eduardo Frei Montalva: un gobierno reformista*. Editorial Universitaria.

Bellei, C., & Vanni, X. (2015). Evolución de las políticas educacionales en Chile: 1980–2014. In C. Bellei (Ed.), *El gran experimento: mercado y privatización de la educación chilena*. LOM Ediciones.

Bellei, C., Contreras, D., & Valenzuela, J.P. (2008). *La agenda pendiente en educación: profesores, administradores y recursos: propuesta para la nueva arquitectura de la educación chilena*. Universidad de Chile.

Bellei, C., Contreras, D., & Valenzuela, J.P. (2010). Fortalecer la educación pública: un desafío de interés nacional. In C. Bellei, D. Contreras & J.P. Valenzuela *(Eds.)*, *Ecos de la revolución pingüina: Avances, debates y silencios de la reforma educacional*. Pehuén Editores.

Bellei, C., Cabalin, C., & Orellana, V. (2014). The 2011 Chilean student movement against neoliberal educational policies. *Studies in Higher Education*, 39(3), 426–440.

Bellei, C., Muñoz, G., Rubio, X., Alcaíno, M., Donoso, M.P., Martínez, J., & Díaz, R. (2018). *Nueva educación pública: contexto, contenidos y perspectivas de la desmunicipalización*. LOM Ediciones.

Berner, H., & Bellei, C. (2011). ¿Revolución o reforma? Anuncios, medidas y compromisos a la espera de la reforma educacional. *Política: Revista de Ciencia Política*, 49(2), 67–96.

Carnoy, M., Gove, A.K., & Marshall, J.H. (2007). *Cuba's Academic Advantage: Why Students in Cuba Do Better in School*. Stanford University Press.

Carrasco, A., Mizala, A., Contreras, D., Santos, H., Elacqua, G., Torche, F., & Valenzuela, J. (2014). *Hacia un sistema escolar más inclusivo: cómo reducir la segregación escolar en Chile*. Informe de Políticas Públicas, 36. Retrieved from www.espaciopublico.cl/media/publicaciones/archivos/25.pdf

Carrasco, A., Bonilla, A., & Rasse, A. (2019). Capital profesional del sector particular subvencionado en Chile: ¿Una oferta diversa o desigual? In A. Carrasco & L. Flores (Eds.), *De la reforma a la transformación: capacidades, innovaciones y regulación de la educación chilena*. Ediciones UC.

Chumacero, R., & Paredes, R. (2008). *Should For-Profit Schools Be Banned?* Documento de Trabajo. Departamento de Ingeniería Industrial, Universidad Católica de Chile.

Contreras, D., Sepúlveda, P., & Bustos, S. (2010). When schools are the ones that choose: the effects of screening in Chile. *Social Science Quarterly*, 91(5), 1349–1368.

Contreras, D., Hojman, D., Huneeus, F., & Landerretche, Ó. (2011). El lucro en la educación escolar: evidencia y desafíos regulatorios. *Trabajos de Investigación en Políticas Públicas*, 10, 1–16.

Cox, C. (2003). *Políticas educacionales en el cambio de siglo: La reforma del sistema escolar de Chile*. Editorial Universitaria.

Donoso-Díaz, S., Frites-Camilla, C., & Castro-Paredes, M. (2014). Los proyectos de ley de fortalecimiento de la educación pública de los años 2008 y 2011: propuestas y silencios. *Pensamiento Educativo: Revista de Investigación Educacional Latinoamericana*, 51(2), 1–18.

Elacqua, G., Martínez, M., & Santos, H. (2011). Lucro y educación escolar. *Claves para Políticas Públicas*, 1, 1–11.

Elacqua, G., Montt, P., & Santos, H. (2012). *Financiamiento compartido en Chile: antecedentes, evidencia y recomendaciones*. Instituto de Políticas Públicas, Diego Portales.

Espínola, V. (1992). *Decentralization of the Educational System and the Introduction of Market Rules in the Regulation of Schooling: The Case of Chile*. CIDE.

Flores, C., & Carrasco, A. (2013). *Preferencias, libertad de elección y segregación escolar*. Reference paper 2. Espacio Público.

Gallego, F., & Hernando, A. (2009). *School Choice in Chile: Looking at the Demand Side*. Retrieved from http://dx.doi.org/10.2139/ssrn.1725911

García-Huidobro, J.E. (Ed.) (1999). *La reforma educacional chilena*. Editorial Popular.

García-Huidobro, J.E., & Corvalán, J. (2009). Obstáculos para el logro de una educación democrática inclusiva. *Perspectivas*, 39(3), 239–250.

Grau, N., Hojman, D., & Mizala, A. (2018). School closure and educational attainment: evidence from a market-based system. *Economics of Education Review*, 65, 1–17.

Hargreaves, A., & Fullan, M. (2015). *Professional Capital: Transforming Teaching in Every School*. Teachers College Press.

Hargreaves, A., & Shirley, D.L. (2012). *The global fourth way: the quest for educational excellence*. Corwin Press.

Jofré, G. (1988). *El sistema de subvenciones en educación: la experiencia chilena (No. 99)*. Centro de Estudios Públicos.

Larroulet, C., & Montt, P. (2010). Políticas educativas de largo plazo y acuerdo amplio en educación: el caso chileno. In S. Martinic & G. Elacqua (Eds.), *Fin de ciclo? Cambios en la gobernanza del sistema educativo*. UNESCO.

Manzi, J., González, R., Sun, Y., Bonifaz, R., Flotts, M.P., Abarzúa, A., & Zapata, A. (2011). *La evaluación docente en Chile*. MIDE UC.

Marcel, M., & Raczynski, D. (Eds.) (2009). *La asignatura pendiente: claves para la revalidación de la educación pública de gestión local en Chile*. Uqbar.

Maroy, C. (2009). Convergences and hybridization of educational policies around "post-bureaucratic" models of regulation. *Compare*, 39(1), 71–84.

Martinic, S. (2010). Cambios en las regulaciones del sistema educativo: hacia un estado evaluador. In S. Martinic & G. Elacqua (Eds.), *Fin de ciclo? Cambios en la gobernanza del sistema educativo*. UNESCO.

Martinic, S., & Elacqua, G. (2010). *Fin de ciclo? Cambios en la gobernanza del sistema educativo*. UNESCO.

Mineduc. (2017). *Cuenta pública de la reforma educacional 2014–2017*. Mineduc.

Mourshed, M., Chijioke, C., & Barber, M. (2010). *How the World's Most Improved School Systems Keep Getting Better*. McKinsey & Co.

Muñoz, G., & Vanni, X. (2008). Rol del estado y de los agentes externos en el mejoramiento de las escuelas: análisis en torno a la experiencia chilena. *REICE: Revista Electrónica Iberoamericana sobre Calidad, Eficacia y Cambio en Educación*, 6(4), 47–68.

Muñoz, G., & Weinstein, J. (2019). The difficult process in Chile: redefining the rules of the game for subsidized private education. In C. Ornelas (ed.), *Politics of Education in Latin America: Reforms, Resistance and Persistence*. Sense-Brill Publishers.

Navarro, L., & Gysling, J. (2017). Educación general en el gobierno de Michelle Bachelet: avances y rezagos. In L. Navarro (Ed.), *Bachelet II: El difícil camino hacia un estado democrático social de derechos*. BPE.

Núñez, I. (1984). *Las transformaciones educacionales bajo el Régimen Militar*. Programa Interdisciplinario de Investigaciones en Educación, PIIE.

Nuñez Prieto, I. (2015). Educación chilena en la República: promesas de universalismo y realidades de inequidad en su historia. *Psicoperspectivas*, 14(3), 5–16.

OECD. (2004). *Revisión de políticas nacionales en educación*. OECD.

OECD. (2017). *Revisión de políticas nacionales en educación*. OECD.

OECD. (2019). *PISA 2018 results (Volumes 1, 2 & 3)*. OECD.

Parcerisa, L., & Falabella, A. (2017). La consolidación del Estado evaluador a través de políticas de rendición de cuentas: trayectoria, producción y tensiones en el sistema educativo chileno. *Education Policy Analysis Archives/Archivos Analíticos de Políticas Educativas*, 25, 1–24.

Prieto Bafalluy, A. (1983). *La modernización educacional*. Ediciones Universidad Católica de Chile.

Raczynski, D., & Muñoz, G. (2007). Reforma educacional chilena: el difícil equilibrio entre la macro y la micro-política. *REICE: Revista Iberoamericana sobre Calidad, Eficacia y Cambio en Educación*, 5(3), 40–83.

Raczynski, D., Muñoz, G., Weinstein, J., & Pascual, J. (2013). Subvención escolar preferencial (SEP) en Chile: un intento para equilibrar la macro y la micro política escolar. *REICE: Revista Electrónica Iberoamericana sobre Calidad, Eficacia y Cambio en Educación*, 11(2), 164–193.

Roje Larreboure, P. (2014). *Segregación escolar por nivel socioeconómico (NSE) y su relación con las políticas educacionales en Chile: el caso del financiamiento compartido (FC) y la subvención escolar preferencial (SEP)*. Master's Thesis, Universidad de Chile.

Treviño, E. (2018). Diagnóstico del sistema escolar: las reformas educativas 2014–2017. In I. Sanchez (Ed.), *Ideas en educación: reflexiones y propuestas desde la UC*. Ediciones UC.

UNICEF. (2014). La voz del movimiento estudiantil 2011. In UNICEF (Ed.), *Educación pública, gratuita y de calidad: algunas lecciones para el sistema educativo chileno*. UNICEF.

Valenzuela, J.P., Villalobos, C., & Gómez, G. (2013). *Segregación y polarización en el sistema escolar chileno y recientes tendencias ¿Qué ha sucedido con los grupos medios?* Espacio Público.

Valenzuela, J.P., Bellei, C., & Ríos, D.D.L. (2014). Socioeconomic school segregation in a market-oriented educational system: the case of Chile. *Journal of Education Policy*, 29(2), 217–241.

Verdejo, M.I.P. (2013). *Las políticas escolares de la concertación durante la transición democrática*. Ediciones Universidad Diego Portales.

Verger, A., Bonal, X., & Zancajo, A. (2016). *Recontextualización de políticas y (cuasi) mercados educativos: un análisis de las dinámicas de demanda y oferta escolar en Chile*. Education Policy Analysis Archives/Archivos Analíticos de Políticas Educativas.

Villalobos, C., & Valenzuela, J.P. (2012). Polarización y cohesión social del sistema escolar chileno. *Revista de análisis económico*, 27(2), 145–172.

Weinstein, J., & Muñoz, G. (2009). Calidad para todos: la reforma educacional en el punto de quiebre. In G. Muñoz (Ed.), *Más acá de los sueños, más allá de lo posible: la concertación en chile*. LOM Ediciones.

Weinstein, J., Muñoz, G., & Rivero, R. (2018). Los Directivos escolares como informantes cualificados de las políticas educativas: sus opiniones bajo el gobierno de Michelle Bachelet en Chile (2014–2017). *REICE: Revista Iberoamericana sobre Calidad, Eficacia y Cambio en Educación*, 16(3), 5–27.

Weinstein, J., Muñoz, G., & Beca, C.E. (2020). Chile: Changing the teaching profession, the most challenging reform. In M. Jones & A. Harris (Eds.), *Leading and Transforming Education Systems*. Springer.

World Bank. (2007) *El diseño institucional de un sistema efectivo de aseguramiento de la calidad de la educación en Chile*. Unidad de Gestión del Sector de Desarrollo Humano/Unidad de Gestión de Países para Argentina, Chile, Paraguay y Uruguay/Oficina Regional para América Latina y el Caribe, Banco Mundial.

Zubizarreta, J.R., Paredes, R.D., & Rosenbaum, P.R. (2014). Matching for balance, pairing for heterogeneity in an observational study of the effectiveness of for-profit and not-for-profit high schools in Chile. *The Annals of Applied Statistics*, 8(1), 204–231.

5 From Political Intentions to Structural Interventions

A Review of Two Decades of Education Policy Reforms in Colombia

Jorge Grant Baxter and Mónica Cristina León Cadavid

Introduction

Like many others in Latin America, Colombia is a country full of contrasts and contradictions. On the one hand, its modern history sways back and forth from violence to peace, deep economic and social inequalities, and imaginaries, perspectives and dualities based on the figures of the drug dealer, the guerrilla and the paramilitary (Melo, 2017). However, on the other hand, recent Colombian history is also notable for its democratic institutions, a relatively stable economy, diverse cultural heritage and resilient people (Cepeda, 2007).

The Colombian Conflict[1] resulted in the death of 262,197 people: 75,587 were deemed missing, 1,500,000 were displaced and 37,000 kidnapped (CNMH, 2018). Sixty years of violence have profoundly impacted and transformed Colombian culture, posing significant political and educational challenges. In many areas of the country, the state's weakness has contributed to the lack of social and educational development. In areas not directly affected, the arrival of displaced persons generated other social and educational challenges associated with integrating children and young people affected by violence. Finally, high levels of inequality and corruption have contributed to widespread distrust of institutions and social groups. Implementing complex educational reforms was challenging in this context, characterized by a lack of trust and institutional weakness.

A fundamental milestone in Colombia's political, social, and educational context was the Political Constitution of 1991, which changed the rules and the relations between national and local governments. The Constitution strengthened the division of powers and empowered other political actors beyond the Executive, such as the Congress, the Constitutional Court, local governments and even ordinary citizens through several mechanisms of participation and justice such as the tutela or action to protect fundamental rights. It also generated high hopes for its articulation of democratic principles with economic and social rights. Furthermore, the 1991 Constitution established education as a fundamental right and made the state responsible for defending and upholding such rights. In addition, the Constitution established freedom of teaching, learning, researching and lecturing in a context that sought to end the Church's interference in school texts and curricula. Finally, it established the principle of free public basic education, university autonomy and the importance of promoting science and technology.

Despite having a relatively advanced legislative framework, effective implementation of national policies in different country regions has proven difficult, given stark differences in local governance capacity and social inequality. A recent study on governance capacity at the department level shows little or no articulation among different sectors and levels and no capacity to monitor and assess the results of implemented policies. It also highlights poor stakeholder participation in creating and monitoring policies and problems regarding transparency and accountability (OECD, 2020). This lack of governance capacity at the local level generates incentives and opportunities for local corruption and political clientelism around federal education subsidies (Melo, 2017). It is worth mentioning some of the territorial entities that have achieved outstanding social policies in poverty reduction, education and health, such as Medellín, Barranquilla, Cali, Tunja and Bogotá. Bogotá, for instance, became a sort of lab for testing education policies that later were adopted nationwide (Herrera & Bayona, 2018).

In the social sphere, Colombia has made progress throughout the period assessed in this chapter. The administrations of Álvaro Uribe Vélez and Juan Manuel Santos managed to reduce poverty from 49.7% in 2002 to 30.7% in 2013 (Molano-Rojas & Salazar, 2018). This resulted from implementing subsidies rather than expanding quality public services, such as health and education (Molano-Rojas & Salazar, 2018). Parallel to poverty reduction, the period has been marked by significant growth of the middle class. However, this emerging middle class in Colombia lives in a vulnerable situation because of their low income and the high rates of informal work in the country, 47% in urban areas and above 82% in rural areas. According to an annual study by Universidad del Rosario, "education has an important effect on the incidence of informality. Achieving a higher educational level reduces informality rates by more than 20%" (Observatorio Laboral, 2018).[2] The COVID-19 pandemic during 2020–21 has likely led to significant reversals of this social progress with increased rates of poverty and inequality.

Finally, in the period studied here, Colombia has been one of the most unequal countries in the world. In 2000, an education analyst wrote, "At the onset of the 21st century, the greatest challenge for the Colombian society is achieving equality" (Sarmiento, 2000). In 2014, Colombia was the second most unequal country in Latin America and fourth worldwide, with a Gini coefficient of 55.4 (UNDP, 2014). Inequalities between regions and groups are replicated in the education sector. In the 2015 PISA tests, rural students got an average of 38 points less than students in urban areas, representing almost a year difference in schooling (OECD, 2018). In 2015, according to the Ministry of Education, the average number of years of education in rural areas was 5.5, compared with 9.2 in urban areas (MEN, 2016).

During the period studied in this chapter, 2002–2020, Colombia had three administrations and five education ministers: Cecilia María Vélez-White in both terms of President Álvaro Uribe Vélez (2002–2010); María Fernando Campo (2010–2014), Gina Parody (2014–2015) and Yaneth Giha Tovar (2015–2018) in the two terms of President Juan Manuel Santos; and María Victoria Angulo, current Minister of Education in the administration of President Iván Duque Márquez. In general, given the four consecutive terms of Uribe Vélez and Santos, there was a common thread in educational plans and processes. Among the five Ministers were two economists, an industrial engineer with postgraduate studies in finance, a lawyer, and a minister who studied conflict resolution, but no formally trained educators. It is worth mentioning that three of these five Ministers of Education came from the Bogotá administrations; Vélez-White and Angulo were Secretaries of Education, and Campo was interim mayor.

Early in the 1990s, boosted by the reform of the Political Constitution in 1991 and the new General Education Law, the country accelerated the education decentralization process, which – with its pros and cons – generated new dynamics within territorial entities and educational institutions throughout the country. Since then, the country has undergone structural changes designed to improve efficiency, equality and quality at several levels. However, these reform efforts occur within a broader political context of political tensions and social turmoil as Colombia attempts to transition to a new post-conflict era.

2002–2010: Education Revolution and Development for All

With the election of the administration of Alvaro Uribe in 2002, the National Development Plan (PND, in Spanish) was developed and aimed at introducing what they called "a revolution in education". The plan aimed to address universal access to primary education, increase efficiency in the system and promote educational quality. At the time, thousands of children and young people were outside the education system, and the results of the national standardized test showed a decline in student performance. Furthermore, regarding governance, there was evidence of "poor coordination among entities, duplication of functions, inflexibility and an institutional organization that failed to generate incentives for efficiency and deeply restricted possibilities of advancing in terms of expanding coverage and improving quality" (DNP, 2003, p. 171). Law 715 of 2001 sought to correct these inefficiency problems and clarify each territorial entity's competencies.

The PND and education policy agenda proposed a variety of specific programs to address access and equity. The first program focused on enrolling 1,500,000 students in kindergarten, primary and high school, prioritizing the most vulnerable populations. In addition, attention was placed on decreasing failure and drop-outs rates. Furthermore, more resources were allocated to the Rural Education Programme to improve access. However, evidence pointed to persistent gaps between groups (socioeconomic, rural versus urban areas, ethnic, among others) (Corpoeducación et al., 2006; PND, 2003).

The government also focused on equity-enhancing policies such as school feeding programs, school transport and early childhood daycare programs led by the Colombian Institute of Family Welfare (ICBF). These actions led to improvements in access and retention at early and basic education levels. In addition, the creation of financing schemes to support entry into universities also bolstered higher education access rates. Other improvements included the modernization of resource allocation to public universities and the strengthening and regulating technical and vocational programs at the higher education level.

Another set of efforts focused on enhancing the quality of education by establishing educational standards and competencies for all levels of education and subject areas. Additionally, assessments were implemented to measure basic skills in language and mathematics and citizenship in school years 5 and 9. The administration developed performance evaluations for teachers and school principals and regulations on the admission and promotion of teachers, tied to quality standards. The strategy included improvement plans focused on students and education institutes identified by those most in need. Emphasis was placed on strengthening school management and managerial skills of school principals, leveraging lessons learned from successful experiences of networking and fostering relationships among teachers (Corpoeducación et al., 2006; PND, 2003; Rivas, 2015).

Given the broader historical context in Colombia associated with conflict, the government developed several curricular innovations on issues related to peace and citizenship. This included new subject areas with innovative competency-based approaches in citizenship, work training, sexual education, violence prevention and substance abuse prevention.

There was a push to strengthen the technological infrastructure of schooling and distance education for both formal and non-formal purposes. This meant ensuring connectivity and distribution of computers and tablets, bolstering educational TV and radio and the creation of audio-visual media and other multimedia quality educational materials. As for higher education, the Labour Observatory was established and the National Accreditation System and the research on higher education were reinforced (OECD, 2016; PND, 2003; Rivas, 2015).

Perhaps one of the most important contributions during this period was improving and modernizing the administrative and management capacity of education secretaries at the national, department and municipal levels. Much of the effort focused on creating management and performance plans and the development of information systems to help track progress. In addition, these actions were meant to foster decentralization with the support of territorial entities in the certification process and "with special emphasis on developing governance skills" (Rivas, 2015, p. 64).

During Uribe Vélez's second term in office, the Ministry focused on improving coverage, quality and efficiency. The greatest challenge of this period was to ensure universal access to basic education (three years of preschool, five years of primary and four years of secondary education) and to reduce gaps between regions and groups. In terms of improving the sector's efficiency, strategies continued to focus on strengthening the management capacity of the National Ministry of Education.

Despite the progress made in expanding coverage in the first period, the number of children outside the system remained high. One of the strategies employed was to promote, among parents, the importance of education for their children and its compulsory nature stipulated by law. Reducing drop-out rates was an equally important challenge, and policy efforts focused on addressing this issue. To that end, the financial incentive scheme (cash-transfer subsidy program) was reinforced and tied to attendance and permanence in schooling. In addition, school-lunch programs and transportation programs continued and parent participation was promoted.

Another goal was to expand coverage in higher education and improve coverage, quality and relevance. Strategies to broaden coverage in higher education were developed through the following programs: promotion and strengthening of technical and technological education; decentralization of higher education options; financing to access higher education focused on vulnerable populations; transformation of public higher education financing; generation of partnerships with other institutions within the system to expand the offering of programs along with the productive sector; and territorial entities and a system of higher education quality assurance. Finally, strategies were generated to consolidate the National System of Education for Work (SNFT, in Spanish).

2002–2010: Critical Analysis

Education Minister Vélez-White held office for eight years, which was unprecedented in Colombia and Latin America at the time. This stability in the ministry allowed for some cohesion and continuity in the proposed educational reforms. Perhaps the main achievements during this period were institutional and administrative, setting the conditions for mid- and long-term educational improvements. Implementing a national information and evaluation system linked to institutional improvement plans was a critical step. Another step forward was creating the General Programme of Transfers, designed for a more equitable allocation of resources based on actual needs. However, the General Programme of Transfers has failed to equalize levels among territories, in part because the differences transferred were minimal (OECD, 2018).

Another aspect worth highlighting during the period was introducing reforms based on competencies, standards and evaluations. In theory, these competency-based policies and programs were introduced to change the dominant pedagogical model based on rote learning. They also were seen as tools to ensure minimum levels of learning for all, given the vast differences in curricula. Unfortunately, they failed to trigger more profound transformations in teaching and learning at the classroom level. Vélez-White's decision to focus on teacher and student evaluations as a key lever of change may have limited more profound transformations at the micro-level in teacher practice. Not enough resources were focused on supporting teacher training processes, school directors' pedagogical leadership, and promoting organizational and collective learning processes between schools and teachers.

In conclusion, the most outstanding achievement of this period was the emphasis placed on organizing the system and establishing institutional mechanisms to drive long-term educational change. Many of these institutional aspects were implemented top-down with the logic that changing the incentives of the main actors would lead to change (see Vélez-White, 2018). However, the strategy left aside the more complicated political, collective, participatory and pedagogical aspects necessary for more profound transformations towards quality.

2010–2018: Prosperity for All and Colombia, the Most Educated

With President Juan Manuel Santos (the previous defence minister of Uribe), there was clear continuity concerning the reform agenda in education. Much of this agenda continued to express an ideological affinity with neoliberal policies to enhance efficiency and boost Colombia's competitiveness through human capital development. In education, this translated into an emphasis on skills development and standardized tests to drive change. In line with the market-oriented logic, the ministry focused on creating national qualification frameworks to align the education sector with the market's needs. In contrast with the previous administration, there was more of a recognition of the role of the teacher in promoting quality.

Throughout the *National Development Plan 2010–2014: Prosperity for All* the skills approach was reinforced, placing particular emphasis on three types of skills: essential,[3] generic[4] and specific.[5] This approach aimed to develop basic and civic skills in students useful for problem-solving and building community. Cross-cutting projects such as Sex Education and Citizenship, Environmental Education and Human Rights Education were strengthened. Early childhood became a focus, as did higher and vocational education.

To complement the focus on skills development, an emphasis was placed on enhancing the assessment regime. This included consolidating and strengthening the National System of Evaluations, strengthening assessment instruments, enhancing the dissemination and use of assessment results and consolidating the teacher evaluation system.

An effort was made to better link school to work. This included designing and implementing a National Qualifications Framework (MNC, in Spanish), which aimed to define and classify the learning outcomes needed in different productive sectors. It also aimed to create more flexibility and links between education levels and schooling, and the outside world. Finally, it was positioned as a tool to promote lifelong learning. The Qualifications Framework approach illustrated the government's overarching neoliberal conceptualization of education quality as meeting market needs.

Perhaps one of the critical assumptions during this period (in sync with global reform discourses) was the need to focus on teacher quality as the critical driver of system improvement measured by standardized tests. To address this perceived need, the government designed a national teacher professional development and mentoring program called *Todos a Aprender* (Let's All Learn). The program focused on providing situated professional development in schools through a system of teacher mentors. The program targeted schools with the lowest performance in the national standardized test (SABER) and with low-income communities with high levels of poverty, year repetition and drop-out rates. Tutors were trained to support schools with education materials focused primarily on language and math.

In its second term, Santos' administration set a goal to turn Colombia into the most educated country in Latin America by 2025 and place the country at the top of the educational rankings. The idea behind the announcement was to set a high expectation that would drive stakeholders to focus even more on quality standards. Despite the competitive framing of the government, some stakeholders framed the goal in terms of rights: "Turning Colombia into the most educated country by 2025 would mean that we have guaranteed the right to education for everyone, offering an education that expands possibilities for people to have a better quality of life in the context of a more democratic society" (Foundation of Businesses for Education, 2018).

A vital part of the strategy to improve quality was to expand the school day and bolster scholarships for teachers to obtain postgraduate degrees in education. The policy also focused on creating incentives for teachers and schools to improve through ongoing assessments of teacher excellence, an annual school-level report card on qualitative improvements and a national day of excellence to highlight teacher and school innovations and promote the diffusion of best practices. Additionally, the government targeted high-achieving students in secondary education and provided them with higher education scholarships. One of the most controversial of these scholarship programs, called *Ser Pilo Paga* (It Pays to Be Smart), provided higher education vouchers to students with the highest test scores. The controversial aspect dealt with the use of public funds to support private higher education institutions.

Another of the focus areas during this period was expanding and improving early childhood education. Emphasis was placed on acknowledging early childhood education as a fundamental basis for success in later stages of academia and life. The main program called *De Cero a Siempre* (From Zero to Forever) focused on articulating efforts between the various agencies and actors involved in early childhood. This program successfully advanced a more integral and holistic framework for early childhood while emphasizing the need to ensure quality management and teacher training at this level.

2010–2018: Critical Analysis

Santos' term in office can be characterized as continuity with the previous approach with new strategic programs that aimed to address the pending issue of quality. During this period, there was more instability at the ministerial level, with three ministers in eight years. This negatively impacted the continuity and depth of the agenda proposed in education. Some ministers, such as Gina Parody, had to resign abruptly due to controversial issues arising from the policies they proposed and broader political dynamics at the time.

Some of the strategic programs designed to improve quality mentioned above, such as Let's All Learn, the Synthetic Education Quality Index, the Education Excellence Day, postgraduate scholarship plans, and the Full-Day Schooling, were vital steps to advance the professionalization of teachers and improve quality. However, they failed to achieve a comprehensive and integral teacher reform at scale. Despite the work carried out, a more substantial investment of resources is needed to extend and deepen these efforts and tie them more directly with institutional improvement processes.

One of the most outstanding achievements of the period was the policy in early childhood *De Cero a Siempre* (From Zero to Forever), which promoted an integral vision of child development and better articulation among institutions. However, despite an essential focus on the poor and most marginalized, it failed to reach scale and expand coverage to all preschool-age children (Revista Semana, 2018).

In short, key achievements in this period were related to the launch of innovative programs that promised to contribute to quality and equality. In the context of decentralization and excessive curricular autonomy, the Ministry of Education tried to circumvent political governance constraints and reach classrooms, schools and families directly with these programs. However, this strategy failed to ensure support from intermediate levels and from actors necessary to carry out these programs and expand them over time at state and municipal levels.

An Open Agenda: Pact for Colombia, Pact for Equality

The goals of the 2018–2022 development plan "Pact for Colombia, Pact for Equality" were to improve quality and fully develop each of the education levels (initial, preschool, basic, secondary and upper secondary), as well as to improve access to and quality of rural education and training for work. As part of the challenges in education, the following goals have been established:

- Expand coverage of quality initial education in the transition year, which currently reaches only 71,500 students.
- Improve the quality of education in public schools (only 14% of students in eleventh grade have an excellent performance in the Saber standardized test).

- Support students' continuance in the system. Out of 100 children entering the first year of education, only 44 manage to graduate from high school.
- Increase net coverage of secondary education, which in rural areas only amounts to 31.41%.
- Increase the coverage rate in higher education, currently at 52.8%.
- Decrease annual drop-out in higher education which, at university levels, reaches 9%.
- Reduce the illiteracy rate, currently at 5.2%.

To achieve these goals, the government suggests the following strategies: expand coverage, allocate more resources to the basic education system, ensure students' continuance in the system by reducing drop-out, design curricula based on the needs and realities of the population, gradually make higher education free, and strengthen the Quality Assurance System in higher education[6] and the Qualifications National Framework.[7] Moreover, finally, continue to build the governance capacity of secretaries and other entities within the sector.

At the time of submitting this chapter, Colombia is facing social turmoil and protest. The education system has been closed down due to the pandemic for almost a year and a half (one of the most extended closures of the education system in the world). Many of the protests have been led by youth who demand the implementation of the peace agreements, a free quality education for all and increased employment opportunities, among other points. Teacher unions, indigenous groups, and other social groups have joined the protests against the Duque government. The pandemic combined with two decades of neoliberal policies has exacerbated inequalities in Colombia. These policies have affected a considerable swath of Colombian society, including low-income urban youth, minority groups, low-wage workers and even middle-class professionals such as doctors who, despite playing the rules of the game (economic and democratic), find that their daily struggle to subsist has increased over time while their dreams of a future with opportunities have diminished. To quell protests, the government announced that all higher education would be free for lower-income groups. It is yet to be seen if some of these concrete measures will be enough to quell the growing frustration and mistrust of the government that is now deep-rooted in many sectors of Colombian society.

The Dilemma of Governance, Participation and Quality Education

Despite a highly complex historical and socio-political context, Colombia has made significant progress in setting up the basic institutional architecture (information, financing, legal) that led to increased coverage and equality in the education system over the last 20 years. During the period, there were also notable curricular, pedagogic and financing innovations that attempted to enhance the quality of education. However, overall, these programs failed to translate into systemic change and improvement. At the local level, there are some cases of sustained improvement over time. However, curiously these cases applied other criteria and policies (see Rivas et al., 2020).

Education Policy Reforms in Colombia 105

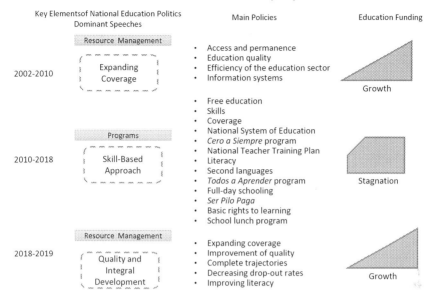

Figure 5.1 Different periods of education reform in Colombia

In the period studied, a series of tensions and paradoxes emerge in the formulation, implementation and evaluation of education reforms. There has been a tendency in Colombia to develop and formulate policies from a top-down and technocratic logic. Reforms focused on standards and assessments are rooted in this logic. The ministers and educational authorities may have opted for more top-down technical approaches due to their conservative political orientation. Nevertheless, they also may have opted for top-down reforms for political expediency in a context of complex relations with teacher unions and lack of local institutional capacity, and broader political dynamics made building consensus difficult.

Some programs and policies have emerged from below with innovations in larger cities with bigger budgets, such as Bogotá and Medellín, such as the school information system and the school feeding program. However, academic experts and technocrats developed many national education policies, and not necessarily in deep consultation with teachers and communities with different needs.

As in many other countries in the region, the paradox in Colombia is that decentralization and autonomy have posed a dilemma for educational policy-makers when attempting to improve quality and equality in education. The principles of autonomy, diversity and relevance are essential to ensure the right to education. However, lack of capacity at different levels, institutions and actors within the system undermines those principles and puts the right to quality education at risk. In some countries of the region, such as Ecuador, governors have used these arguments to regain control over the system, with the idea of making it fairer, and to grant autonomy to local entities and schools gradually:

> Autonomy must be earned. Driving accountability toward schools is critical for a long-term sustainable change. However, this is a gradual process of orientation and supervision and, ultimately, implies granting autonomy when specific benchmarks have been achieved. This may be a challenging process in societies with authoritarian traditions and some of the long-term perverse policy effects of a welfare state. Local communities have become dependent on the central administration to receive instructions and resources.
>
> (Baxter, 2016, pp. 203–204)

In the case of Colombia, it is evident how this tension between decentralization and education reforms has conditioned the scope and results of education policies. The short-term solution for many countries is to recentralize critical aspects of the system and use market mechanisms to control local actors from afar (assessments, standards, competencies). However, recent history in Colombia and the region shows us that these mechanisms have failed to produce transformations in classroom practices in many countries. Therefore, education quality remains a challenge.

Generating a new political dynamic to formulate and implement education policies is, in many aspects, one of the most demanding challenges for Colombia. This would imply promoting the conditions to develop more inclusive ways to generate education policy at all levels, particularly in contexts with high inequality and distrust between state and local actors. In addition, there is a critical need to open more public spaces for political, social and union dialogue and individual, organizational and systemic learning.

This inclusive approach to policymaking will require changing policymakers' perceptions of teachers, who should not be seen as a problem or obstacle to driving changes but acknowledged for their existing capacities. Similarly, Ossenbach (1999) argues that the emergence of the technocratic approach in the early 1950s shifted the decision-making process around crucial education aspects (policy formulation, curriculum and evaluation) away from teachers. Technocrats in the Ministry of Central Planning and international organizations began to be responsible for all the decision-making. As a result, teachers lost their leading role and gave up the fight for education change and reform (Ossenbach, 1999).

In this sense, the challenge is to rethink education policy (its formulation, implementation and evaluation) in a way that combines more participatory perspectives with informed technical rigor, bearing in mind that for a public policy to be feasible, sustainable and meaningful, it must be developed with actual participation of the parties involved but also considering evidence from different contexts and realities (Baxter, 2016).

Notes

1 The Colombian Conflict refers to "military actions, attacks in small towns, targeted killings, massacres, terrorist attacks, kidnappings, forced disappearances, sexual violence, damages to civil property; recruiting and exploitation of boys, girls and teens; anti-personnel mines and unexploded munitions." Victims are attributed to paramilitary groups, the guerrilla and state agents (CNMH, 2018).
2 www.urosario.edu.co/Periodico-NovaEtVetera/Documentos/Reporte-LaboUR-Informalidad-Mayo-2018-PERFIL-ACTUA.pdf
3 Essential skills: basic, communicative and arithmetic skills, using technology, mastering a second language.
4 Generic skills: common to a range of sectors.
5 Specific skills: knowledge, skills and attitudes for a particular professional activity.
6 This system was created to allow Higher Education Institutes (IES, in Spanish) to automatically do the paperwork related to the process of registering Qualified Programmes and other institutional processes such as recognition of legal status, approval of feasibility studies for public Higher Education Institutions, change of character, recognition as a university, redefinition for the offering of propaedeutic cycles and authorization to create branches (National Ministry of Education, 2017).
7 The Qualifications National Framework is an instrument to classify and organize in a level scheme knowledge, skills and competencies, based on criteria related to the lessons learned by people (National Ministry of Education, 2017).

References

Baxter, J. (2016). *Who Governs Educational Change? The Paradoxes of State Power and the Pursuit of Educational Reform in Post-Neoliberal Ecuador (2007–2015)*. Doctoral Dissertation, University of Maryland.

Centro Nacional de Memoria Histórica. (2018). *262.197 muertos dejó el conflicto*. Retrieved from www.centrodememoriahistorica.gov.co/noticias/noticias-cmh/262-197-muertos-dejo-el-conflicto-armado.

Cepeda Ulloa, F. (2004). *Fortalezas de Colombia*. Ariel and Banco Interamericano de Desarrollo.

Corpoeducación, Fundación Corona, Fundación Empresarios por la Educación, Programa de Promoción de la Reforma Educativa en América Latina y el Caribe — PREAL. (2006). *Hay avances, pero quedan desafíos*. Informe de progreso educativo de Colombia.

Departamento Nacional de Planeación. (2003). *Plan nacional de desarrollo 2002–2006: hacia un estado comunitario*. Retrieved from https://colaboracion.dnp.gov.co/cdt/pnd/pnd.pdf.

Departamento Nacional de Planeación. (2007). *Plan nacional de desarrollo 2006–2010. Estado comunitario: Desarrollo para todos*. Retrieved from https://colaboracion.dnp.gov.co/CDT/PND/PND_Tomo_1.pdf.

Departamento Nacional de Planeación. (2011). *Plan nacional de desarrollo 2010–2014: prosperidad para todos*. Retrieved from https://colaboracion.dnp.gov.co/CDT/PND/PND2010-2014%20Tomo%20I%20CD.pdf.

Departamento Nacional de Planeación. (2015). *Plan nacional de desarrollo 2014–2018: todos por un nuevo país*. Retrieved from https://colaboracion.dnp.gov.co/CDT/Prensa/PND%202014-2018%20Bases%20Final.pdf.

Departamento Nacional de Planeación. (2018). *Plan nacional de desarrollo 2018–2022: pacto por Colombia, pacto por la equidad.* Retrieved from https://colaboracion.dnp.gov.co/CDT/Prensa/Resumen-PND2018-2022-final.pdf.

Fundación Empresarios por la Educación. (2018). *Ideas para tejer: reflexiones sobre la educación en Colombia 2010–2018.* Fundación Empresarios por la Educación.

García, M., Espinosa, J., Jiménez, F., & Parra, J.D. (2013). *Separados y desiguales. Educación y clases sociales en Colombia.* Colección De Justicia. Ediciones Antropos.

Herrera, J.D., & Bayona, H. (2018). *21 voces: historias de vida sobre 40 años de educación en Colombia.* Ediciones Uniandes-Universidad de los Andes.

Melo, J.O. (2017). *Historia mínima de Colombia.* El Colegio de Mexico AC.

Ministerio de Educación Nacional. (2006). *Plan nacional decenal de educación 2006–2010.* Retrieved from www.plandecenal.edu.co/cms/media/herramientas/pnde_2006_2016_cartilla.pdf.

Ministerio de Educación Nacional. (2015). *Colombia, la mejor educada en el 2025: líneas estratégicas de la política educativa del Ministerio de Educación Nacional.* Retrieved from www.mineducacion.gov.co/1759/articles-356137_foto_portada.pdf.

Ministerio de Educación Nacional. (2016). *Plan nacional decenal de educación 2016–2026.* Retrieved from www.plandecenal.edu.co/cms/images/PLAN%20NACIONAL%20DECENAL%20DE%20EDUCACION%202DA%20EDICION_271117.pdf.

Ministerio de Educación Nacional. (2017). *Introducción al MNC. Marco nacional de cualificaciones: Colombia.* Retrieved from www.mineducacion.gov.co/1759/articles-362828_recurso.pdf.

OECD. (2020). *Public Governance Scan: Colombia.* OECD. Retrieved from www.oecd.org/gov/Colombia-Scan-Final-English.pdf

Ossenbach, G. (1999). La educación en el Ecuador en el período 1944–1983. *Estudios interdisciplinarios de América Latina y el Caribe,* 10(1), 37–60.

Redacción Portafolio. (2010). Durante la era Uribe el país se rajó en educación: aumentó la inversión, pero disminuyó la calidad. *Revista Portafolio.* Retrieved from www.portafolio.co/economia/finanzas/uribe-pais-rajo-educacion-aumento-inversion-disminuyo-calidad-426896.

Rivas, A. (2015). *América Latina después de PISA: lecciones aprendidas de la educación en siete países (2000–2015).* CIPPEC-Natura-Instituto Natura.

Rivas, A. et al. (2020). *Las llaves de la educación: Estudio comparado sobre la mejora de los sistemas educativos subnacionales en América Latina.* Fundación Santillana.

UNESCO. (2013). *Situación educativa de América Latina y el Caribe: hacia la educación de calidad para todos al 2015.* Oficina Regional de Educación para América Latina y el Caribe (OREALC/UNESCO Santiago). Retrieved from www.unesco.org/new/fileadmin/MULTIMEDIA/FIELD/Santiago/images/SITIED-espanol.pdf.

6 The Educational Policy Agenda in Mexico (2000–2020)

A Time of Continuities and Political Shocks

Juan C. Olmeda and Valentina Sifuentes

This chapter proposes an analysis of the educational policy agenda in Mexico during the 2000–2019 period. In this sense, we review the educational initiatives promoted by the federal government, based on a periodization organized around the presidential administrations. The year 2000 is considered its starting point since political alternation in the presidency took place then. As a result, after seven decades of PRI hegemony, an opposition candidate took office. The analysis presents results from a qualitative study based on the analysis of official documents and the review of academic articles on the subject. Thus, it reconstructs the panorama of national policies implemented during the period of study, outlining the national scenario in which the improvements registered in the subnational cases studied for the research project took place.

The year 2000 was a turning point in the modern political history of Mexico, as, after 70 years in the presidency, the Institutional Revolutionary Party (PRI, in Spanish) was defeated in the elections, which took place in July of that year. The opposition candidate, Vicente Fox of the National Action Party (PAN, in Spanish, center-right), was proclaimed president. The decline in PRI's hegemony had begun several years before: in 1989 an opposition candidate had been elected in a government election after several decades, and in 1997 the PRI had lost its majority in the Chamber of Deputies. The PRI leaving the presidency was proclaimed by many analysts as an irreversible change. Many thought that political alternation would be helpful to promote essential changes in the quality of life of Mexicans, which was encouraged by Fox's discourse during the campaign.

This vision was deepened during the early days of the new government when the incoming president aimed to install the idea that he would rule differently. This meant, for instance, the incorporation of both mechanisms and prominent leaders from the business world. The fact that a head-hunting company was requested to identify potential candidates for the cabinet was much commented on. At the same time, an agenda aimed at promoting a series of structural reforms to the Mexican economy was added. However, Fox confirmed immediately that there were structural limits to his attempts at reform. His party did not have a majority in either house of Congress and was supported only by a few governors. In addition, the search to generate

DOI: 10.4324/9781003225782-6

agreements with a sector of the PRI was overthrown after a failed attempt to promote a reform aimed at extending the scope of VAT to food and medicines, which are still exempted today. On the economic level, the first years of the Fox administration coincided with a fall in oil prices, one of Mexico's main exports and a central source of resources for the public sector, which affected government finances. Due to the Mexican productive matrix and its close ties to the United States, the country was also unable to take advantage of the so-called "commodities boom" from which South American countries benefited.

This essentially explained why, during the last years of the six-year term, Andrés Manuel López Obrador, then Chief of Government of Mexico City, began to gain strength and eventually became the candidate of the Democratic Revolution Party (PRD, in Spanish, center-left). Lopez Obrador ended up competing against the ruling party candidate Felipe Calderón in the 2006 elections. The elections were defined by a narrow margin in favor of Calderón (only a 0.56% difference). However, they were followed by fraud accusations that almost paralyzed the country for several weeks.

Faced with accusations of a lack of legitimacy at the beginning of his term, President Calderón tried to promote policies that would strengthen his leadership and put the "war on drugs" at the center of his agenda. The involvement of the armed forces in internal security tasks, the strengthening of the police, and the focus on the fight against drug cartels defined the policy of his six-year term. However, poor economic growth caused mainly by the 2007–2008 global financial crisis that particularly affected the country and the steady increase in violence made the PRI gain strength again as the 2012 presidential elections approached. In the end, its candidate, Enrique Peña Nieto, won the contest, followed by López Obrador, who ran for office for the second time.

The Peña Nieto six-year term began with the negotiation of the so-called Pact for Mexico, an agreement signed by the three main political forces (PRI, PAN and PRD) aimed at promoting a series of structural reforms in different public policy areas that were supposed to allow the country to gain dynamism and improve economic growth. Education stood out among the areas on which agreements were reached, and a reform bill was submitted to Congress a few days after the new president took office. The dynamism that this agenda of transformations generated during the first years of the Peña Nieto administration began to decrease when implementing many of these measures, evidenced by their problems. The Mexican agenda was highlighted as an exemplary case by publications such as *Time Magazine* or the *Economist*. However, despite the government's efforts to downplay the importance of security policy, the sustained increase in violence and murders linked to drug trafficking negatively affected the president's popularity. The disappearance and alleged murder of 43 students from the Ayotzinapa School in Guerrero by a group that included drug traffickers and security forces became a turning point. Protests demanding justice multiplied throughout the country, and the federal government was slow to understand the relevance of the issue. This led to a sustained deterioration of Peña Nieto's image, which deepened with the emergence of corruption allegations involving Peña Nieto and his wife. In addition to this and the lack of improvements derived from the reforms implemented and the low economic growth, the last years of his mandate were defined by growing citizen discontent.

This explains why, as the 2018 presidential elections approached, López Obrador regained strength as an alternative. As a candidate for president for the third time, he designed a campaign centered on the need for change and the promise to re-found the country. He openly attacked the reforms promoted by Peña Nieto, proposing that if elected, he would reverse many of the measures derived from them, particularly in education. The elections sealed an overwhelming victory for López Obrador, who obtained 53% of the votes, an unprecedented event since the early 1980s. For the first time since 1997, the newly elected ruling coalition also achieved a majority in both legislative chambers, something which Fox, Calderón and Peña Nieto had lacked. This concentration of power allowed him to reverse several of the policies of his predecessors during his first year in office.

Educational Administration

In Mexico, the Secretariat of Public Education can be compared to what in other countries is known as a Ministry of Education. However, Mexico only has state education secretariats at the subnational level, as municipalities do not have relevant powers, unlike other education systems where the local level is the most important (Matínez Rizo, 2018a). For most of the period under analysis, another quality of the Mexican education system was the existence of self-governed bodies such as the National Institute for Educational Evaluation (INEE, in Spanish), which in 2019 was dissolved to create the National Center for the Revaluation of the Teaching Profession.

In the last 18 years of government, eight secretaries of education have succeeded one another. However, in terms of tenure in office, only one of those who held this position remained for the six-year presidential term (Reyes Tamez Guerra). In the rest of the cases, the average period was around three years. As for the profiles, it is worth mentioning that only one of them had previous experience in the educational sector: Reyes Tamez Guerra had previously held various positions at the Universidad Autónoma de Nuevo León, in which he became the rector. Regarding the others, the predominant profile was that of people with broad experience in politics and/or public administration, although in positions not necessarily related to education. This suggests that they were chosen for their positions probably because of their negotiating skills or their experience in managing government areas and implementing public policies. For instance, both Emilio Chuayffet and Otto Granados had a broad political career within the PRI before taking office. This led the former to hold different positions in the government of the State of Mexico until he became its governor in 1993. Then, in 1995, he became the Secretary of the Interior in the federal administration, a position that was then considered one of the most powerful in the cabinet.

Therefore, it is not surprising that Peña Nieto chose him to carry out one of the most critical reforms promoted by his government. Otto Granados also had a broad political career before becoming Secretary of Education, holding various positions in the federal public administration, and serving during the 1992–1998 period as governor of Aguascalientes, a position from which he promoted various educational policies that became a reference for the rest of the country. José Ángel Córdova, Aurelio Nuño, Josefina Vázquez and Esteban Moctezuma are part of this group, although unlike the previous two, they did not hold elected positions in the executive branch: Córdova served as a deputy for one term before becoming Secretary; Vázquez Mota was also a deputy before and after heading the SEP; Moctezuma held a seat in the Senate, although it was only for one year. It is also worth mentioning that Cordova previously served as Secretary of Health (his area of expertise) and was appointed to education because of Alonso Lujambio's health problems that made him step away from the position.

A common element to the first three is that they never hid their political ambitions. Córdova left the Secretariat of Health to become a candidate for governor of the state of Guanajuato (an electoral battle in which he was defeated), and Nuño left his position in education to try to become a candidate for the presidency (something he did not achieve). Vázquez Mota served as Secretary of Social Development during the Fox administration and played an active role in promoting Calderón's candidacy in 2006. As a result, she was appointed Secretary of Education when Calderon took office. After stepping away from that position and from the Chamber of Deputies, Vázquez Mota saw a boost in her image. Vázquez Mota's increasing notoriety led to her becoming the PAN candidate to run for president in 2012. Moctezuma, in contrast, developed an intense political life in the 1990s, which allowed him to become Secretary of the Interior and then Secretary of Social Development. However, at the beginning of this century and with the alternation of power, he distanced himself from politics. Instead, he performed various activities in the private sector – the most outstanding one was being Executive Director of Fundación Azteca, a philanthropic organization linked to one of the most important economic groups in the country until López Obrador called him to lead the educational portfolio. On the other, Alonso Lujambio built an academic profile in the university field throughout his professional life with a specialization in electoral studies. The latter led him to become General Counselor of the Federal Electoral Institute (IFE, in Spanish) from 1996 to 2003. Subsequently, between 2005 and 2009, he was a named Commissioner and President of the Federal Institute of Access to Information.

However, the dynamics of educational administration in Mexico cannot be understood without considering another relevant actor: the National Union of Education Workers (SNTE, in Spanish) and its leader for most of the period under analysis, Elba Ester Gordillo. During PRI hegemony, the SNTE played a central role in the party's corporate network, being the union with the most significant number of members and the broadest territorial deployment. Its strength became evident in 1992 when the transfer of education from the central government to the states was carried out. Even though some of the promoters of decentralization believed that the initiative would serve to de-structure the union and take labor negotiations to the state level, the SNTE managed to resist and remained unified. Its power was even greater after the alternation of administrations. Both Fox and Calderón tried to establish alliances with Gordillo to count on her support in the educational field, promote reforms at other levels and even use union networks for electoral purposes. For instance, some believe the SNTE played an essential role in mobilizing voters in favor of Calderón in 2006. One of this administration's pillars was the vast number of resources managed by the union, in many cases used in a non-transparent manner and outside the scope of the law. This central position was further defined when, after several conflicts with different leaders within the PRI, Gordillo decided to promote the creation of a new political party (Partido Nueva Alianza; PANAL, in Spanish). In addition, the union managed to control several vital offices both in the Federal Congress and in the states.

With these power resources, the SNTE and Gordillo were able to play a relevant role in national politics, especially during the 2000–2012 period, obtaining necessary concessions from the government concerning decisions related to the filling of positions in schools, having de facto power over the appointment of those who should occupy them (in many cases in exchange for money) as well as in positions of power in both the federal SEP and state education secretariats. Thus, from 2006 to 2011, the federal Undersecretary of Basic Education was led by Fernando González, Gordillo's son-in-law.

However, a significant break occurred towards the end of 2012 due to a growing confrontation between the SNTE and the federal government. The altercation concerned the educational reform proposed by Peña Nieto. Within this framework, through the Federal Attorney General Office, the government arranged for his arrest in February 2013 when he returned in a private jet owned by the union from his home in San Diego (United States). The accusations included references to crimes such as money laundering and the use of resources of illicit origin. As a result, the leader was detained, first in jail and then on house arrest, for five years until the justice system determined in favor of his release in August 2018 due to legal weaknesses in the prosecution's case (this took place on the same day that López Obrador received his confirmation as President-Elect). His arrest led the government to discipline the union leadership, supporting the proposed reforms.

t is essential to point out that the SNTE is not a monolithic body. On the contrary, the local sections are dominated in different states by more radical internal currents with great mobilization capacity. The most important one is the National Coordination of Education Workers (CNTE, in Spanish), founded in 1979 by a group of dissidents to promote the democratization of the SNTE. The teachers in the CNTE, which is dominant in Oaxaca, Guerrero, Chiapas and Michoacán have recurrently confronted the government and its various reform projects and the authorities of the SNTE.

The Education Agenda during the 2000–2019 Period

In order to understand the evolution of education policy in Mexico since the beginning of the century, it is essential to point out that decades earlier the country had managed to expand the scope of the educational system to achieve high levels of coverage. In this sense, by the end of the 1980s, universal coverage in elementary school had already been achieved. The need to focus on other aspects, such as dealing with inequality and promoting quality, began to be considered. The type of reforms that, according to Grindlee (2004), can be considered *easy* were replaced by those that we can define as *difficult* because, as Martínez Rizo (2018a, 2018b) argued, they involved long chains of decisions and actions that must be adopted in the classroom with many levels of implementers. Other roadblocks include laziness, misjudgment, organizational jealousy and logistics, all of which make it much more challenging to achieve the objectives that were set out.

Decentralization as a Precedent

One of the first strategies within the framework of this new stage initiated in the early 1990s was to move towards decentralization. This action was materialized through the National Agreement for the Modernization of Basic Education (ANMEB, in Spanish), signed in 1992 by the state governors, the President of the Republic, and the leadership of the SNTE (Arnaut, 1998), represented a pact between the real powers of the educational system: the federal government, which reserved decision-making powers over educational services, and the SNTE, which retained the ownership of representation and the labor relationship with the SEP (Fierro et al., 2009).

The decentralization model outlined in the ANMEB resulted from certain political and structural conditions in Mexico at the end of the century: a single-party-hegemonic presidential regime and a corporative-clientelist structure. Consequently, the fundamental political agreements resulted from negotiations between the Federal Executive and the SNTE rather than with the state governments (Fierro et al., 2009). Therefore, the path towards educational decentralization was controlled by the federal government, which maintained the central powers, such as the design of curricula and programs, salary negotiation, substantive aspects of the teaching career and control over the allocation of fiscal resources. Local governments were delegated strictly operational aspects and proposed their curriculum content (Messina, 2008). It is essential to point out that at that time, there were significant differences among the states concerning the management capacities of the education system, mainly linked to whether there was a developed state education sector at the time of decentralization or not.

The Agreement proposed four strategies. The reorganization of the education system along two axes: educational federalism, in which the administration of school resources and establishments was transferred to state governments and the drafting of State Education Laws was promoted; and social participation, in which teachers, parents, and authorities would be integrated into school decision-making. It also proposed the increase in educational expenditure, the reformulation of educational content and materials, the revaluation of the teaching profession and the creation of the teaching degree program. In addition, although the extension of compulsory education up to the third year of secondary school was not formally included in the Agreement, it was officially announced, which was constitutionally established the following year.

As a result of the ANMEB, around 100,000 schools administered by the Federal Government were transferred to state governments in a generalized and unilateral manner to all the federative entities. This transfer was done without considering the differences concerning local educational systems' management capacity; hence, the result of the transfer was heterogeneous. While five already had state education secretariats, the other 26 needed to create decentralized local administration organizations to manage the new functions (Fierro et al., 2009).

In order to provide this reform with legal support, the Third Constitutional Article was modified in 1993. The General Education Law (LGE, in Spanish) was enacted. In eight chapters, this law sought to specify the distribution of the social function of education among the different levels of government (federal, state and municipal). It also established norms regarding equity in education, the educational process, education provided by private entities, the official validity of studies and social participation in education. It included infringements, sanctions and administrative procedures. The *Carrera Magisterial* (teacher training) program was also implemented, which was considered a salary mobility modality based on a horizontal scale (Latapí, 2008) and which introduced an assessment system involving large-scale tests to assess student learning (Martínez, 2013).

It is essential to highlight that the LGE strengthened the leading role of the SEP attributions concerning the direction and administration of the national education system, delegating to the entities accessory and merely operational functions, almost totally conditioned and subject to the approval and supervision of the SEP itself. Therefore, as pointed out by several authors, the educational decentralization model of the Mexican system centralizes power and decentralizes administration (Di Gropello, 1999; Fierro et al., 2009; Latapí & Ulloa, 2000; Ornelas, 1998; Zorrilla & Barba, 2008). However, this decentralization as federalization only transferred the operation and responsibility for educational services to the entities.

In the following years, the educational policy continued to boost the same decentralization model with the arrival of the Secretary of Education, Ernesto Zedillo, to the presidency. During this period, work teams led by Olac Fuentes Molinar and made up of academics, specialists and researchers were promoted to improve printed materials and textbooks free of charge.

On the other hand, with Mexico joining the OECD in 1994, the need to participate in assessment projects at the international level that would make it possible to know the state of various aspects of the educational system was raised (Martínez, 2013). Thus, in 1997, it was decided that Mexico would participate in the PISA tests.

2000–2006 Vicente Fox: 12-Year Basic Education and the School Management Transformation

Fox's arrival to the presidency was presented as a break-up with the past at the political level. The new government did not hide its objective of promoting far-reaching changes in different aspects of the lives of Mexicans. At the educational level, during his electoral campaign, Fox emphasized the need to promote modernization to improve the quality of education through measures such as the introduction of technology in the classroom and the promotion of English language teaching. However, work in general continued along the same axes adopted during the presidencies of Salinas de Gortari (1988–1994) and Zedillo (1994–2000), for instance the emphasis on quality and reduction of inequalities.

From the beginning of his mandate, it was evidenced that the focus would be on placing the school as the center and object of educational transformation actions. In the National Education Program 2001–2006, launched in September 2001, a change in school organization and management was suggested. New technologies to increase school learning were incorporated, and the twelve grades of basic education became compulsory. In 2002 this led Congress to establish preschool education as compulsory. Compulsory basic education consisted of three years of preschool education, six years of primary education and three years of secondary education. Thus, the importance of the school and arising from the transformation of its management to achieve the goals set is established as the starting point and target of the general processes of promoting and carrying out planning and evaluation and updating.

In this context, learning assessment became relevant as a tool for the educational policymaking process.[1] It is also worth pointing out the creation, through a presidential decree, of the National Institute for the Evaluation of Education (INEE, in Spanish) in 2002, to evaluate the functioning of the Mexican educational system in basic and high school education (Martínez Rizo & Blanco, 2010). For this purpose, it was proposed to develop national evaluation schemes that had their first expression in the Examination for Educational Quality and Achievement (EXCALE, in Spanish), focused on primary education, which began to be applied in 2005. This also led Mexico to participate in the UNESCO Second Regional Comparative and Explanatory Study (SERCE, in Spanish) in 2006.

The incorporation of technology into school life also played an essential role in government priorities. The most critical program in this area was the *Enciclomedia* program. This program aimed to provide fifth- and sixth-grade classrooms with a computer, a projector and an electronic board, together with an electronic database and software included on a compact disc for teachers' use.

During the second half of the Fox administration, the program was developed intensively. Then, it continued for some years during the Calderón administration, when it was discontinued amid allegations of irregularities in the bids and contracts to acquire the equipment.

Another flagship program during the period was the so-called Quality Schools, a compensatory scheme that started in 2001. It aimed to provide exceptional support, both in human and material resources, to schools with the most significant lack of educational achievement and/or which were located in highly social marginal areas (Álvarez Gutiérrez, 2003). The program's implementation implied that the selected institutions were granted a sum of money for a specific period of years to purchase both didactic materials and technical equipment and strengthen the pedagogical strategies to promote academic achievement and the training of teachers and administrators. At the same time, the Program to Reduce the Gap in Initial and Basic Education (PAREIB, in Spanish) continued. It had a similar purpose but with a broader scope.

Apart from promoting new initiatives, during the Fox administration, a series of reforms were carried out (or at least proposed) both in terms of curriculum and the institutional design of the system's governance. Regarding the former, the reform of preschool education (which followed the declaration of its compulsory nature) and the proposal for the Comprehensive Reform of Secondary Education (RIES, in Spanish) aimed at the articulation of basic education. Nevertheless, the vision of the competency-based learning model prevailed.

Regarding the latter, the Secretariat of Public Education structure was reformulated to meet the new characteristics of the system in 2005. Thus, the three main offices within the SEP became the Undersecretary of Basic Education, the Undersecretary of Upper Secondary Education and the Undersecretary of Higher Education.

Regarding teacher training, the State Strengthening Program for Teacher Training Colleges was developed (starting in 2005), aimed at strengthening the teaching staff of these institutions throughout the country. However, although the Secretary of Education proposed the need to review the teaching career, this project never had an impact (Ornelas, 2010).

In order to understand this, it is worth mentioning a dynamic that, although registered outside the educational level, had direct effects on it. On the one hand, the situation resulted in the weakness of the ruling party in Congress (where the PRI continued to dominate the Chamber of Deputies and the Senate), which encouraged Fox to look for allies. On the other hand, Elba Gordillo began to play a prominent role as the head of the SNTE. The role helped her become Secretary-General in 2002 and head of the PRI bench in the Chamber of Deputies from 2003. This combination resulted in a closer relationship between the union leader and the president, to the extent that Gordillo became an advocate of the government agenda in Congress. In return, the SNTE gained influence over the definition of the government educational policy and was able to limit any attempt to reform the structure of the teacher's union. However, Gordillo's pro-government stances led to a growing confrontation with sectors of her party, which broke out during voting on a fiscal reform promoted by Fox on which the PRI vote was divided.

The situation increased the pressure against the leader. This pressure led her to resign from the PRI bench and her position in the party. As a result, Gordillo also promoted a new party force, the New Alliance Party (PANAL, in Spanish), which began to move as a political branch of the SNTE.

2006–2012 Felipe Calderón: The Alliance for the Quality of Education

Felipe Calderón's disputed victory in the 2006 presidential elections determined the continuity of the PAN in the federal government, but not the direction of educational policies. The new mandate began with changes in most of the most relevant positions in the public administration (and the Secretariat of Education was no exception). Although educational policies continued to emphasize the concept of quality, there were essential changes in their perspective.

The National Development Plan 2007–2012, launched a few months after the beginning of the Calderón term in office, stated in its diagnosis of the educational system a state of severe obstacles to achieving the planned development, despite the progress made during the previous six-year term. These included a low national scope with significant differences per educational level and region, low school performance levels with significant achievement gaps, lack of technological tools, inequalities in the system reflected in school infrastructure and equipment, and teacher training and professionalization. In response to this situation, it was suggested that the main objectives of the educational transformation should be to raise the quality of education through the competency-based model and reduce regional, gender and socioeconomic inequalities, as well as to promote the use of new technologies and to expand the scope of higher education. Furthermore, Calderón strengthened the political alliance with Gordillo, who, according to some journalistic articles, had played a key role in mobilizing votes that ensured his victory in 2006. This led not only to the fact that the central policies of the six-year term were agreed with the SNTE but also to the fact that from the beginning of the administration, the Undersecretary of Basic Education was in charge of the union leader's son-in-law.

This explains why the main initiative of the Calderón administration, the Alliance for Quality Education (ACE, in Spanish), launched in 2008, was the result of an agreement signed between the federal government and the SNTE leadership. It is worth mentioning that this link was built on the direct relationship between the President and Gordillo, despite the fact that the Secretary of Education, Josefina Vázquez Mota, was reticent in this regard and never managed to establish a good relationship with the leader.

The explicit objective of the ACE was "to encourage and induce a broad mobilization around education, so that society could monitor and embrace the commitments demanded by the profound transformation of the national education system" (SEP, 2008, p. 3). Accordingly, it was structured along five main axes: (1) modernization of schools; (2) ensuring the well-being and integral development of students; (3) integral training of students for life and work; (4) evaluation for improvement; and (5) continuous professionalization of teachers and educational authorities.

Unlike other administrations, the strategy to achieve these objectives did not lead to constitutional reforms but to the implementation of a series of programs. The modernization of schools was planned from the point of view of infrastructure, equipment and modern technology. For this purpose, the Better Educational Spaces Program was created, which was in charge of the National Council for the Promotion of Education (CONAFE, in Spanish), coordinating with school authorities. In addition, to improve children and young people's well-being and integral development, attention was focused on inequality of opportunities, safety and learning. For this reason, the number of scholarships granted to low-income students through the Opportunities Program (under the responsibility of the Secretariat of Social Development) was increased, the School Breakfast Program was strengthened and assistance was given to children living in food poverty or vulnerable conditions through the Social Development Program. At the same time, we continued with the Quality Schools Program, which had begun during the previous administration.

Student safety in schools – relating to places where violence is prevalent – was an issue addressed with the help of the Safe School Program. Finally, to improve learning opportunities, the Full-Time School Program was implemented, through which public elementary schools extended their school day.[2] At the same time, the School Always Open Program was implemented to include extracurricular activities after the end of the school day.

Progress was made with the idea that in order to achieve a comprehensive preparation of students for life and work, "schools must ensure a formation based on values and a quality education, which favors the construction of citizenship, the promotion of productivity and the promotion of competitiveness so that people can develop their full potential" (SEP, 2008, p. 21). Therefore, the reform of approaches, subjects and contents of basic education was promoted based on the competence-based model. According to some researchers, this has allowed the return of a behavioral and efficiency-based perspective of education. Although it is stated that the development of curricula responds to a vision of learning as a process, results are measured only through large-scale examinations and the comparison of scores (Díaz-Barriga, 2014).

Regarding the fourth axis, the ACE stated that "evaluation should serve as a stimulus to improve the quality of education, favor transparency and accountability, and serve as a basis for the adequate design of educational policies" (SEP, 2008, p. 12). In line with what has already been detailed concerning the Fox administration, national and international tests, such as PISA and ENLACE,[3] continued to be used to measure the learning process performance. The creation of a National Assessment System was also suggested to carry out an exhaustive and periodic assessment to establish performance standards based on students' results and, through them – as established in the last axis of the Alliance – of teachers.

The proposals regarding the continuous professionalization of teachers and school authorities were aimed at tying the granting of economic incentives to teachers to the "educational achievement of children and young people" (SEP, 2008, p. 7), according to the results obtained in the standardized evaluations approved by the National Institute for the Evaluation of Education (INEE, in Spanish) (Ornelas 2010). Furthermore, based on the idea that assessment is a stimulus to improve the quality of education, it was also suggested that all new or permanent positions would be carried out through a national public competitive examination. Thus, as of 2008, the National Call for the Awarding of Teaching Positions at the elementary level was implemented.[4]

In general terms, the ACE, as a strategy that guided educational policy during the period, once again focused on the notion of quality with the same connotations as in previous administrations: relevance, efficiency and usefulness. However, at the same time, it carried similar limitations because the advances or delays in terms of quality continued to be thought of concerning educational achievement based on students' results in standardized tests. This mechanism has been highly criticized for setting aside the importance of understanding assessment as a process.

It is also worth adding some other actions that became relevant during the period. First, several curricular reforms took place in the different stages of basic education during these years. Thus, in 2006 and 2007, the changes arising from the preschool and secondary education reform processes began to be implemented. Second, in 2008, an update of primary education and the comprehensive reform of secondary education were undertaken. These elements served, among other things, to strengthen the focus on the development of competencies and define the graduation profiles and the expected learning to be achieved at each stage. These processes served as a background for the comprehensive reform of basic education suggested in 2009 and resulted in new curricula for the different stages in the following years. In addition, the work teams formed by Fuentes and maintained by Gómez Morín were broken up.

Before the end of his administration, Calderón promoted the inclusion of secondary education in basic education. As a result, in February 2012, Congress voted in a reform to Article 3 of the Constitution that set forth the compulsory nature of this stage of education, establishing a 15-year-period of compulsory education in Mexico. At the same time, during the 2007–2012 period, a comprehensive reform process of general education was carried out.

Finally, it is worth mentioning that in 2011 Congress sanctioned a series of changes to the tax legislation at the initiative of the Executive Branch, among which was included the possibility of deducting taxes for those citizens who send their children to private schools. Although at the time this measure generated some criticism from those who pointed out that it could mean moving towards the privatization of education, this change did not result in significant growth of private education (which in primary and secondary education is less than 10% of enrollment, and in preschool and high school education is around 15%), and this remains the same today.

2012–2018 Enrique Peña Nieto: Pact for Mexico and Education Reforms

Education was placed at the center of the government agenda when Peña Nieto took office and signed the Pact for Mexico and the series of suggested structural reforms. During this six-year term, measures were taken that weakened the federalism promoted by the 1992 ANMEB and repealed provisions that had been in force for more than 50 years. In addition, the new government diagnosis proposed that the repeatedly emphasized educational quality could not be achieved if the balance of power between the Secretariat of Public Education and the SNTE were not redefined. In short, the approach assumed that the union had subdued the institutions in charge of the system governance, both at federal and state levels, and unilaterally controlled all aspects related to the teaching career: admission, tenure and promotions. Therefore, any progress started with taking power away from the union (Ornelas, 2018).

Consequently, the document in which the pact agreements were laid down established three objectives for the educational area: (1) to increase the quality of basic education, which would be shown in the results of international evaluations such as PISA; (2) to increase enrollment and quality of secondary and higher education; and (3) to recover the leading role of the Mexican State in the national education system. This last point expresses what would be the fundamental difference concerning previous educational reforms and which, in time, would become the leading cause of their failure. Specifically, this explains the idea that in previous governments, the emphasis on quality (which the new president shared) had focused on student assessments but had neglected teacher evaluations. Thus, assessment was established as an accountability tool (Martínez Rizo & Blanco, 2010). From this conception, a strict teachers' assessment both at entering the teaching career and at tenure was assumed as a mechanism that would guarantee that only the most qualified teachers would be in charge of the education of children and young people. This would result in students acquiring better learning (which would be shown in better results in standardized evaluations). Granados (2018) and SEP (2018) present the official position in this regard.

It was not by chance that the education reform was the first of the structural reforms sent to Congress to comply with the Pact's objectives. It involved amendments to Articles 3 and 73 of the Political Constitution of the United Mexican States and was passed after some amendments in February 2013. The constitutional change was followed, in September 2013, by the approval of three secondary laws. Firstly, the National Institute for Educational Assessment Law turned the INEE into a self-governed constitutional body, granting it independence from the federal Executive Branch in its operation and the power to administer its budget.[5] Secondly, the Professional Teaching Service

Law created the Professional Teaching Service, which redefined the teaching career by highlighting the evaluation by the state as a central requirement for entry, tenure and promotion. The last one was a reformed version of the General Education Law, adapted to the new reality arising from the reform.

However, the regulatory changes were the first step. Implementing the core aspects of the reform (basically the evaluations to which teachers were to be subjected) meant deploying a careful political strategy, taking into account that this was an issue that had historically generated conflicts with the SNTE and, unlike previous reforms, it had not been previously negotiated with the union. It was not surprising that during the months in which several of the initiatives were discussed, Gordillo expressed her disagreement with this initiative, making it possible to foresee a confrontation with this organization. In February 2013, the government took another step forward in its decision to confront the union openly when the Attorney General's Office arrested Gordillo.[6] Apart from the suspicions that had existed for a long time about managing the union resources, the arrest was interpreted as a political act intended to make the SNTE lose strength in the framework of the negotiation of the secondary laws. Particularly of one law that would establish the Professional Teaching Service, mentioned before. Not surprisingly, shortly after this event, the Secretary-General and new President of the union, Juan Diaz de la Torre, declared that the organization would support the reform.[7]

The emphasis placed on recovering the state's steering role also led to other complementary measures based on the diagnosis that the colonization of the system by the SNTE had resulted in a considerable increase in the number of teachers who had accumulated tenures that were incompatible with each other or who were exempted from being in front of the classroom due to union leaves. Two actions were relevant in this regard. First, the SEP conducted a census in all schools in Mexico to gather essential data regarding their operation.[8] One of the unstated objectives of the exercise was to confirm whether the teachers listed as appointed to such entities were working. Second, there was a decision to concentrate the management of teachers' salaries throughout the country within the Secretariat of Finance of the federal government. All these actions led to a sort of re-centralization. The federal government gained power over the definition of the main lines of educational policy and the management of the system. This had never been done before.

Although the government made progress in activities of a more pedagogical nature, which are taken up again later, the evaluation of teachers became the central theme during the six-year term because of several issues. First, because for the president it became the main objective with which he wanted to show that his education reform was moving forward. Secondly, because of the logistical challenges that were generated in the process of implementing the reviews.[9] Thirdly, because of the growing resistance observed in some states of the country by the most combative union sections, which mobilized their affiliates to oppose the proposed changes and to boycott and prevent the carrying out of examinations. In this regard, the cases of the states of Guerrero,

Oaxaca and Michoacán were highlighted. Finally, because the voices of academics and opponents of the measure grew, denouncing that it did not represent an educational reform but a labor reform, in which the technical argument was the search for quality to legitimize evaluation as a mechanism for selection and permanence of teachers (Gil-Antón, 2018).

In this context, the INEE was considered a fundamental actor since it bore the responsibility for coordinating teachers' assessments,[10] along with the SEP (Martínez Rizo, 2013; Martínez Rizo & Blanco, 2010). This also placed it in the storm's eye and turned it into an object of profound criticism from dissatisfied teachers. This led to a decline of the institution and a shift in the functions assigned to the organization at the time of its creation, which led to its dissolution under the López Obrador government.

In the second part of Peña Nieto's six-year term, progress was made in developing actions that were more focused on the pedagogical aspect. In March 2017, the so-called New Educational Model (NME, in Spanish) was launched, which emerged from a consultation process with the most relevant system actors and that continued previous trends, although it was presented as innovative. This supposed new model would articulate compulsory education to put an end to rote learning, reduce the amount of content, retake constructivism and leave out the competence-based approach, encourage collaborative work and the use of technologies, and also incorporated exciting but challenging to implement elements, such as curricular flexibility and autonomy and the learning of socio-emotional skills. It also established the inclusion of English as a compulsory subject (Díaz-Barriga, 2018).

Similar to what had been the norm during previous six-year terms, the NME suggested the need to place the school at the center of the educational system, promoting a school reorganization to adapt it to the new model with more significant margins of autonomy (Mejía, 2017). This was combined with the development of school infrastructure improvement programs (such as *Escuelas al CIEN*) that promoted the transfer of resources directly to schools to deal with minor maintenance and equipment issues. Finally, in this period the Full-Time School Program was expanded. Unfortunately, not all of the above happened due to the delayed start and the new administration's arrival.

2018–Present: Andrés Manuel López Obrador: Backtracking on Reforms and Prioritizing Inclusion

From the beginning of his government, Peña Nieto's central objective was to move forward with structural reforms, putting education in a prominent place. Meanwhile, López Obrador proposed in the campaign that brought him to the presidency that one of his priorities upon coming to power would be to reverse most of the changes. Thus, the repeal of the educational reform became one of the main points of the candidates' discourse, which, in addition, resulted in public outreach with the CNTE (and also with Gordillo, who regained her freedom shortly after the elections). Among the main criticisms was the claim that the teacher assessment had pursued a purely punitive purpose and that it had been more a labor reform than an educational one. This was also connected to the belief that quality should no longer be the primary concern and, therefore, that standardized evaluations and the results obtained by students should no longer be relevant.

The above explains why during the first year of the mandate that started in December 2018, López Obrador promoted a new constitutional reform which reversed several of the changes approved in 2013. The new reform reinforces the state's role, making it responsible for providing teaching materials and infrastructure safeguarding. In addition, free of charge state education at all levels, including higher education, is pointed out.

The reforms and the secondary laws that followed them also advanced on the two points that had been at the center of Peña Nieto's education policy. Thus, the Professional Teaching Service was rolled back, and the Teacher Career System was established, which suggested a reversal of the most questioned aspects of teacher assessment. Since the arrival of the new government, the SEP stopped implementing the evaluations that had already been programmed. On the other hand, the INEE was dissolved and replaced by the National Center for the Revaluation of Teachers and the Continuous Improvement of Education.

These measures were taken within the framework of a change in the conceptualization of the educational field, in line with the foundational discourse with which López Obrador came to power to produce deep transformations that improve the situation of the most vulnerable and traditionally neglected sectors. Hence, it was suggested that educational policy should stop prioritizing quality and shift to emphasizing inclusion. This vision was embodied in the guiding document for the area: the National Strategy for Inclusive Education. This document was considered "a response to the logic of social and educational exclusion that has prevailed for decades" (SEP, 2019, p. 4). Thus, the new government's approach to the problems of the education sector is more than evident when it states that:

> the objective is clear: to progressively convert the current National Education System characterized by being standardized, centralized, inflexible, inequitable and fragmented, into an inclusive, flexible and relevant system that favors access, advancement, permanence, learning, participation and completion of studies for girls, boys, adolescents and young people throughout the country, in their wide diversity, under equal conditions and opportunities.
> (SEP, 2019, p. 5)

Progress in the materialization of these lines in the country was undoubtedly affected by the Coronavirus pandemic in the first months of 2020, and the measures taken to restrain it. One of the most relevant sectors was the suspension of face-to-face classes in March 2020.

Despite the above, it must be pointed out that the new agenda in terms of educational policy had not registered significant advances in the year before the pandemic. Perhaps the most outstanding feature of the López Obrador administration was the implementation of a broad scholarship scheme for education, called "Scholarship Program for the Welfare of Benito Juarez," which replaced the most relevant social program of the previous administrations ("Progress-Opportunities-Prosper"). The program has different components that reach families with children in initial, preschool, primary, secondary, upper secondary and higher education.[11]

The other relevant aspect has to do with the decision to suspend teacher assessments, which had become the flagship of the Peña Nieto administration, in the context of broad criticism of the previous model, highlighting its punitive intention rather than its concern for training, as previously mentioned.

This stagnation in the consolidation of a new agenda for the sector was not only a result of the pandemic. However, it was also related to the change of the Education Secretary Moctezuma, who was formally appointed as Mexico's Ambassador to the United States at the beginning of 2021. He was replaced at the head of the SEP by Delfina Gómez Álvarez, who has a background as a teacher but has been involved in party politics in recent decades.

Conclusions

The agenda that has prevailed in the education area since the beginning of the 2000s in Mexico cannot be understood without referencing two main events during the last decades of the previous century. On the one hand, the policies that during most of the 20th century gave priority to the expansion of the system reached their goals once coverage became universal (especially for primary education). On the other hand, decentralization reforms enacted in the first part of the 1990s transferred management responsibilities to state governments and, as a result, gave the federal Secretary of Education more room to focus on regulation and coordination across the territory.

As a result, it is not surprising that quality emerged as the concept that gained centrality in the agenda pursued by the federal government in the educational area. Many initiatives adopted by the administrations of presidents Fox, Calderón and Peña Nieto were oriented to consolidate a system to assess students' learnings and, later, teachers' knowledge, using the standardized test in both cases. In addition, a particular institutional framework, led by the National Institute for the Evaluation of Education (INEE), was built to advance this line of work.

In this sense, during the period 2000–2018, a sense of continuity defined education policy. For example, the INEE, created during the Fox administration, remained important during the following years but was strengthened. That institution became a central actor and even acquired constitutional autonomy during Peña Nieto's presidency.

Continuity was also stressed because in pursuing this agenda, the federal government was involved in constant negotiations with another central actor in the Mexican educational landscape: the National Teachers' Union (SNTE). Being the largest labor union in Latin America, the SNTE acquired political and financial power throughout most of the 20th century and even became a central partner to the hegemonic PRI, trading resources and prerogatives in exchange for mobilizing its affiliates during electoral processes to favor *priista* candidates. Once this party was removed from the presidency in 2000, the union re-adjusted to the new political scenario and used its power to maintain its bargaining position. As a result, both Fox and Calderon agreed to negotiate part of their agenda with the SNTE and conceded fundamental benefits in exchange. The latter included financial resources for the union and the informal prerogative to appoint officials in critical positions within the Secretary of Education. This also became the rule at the state level. SNTE's historical leader, Elba Esther Gordillo, even emerged as an essential political partner of both presidents.

Peña Nieto's administration kept quality at the center of its agenda and attempted to expand evaluations to include teachers. The educational reform bill passed by Congress at the beginning of his presidency was not only a centerpiece of Peña Nieto's *modernizing* program but also contained an ambitious scheme to make teachers accountable to regular evaluations and impose sanctions on those who were not able to meet minimum requirements. Of course, this initiative was openly opposed by the SNTE and especially by Gordillo. However, unlike his predecessors, Peña Nieto chose to confront them, using old *priista* tactics: Gordillo was accused of corruption and money laundering and arrested. Rapidly, other SNTE leaders declared their support for the reform.

It is necessary to mention that this emphasis on quality was accompanied by compensatory policies and programs focused on poor schools. In addition, during those years, Mexico became a champion of conditional cash transfer initiatives in the social policy area that included education as its central component.

The arrival of Lopez Obrador to the presidency marked a substantive change in the educational agenda in the country. In the past, he had been a fervent opponent of Peña Nieto's reforms and, during the 2018 campaign, openly proposed that if elected president, he would reverse most of those changes. In the educational area, Lopez Obrador argued for the need to move the emphasis from quality to inclusion and considered that previous governments had promoted a neoliberal agenda that should be stopped. Therefore, it is not a surprise that during his first year in office, most legislation enacted during the previous administration was eliminated and supplanted by new regulations. One of the most critical changes has been observed in teacher evaluations since the previous scheme disappeared.

To conclude, it is necessary to stress that even when it is clear that the model that prevailed during the first two decades of the century was already behind, the consolidation of the new model is still pending.

Notes

1 In this area, work continued following what was proposed by the previous government, which in 1997 had decided that Mexico should be included in the PISA test and organized the first application of the test in the country, which took place in May 2000.

2 Assuming that the extension of the school day implies the possibility of raising educational results allows us to observe that the perspective on which the Alliance for Quality Education is based confirms that educational quality is directly proportional to school achievement, which is understood as the results obtained in standardized tests.
3 The National Assessment of Academic Achievement in Schools (ENLACE, in Spanish) began to be conducted in 2006 on an annual basis for students in sixth grade, the third year of high school (as of 2009) and last year of high school (as of 2009). It was a critical assessment that was carried out between 2006 and 2013 with no interruptions. As of 2005, a representative sample of students sat for the the Educational Quality and Achievement Exams (EXCALE, in Spanish).
4 Since 2007, the SEP has established that school heads in upper secondary education would be hired through competitive examinations.
5 The figure of a constitutionally self-governed body became popular in Mexico in the 1990s to protect certain state agencies from political parties and interests. Among the first institutions to acquire such status were the Bank of Mexico, the National Human Rights Commission, and the Federal Electoral Institute (the National Electoral Institute). This status confers the INEE its legal personality and assets, with full technical, managerial, and budgetary autonomy, to determine its internal governance and organization. It also has powers regarding its purpose (educational evaluation).
6 On the same day that the arrest took place, the educational reform was published in the Official Journal of the Federation, coincidentally or not. As previously mentioned, Gordillo remained under arrest for five years. However, towards the end of Peña Nieto's six-year term, she was released due to procedural errors that led to the dismissal of the accusation.
7 This position contrasted with that of the CNTE and the most radical sections, which mobilized in different states during the legislative debate. A permanent camp was even set up in Mexico City's Zócalo in opposition to the reform.
8 It was called Census of Schools, Teachers, and Students of Basic and Special Education (CEMABE, Spanish). However, in some states (Chiapas, Guerrero, Michoacán, Oaxaca), the local unions' collection of information was blocked, and the data collected were partial.
9 The first evaluation was conducted from November 14 to December 13, 2015. According to Granados (2019), in the period 2015–2018 the evaluation of 1,200,000 teachers was carried out.
10 The INEE also continued to be in charge of student assessments. In 2014, the ENLACE and EXCALE tests were replaced by new assessments generated within the National Plan for the Evaluation of Learning (*Planea*, in Spanish). A significant change was that it was decided that the results would not be used to rank the performance of schools and students, nor would they be considered for additional payments to teachers (see Flamand et al., 2020).
11 The objective is to reach almost six million families through these programs.

References

Álvarez Gutiérrez, J. (2003). Reforma educativa en México: el programa escuelas de calidad. *REICE: Revista Iberoamericana sobre Calidad, Eficacia y Cambio en Educación*, 1(1), 11.

Arnaut, A. (1998). *La federalización educativa en México: historia del debate sobre la centralización y descentralización educativa (1889–1994)*. CIDE Colmex.

Bracho, T., & Zorrilla, M. (2015). *Perspectiva de un gran reto*. INEE, Reforma Educativa; Marco Normativo.

Di Gropello, E. (1999). Los modelos de descentralización educativa en América Latina. *Revista de la CEPAL*, 68, 153–170.

Díaz-Barriga, Á. (2014). Construcción de programas de estudio en la perspectiva del enfoque de desarrollo de competencias. *Perfiles educativos*, 36(143), 142–162.

Díaz-Barriga, Á. (2018). "El que mucho abarca…". *Revista Nexos*. October 1. Retrieved from www.nexos.com.mx/?p=39535.

Fierro, M., Tapia García, G., Rojo, F. & Education, OECD. (2009). *Descentralización educativa en Mexico: un recuento analítico*. Retrieved from http://lst-iiep.iiep-unesco.org/cgi-bin/wwwi32.exe/[in=epidoc1.in]/?t2000=028323/(100).

Flamand, L., Arriaga, R., & Santizo, C. (2020). Reforma educativa y políticas de evaluación en México ¿Instrumentos para abatir el rezago escolar y promover la igualdad de oportunidades? *Foro Internacional*, 60(2), 717–753.

Gil-Antón, M. (2018). La reforma educative: fracturas estructurales. *Revista Mexicana de Investigación Educativa*, 23(76), 303–321.

Granados, O. (2018). *Reforma educativa*. Fondo de Cultura Económica.

Grindle, M.S. (2004). *Despite the Odds: The Contentious Politics of Education Reform*. Princeton University Press.

Latapí, P. (2012). *Andante con brío: memorias de mis interacciones con los secretarios de educación. 1963–2006*. Fondo de Cultura Económica.

Latapí Sarre, P., & Ulloa, M. (2000). *El financiamiento de la educación básica en el marco del federalismo*. Centro de Estudios sobre la Universidad de la Unam.(Sección de Obras de Educación y Pedagogía).

Martínez Rizo, F. (2013). El futuro de la evaluación educativa. *Sinéctica*, 40, 1–11.

Martinez Rizo, F. (2018a). Reflexiones sobre las políticas educativas. *Revista Latinoamericana de Estudios Educativos*, 48(2), 71–96.

Martínez Rizo, F. (2018b). Las evaluaciones y su uso para sustentar políticas: el caso de PISA y el Informe McKinsey. *Reformas y Políticas Educativas*, 3, 53–74.

Martínez Rizo, F. & Blanco, E. (2010). La evaluación educativa: experiencias, avances y desafíos. In A. Arnaut & S. Giourguli (Eds.), *Los grandes problemas de México: educación*. El Colegio de México.

Mejía-Botero, F. (2017). *Cuatro años de desencuentros: recuento y reflexión sobre la reforma educativa*. ITESO.

Messina, G. (2008). Análisis comparado sobre experiencias de descentralización y gestión educativa municipal. A. Didrikson & M. Ulloa (Eds.), *Descentralización y reforma educativa en la Ciudad de México*. Secretaría de Educación del Gobierno del Distrito Federal.

Ornelas, C. (1998). La descentralización de los servicios de educación y salud en México. In E. Di Gropello & R. Cominetti (Eds.), *La descentralización de la educación y la salud: un análisis comparativo de la experiencia latinoamericana*. CEPAL.

Ornelas, C. (2008). *Política, poder y pupitres crítica al nuevo federalismo educativo.*. Siglo XXI.

Ornelas, C. (2019). *La contienda por la educación: globalización, neocorporativismo y democracia*. Fondo de Cultura Económica.

Secretaría de Educación Pública (SEP) (2008). *Alianza por la calidad de la educación*. SEP

Secretaría de Educación Pública (SEP) (2018). *El libro blanco de la reforma educativa*, SEP
Secretaría de Educación Pública (SEP) (2019). *Estrategia nacional de educación inclusiva*. SEP.
Zorrilla, M., & Barba, B. (2008). Reforma educativa en México: descentralización y nuevos actores. *Sinéctica, Revista Electrónica de Educación*, 30, 1–30.

7 The Slow Development Process of Educational Policies in Peru

María Balarin with the collaboration of Manuela de Szyszlo

This chapter presents a synthesis of the educational policy agenda in Peru during the 2001–2019 period. It also examines educational policies promoted by the Peruvian state, based on a periodization organized around the different presidential administrations of the period. The synthesis stems from a qualitative study based on the analysis of official documents and the review of academic articles on the subject. The chapter thus reconstructs the scenario of national policies implemented during the period of study. Besides, it outlines the national scenario in which improvements registered in the subnational cases studied in this research project took place.

At the beginning of the first decade of this century, Peru was undergoing a transitional stage. After the fall of the authoritarian government of Alberto Fujimori, who was seeking his third term in office amidst evidence of corruption and human rights violations, Valentín Paniagua took office as interim president. The population demanded a country with more solid democratic and institutional foundations and a more serious commitment to decentralization.

One year after the fall of Fujimori, the electoral process organized by the transitional government culminated in the election of Alejandro Toledo as president (2001–2006). Toledo came to power with a discourse that emphasized the need to strengthen democracy and the importance of implementing reforms to end the strong centralism that characterized the country. To this end, he outlined a series of regulatory reforms aimed at decentralizing government and public administration. These reforms sought to bring the government closer to the people, improve the delivery of public services and democratize government processes by making them more participatory, under the premise that "decentralization of power is the modern face of democracy" (Castells, 1998).

In 2001, the regulatory framework for decentralization was designed with constitutional reform.[1] The "Law on the Bases of Decentralization" (LBD, in Spanish) was passed, which established the new administrative divisions consisting of 25 self-governed Regional Governments, one for each department of the country, and a regional government for the Constitutional Province of Callao. In 2002, the decentralization process formally began with creating these governments and the election of their regional governors.

DOI: 10.4324/9781003225782-7

The decentralization process in Peru has been burdened with problems related to both their institutional design and transference of governmental capacities to the Regional Governments. Regarding the design, although the LBD established the autonomy of the three levels of government, the Organic Law of the Executive Branch granted the different ministries a guiding role both in the administrative systems and in the design and supervision of national and sectoral policies to ensure the functioning of the state "as a coherent and articulated whole" (Comptroller General of the Republic, 2014, p. 375). However, the mechanisms (coordination, incentives, supervision, among others) to ensure adequate governance of the system were not strong enough, and they weakened over time. This led to a series of problems, such as the existence of regional authorities that do not agree with the national government decisions in different matters, including the design of sectoral policies that do not consider the Regional Governments' contributions. Besides, the process of transferring capacities to the Regional Governments did not take place through a gradual and phased progression, as stipulated in the LBD, but through "an accelerated process" in which "accreditation was a formalism rather than a mechanism… to adequately identify the capacity gaps that existed in the regions and municipalities" (Comptroller General of the Republic, 2014, p. 371). This led to subnational governments "suddenly [receiving] a massive burden of functions and powers without the necessary resources or adequate capacities for a timely, effective and efficient provision of services" (Comptroller General of the Republic, 2014, p. 371).

For some specialists, weaknesses in the institutional design and transference process resulted in a "Frankensteinian model" of decentralization that was "destined to fail" (IDEHPUCP, 2017). In this context, a series of problems emerged, such as high levels of corruption, the influence of organized crime, and low spending levels in several Regional Governments.

In the education sector, the decentralization of educational management to the Regional Governments coincides with what has been described so far. However, since 2011, amid the governance crisis and corruption evident in several regional governments, a gradual weakening of the decentralization process began. There has been "a trend towards the reconcentration of budgetary decisions that is reflected in the conduct of large national programs" (UNESCO & CNE, 2017, p. 82), which are designed and managed directly by MINEDU and have been gaining increasing weight in the education budget (Balarin & Saavedra, 2021).

Apart from the institutional and political reforms, the period under study was also a time of significant economic and social transformations. Between 2002 and 2013, Peru's economy grew at an average annual rate of 6.1%, making it one of the countries with the steadiest and most accelerated growth in the region. This was primarily the product of a favorable international environment, characterized by the commodity super-cycle in the global economy and the adoption of macroeconomic policies that contributed towards "a scenario of high growth and low inflation" (World Bank, 2019). Since 2014, however, economic growth has slowed to an annual average of 3%, mainly due to the fall in the international price of raw materials (especially the price of copper, Peru's main export product), and 2018 ended with a 4% GDP growth.

A consequence of economic growth during the period under study was poverty reduction (defined as the percentage of the population living on less than USD 5.5 a day), which fell from 52.2% in 2005 to 20.7% in 2017.[2] This change can also be attributed to the implementation of critical social programs: the *Juntos* program, created in 2005, which provides conditional transfers to the poorest households in the country, and the National Solidarity Assistance Program *Pension 65*, created in 2011, which provides a solidarity pension to elderly adults from poor households (Perova & Vakis, 2010).

Despite these improvements, Peru is a country with significant inequality gaps – a common trend in the Latin American region. Although the Gini coefficient, which measures economic inequality, decreased from 0.41 in 2007 to 0.35 in 2017, it has remained relatively high. Herrera (2017) also shows that the gap in the average expenditure of the richest and poorest quintile decreased between 2007 and 2011, but it remained relatively stable after this period. Inequality is particularly marked between geographic areas: by 2017, around 44% of the population in rural areas lived in poverty, compared to only 15% of the population located in urban areas.

A significant problem that has affected the possibilities of more inclusive development in the country is the high rates of informality in the Peruvian economy. According to figures from the National Institute of Statistics, in 2016, the informal economy represented 18.4% of GDP, and informal employment reached 72% of the Economically Active Population (INEI, 2017). Informal employment poses challenges not only for tax collection but also for the quality of employment and social security, especially among the most vulnerable population and young people (CEPLAN, 2016).[3]

Socioeconomic inequalities and the nature of the economic growth model, heavily based on extractive industries, have also given rise to significant problems, such as a lack of social cohesion, high crime rates and urban violence, and increasing social conflict. Peru, as Hernández (2016, p. 148) points out, is a country that "has grown economically with violence," which has given rise to what the author describes as an "urban dilemma." Moreover, "the extractive development model, based on attracting foreign capital while attributing the state a subsidiary role, has been maintained despite it generating strong social conflict and the reproduction of social inequalities" (Damonte, 2014, p. 38).

A final issue that has strongly marked the period under study, especially the last five years, is corruption and its impact on democratic governance. Corruption in Peru is not a new phenomenon; however, its current form is. The reforms implemented after the fall of the Fujimori government placed great emphasis on strengthening state control and citizen surveillance. However, the interests of governments were focused "on economic stability and the management of social conflicts, leaving aside the fight against corruption" (Panfichi & Alvarado, 2011, p. 18). In a context in which regional and local governments acquired greater power and resources, without adequate control, corruption became more "dispersed and contained in numerous entities and specific areas that cover almost the entire state system" (p. 18). In 2014, official figures showed that 92% of provincial mayors in the country were under investigation for crimes against public administration, and by 2017, five regional governors had been sentenced for corruption offenses. By that year, corruption had also become the primary concern of citizens (Bigio & Ramírez, 2017, p. 2).

Since 2016, investigations related to the Lava Jato case have evidenced the level of corruption in the country. The financing of political parties, public bidding processes, bribery of judges and magistrates are just some of the areas in which grand corruption has operated and which have resulted in several former presidents, high-ranking officials and political figures facing investigation, some under preventive detention, house arrest or barred from leaving the country.

These processes have led to a robust governance crisis. 2018 began with protests over the pardon granted to Fujimori – imprisoned for corruption and human rights crimes – by then-President Pedro Pablo Kuczynski.[4] Just three months later, in March 2018, Kuczynski resigned from the presidency after Congress launched a second vacancy process against him over corruption allegations. Following his resignation, Vice President Martin Vizcarra took office.

Vizcarra's mandate was marked by an intense confrontation with a Congress led by Fujimori opposition and facing several reform processes and investigations for several corruption cases. In this context, at the end of 2018, Vizcarra called for a referendum to carry out political reform. Successive congressional blockages to the proposed reforms led Vizcarra to propose the advancement of presidential elections in July 2019, which resulted in the dissolution of Congress. The crisis of governance that these events caused has revealed the degree of penetration of corruption and the institutional weakness that characterizes the country.[5]

This is the context in which educational policies took place in Peru during the 2004–2019 period. During this time, the education sector has been led by nine ministers, which has resulted in a great diversity of political discourses on how to carry out educational reform processes.

Despite the ministerial changes, the period can be subdivided into four major stages that coincide with the presidential terms. The 2001–2006 period, during which four ministers were in charge, was a period of significant laws and transformations regarding the management structure of the sector. 2006–2011 was a period of high ministerial stability and idiosyncratic reforms that marked important breaks with existing laws and political agreements. The 2011–2016 period was in the hands of two ministers and saw the launch of large educational programs, the consolidation of the teachers' reform and a progressive recentralization of the system's management. Finally, the period from 2016 to the present has been one of strong political instability and permanent changes in the management of the education sector.

Periodization of Peruvian Education Policy Agendas

2001–2006 – Alejandro Toledo: Great Laws and Transformations in the Management Structure of the Education Sector

In 2001 Alejandro Toledo's predecessor, Valentín Paniagua[6] had considered the importance of a thorough educational reform that would respond to the evident democratic deficit in the country. The starting point for this reform was a national consultation process, which resulted in a National Agreement for Education. The Agreement established, as key reform objectives, the reform and reassessment of the teaching career, an increase in educational investment, the improvement of secondary education, and the decentralization of educational management.

These agreements guided the educational policies implemented during the Toledo administration (2001–2006), a period in which there were four education ministers: Nicolás Lynch (July 2001–July 2002), Gerardo Ayzanoa (July 2002–June 2003), Carlos Malpica (June 2003–February 2004) and Javier Sota (February 2004–July 2006). At the beginning of his mandate, Toledo promised to double the national education budget from 2.4% to 4.9% of GDP and double teachers' real salaries, among other issues.

The main milestone of this period was the enactment of a new General Education Law (#28044) in 2003, which emphasized decentralization and participatory management processes. In addition, the National Education Council was created in 2002 as a specialized advisory and self-governed body of the Ministry of Education, which was in charge of the development, coordination, follow-up and assessment of the National Education Project, which would guide educational policies in the medium and long term. Another important set of education policy guidelines which was approved during this period was the "National Education for All Plan 2005–2015," with proposals for achieving the six objectives set forth at the World Education Forum in Dakar in 2000 (UNESCO, 2000).[7]

From the beginning of this period, much of the policy debate was focused on teachers. The first administration of the period, led by Minister Nicolás Lynch, called a team of specialists to prepare a diagnosis and proposals for improving the teaching career (Rivero, 2002). The main reform proposals that arose from this diagnosis focused on establishing a new merit-based teaching career law, which would be based on teacher performance assessment and would be accompanied by coherent training strategies. However, political instability and changes in the sector's management hindered progress towards this aim (Cuenca, 2011). Thus, during this period, what can be found are mainly strategies aimed at in-service teacher training, such as the National In-Service Training Plan (2001). The latter incorporated the skills from the National Teacher Training Plan (PLANCAD, in Spanish) developed during the 1990s and the pilot plan of Amauta Centers in 2005, which was created to consolidate the country's in-service teacher training model. In addition to this, the program "Better Education through More Time in the Classroom" (META, in Spanish) was included. It was launched in 2003, and it offered incentives for teachers to remain in the classroom. These initiatives, however, ended up working only as specific or pilot strategies, which failed to become a coherent and sustainable training program over time and, above all, did not focus on generating changes in teacher's initial training.

During Toledo's administration, a change in the discourse regarding educational policies also began to occur: greater emphasis was placed on learning achievements measured by performance evaluations, a move led by the Learning Quality Measurement Office (UMC, in Spanish) of the Ministry of Education. In November 2001, Peruvian students sat for the Organization for Economic Cooperation and Development (OECD) Program for International Student Assessment (PISA) test for the first time. They also participated in the National Student Achievement Assessment that year, which was repeated in 2004. Both evaluations revealed a pattern of deficient performance among Peruvian students. These results led Toledo to declare an "Educational Emergency" in 2003 and draft a National Plan to address the situation. According to Rivero (2007), however, the plan lacked proposals for concrete actions, and it did not include "additional funds, which made any transcendent action and any essential change impossible" (p. 82).

During this period, policy discourses also emphasized the importance of promoting innovation and incorporating educational technology. The "Huascarán" Project was a government "flagship" program, which aimed to incorporate and encourage the use of information and communication technologies (ICT) in pedagogical practice to improve the quality of education in rural and urban areas of the country. The lack of funding and management changes made it difficult to achieve the project's objectives, and it never went beyond the pilot phase. The project focused more on the provision of computers than on promoting the use, appropriation and sustainability of ICT in schools (Balarin, 2013). In addition, in 2004, the National Fund for the Development of Peruvian Education (FONDEP, in Spanish) was created with the aim of financing innovation and knowledge management projects that sought to improve learning and close learning gaps, and which promoted collaboration between public, private and international cooperation entities.

This period was also characterized by a series of advancements in the improvement of education in rural areas. A significant milestone in this regard was the approval of the Law for Intercultural Bilingual Education in 2002. During this period, the Education in Rural Areas Project (PEAR, in Spanish) was also launched, with financing from the World Bank. This sought to promote the growth of the educational supply in preschool and secondary education in rural areas, the improvement of educational quality in primary education and the institutional consolidation of rural educational institutions. The PEAR program also sought to facilitate the articulation of efforts regarding access, quality and management of the education sector in rural areas of the country. However, the PEAR program was canceled because of an unfavorable political and institutional context, and its expected results were only partially achieved (Ames, 2015).

Although this period began with an essential boost to educational reform, which resulted in the approval of the new General Education Law, the government did not achieve significant progress in crucial issues raised by that law, such as the reform of the teaching career, the improvement of the educational budget or an effective transfer of functions to regional governments within the framework of the decentralization process (Defensoría del Pueblo, 2009; Rivero, 2007).

2006–2011 – Alan García: Partial Progress in Teacher Reform and Cosmetic Reforms

One of the most notorious characteristics of this period was the great ministerial stability. Minister José Antonio Chang (July 2006–March 2011) was in charge of the portfolio for almost the entire government period. He was only succeeded by Víctor Raúl Díaz (March 2011–July 2011) during the last months of the García administration. This government period was inaugurated with the approval of the National Education Project to 2021: "The education we want for Peru" in 2007, which should have served to organize the policy agenda. The period, however, was characterized by a substantial degree of policy dispersion, the introduction of a series of policy measures that contradicted the priorities defined in the National Education Project, and various policies that were rather cosmetic.

The reform of the teachers' career, channeled through the slogan "better teachers, better students," was undoubtedly the policy area that concentrated the most significant efforts during this period. In mid-2007, amid protests by the teachers' union and while "the technical discussions of the draft bills were abandoned" (Cuenca, 2011, p. 22), the national Congress enacted a new Public Teaching Career Law (LCPM – 29062). The Law aimed to reform the teaching career to be based on merit and not on career trajectory. To this end, it introduced teacher assessment as the primary mechanism for career promotion.

Although the law was an important milestone towards the establishment of a meritocratic teaching career, the confrontational approach adopted by the government concerning the teachers' union, the characteristics of the LCPM and how it was passed, as well as the nature of teacher assessments, made it difficult to achieve substantial progress in this regard (Cuenca, 2009). The main problem with the Law was that the transition to the new teaching career was voluntary, and the 1984 Teachers Law remained valid as the new law was implemented, thus creating two career paths. Although the government expected a massive migration of teachers to the LCPM, the process was relatively slow, and by the end of the period, only one out of four teachers had joined the new teaching career. This is partly explained by the fact that the new career law did not include salary improvements and because there were a series of problems in the technical quality of teacher assessments. The latter focused on the assessment of basic knowledge, rather than on teaching practices, and reproduced a very traditional notion of "education as instruction," centered on "a sort of minimum curriculum" that focused only on two areas (communication and mathematics) (Guerrero, 2009, p. 35). This generated a firm rejection of assessments and weakened the legitimacy of this mechanism.

The other significant measure for improving teaching quality during this period was introducing the Continuing Education and Training Program (PRONAFCAP, in Spanish). The scope of this program, however, was limited. One of its main characteristics was what Cuenca (2017) describes as its punitive nature. The program was intended only for teachers who had agreed to participate in the Teacher Census-Based Assessment, the same for admission to the LCPM. Some of the criteria for entering the program were modified over time; however, the training only reached 26% of the national teaching profession.

Apart from reforming the teacher career, García's administration emphasized the decentralization process, announcing at its inauguration that it would implement a decentralization shock. As a result, the Organic Law of the Executive Branch (LOPE in Spanish) was passed in 2007. It defined the functions of the national government within the framework of its exclusive and shared competencies. In 2009, Supreme Decree 047–2009-PCM was also approved, which established the guidelines for the development of decentralized management and proposed an "Annual Plan for the Transfer of Sectorial Competencies to Regional and Local Governments for 2009." During this period, there was progress in the education sector, and it ended with the formal process of transferring powers to regional governments which had begun in the previous period. However, according to Valdivia et al. (2018), this process had "a purely administrative and bureaucratic bias" (p. 12), as it was not accompanied by adequate funding or a capacity-building strategy that would allow subnational governments to take over their new functions adequately. The government also chose, in clear contradiction with what was established in the General Education Law, to implement a Pilot Plan for Educational Municipalization (2007), "an improvised initiative, without further justification or strategic sense," and that, when it was evaluated some years later, did not show any positive impact (Valdivia et al., 2018, p. 12).

An important issue to point out during this period is the postponement of policies to address education in rural areas and the bilingual population (Ames, 2009; Trapnell & Zavala, 2009). On the one hand, the government ended the Education in Rural Areas Program (PEAR) in 2007. Although the PEAR program had faced several design and implementation problems, there were no efforts to improve it, nor was there a different proposal to assist students in rural areas. On the other hand, the teacher training provided by PRONAFCAP did not contemplate the different strategies required for teachers in rural or multi-grade schools. Something similar happened with intercultural bilingual education, which was abandoned during this period.

The focus of the period was instead on the implementation of a series of specific initiatives, such as the improvement of the infrastructure of 47 "Emblematic

Educational Institutions" (2009) nationwide; the creation of the first high-performance secondary school "Colegio Mayor Secundario Presidente del Perú" (2009); the implementation of the "One Computer Per Child Program"; the launching of the Mobilization for Literacy Program (PRONAMA) in 2006; and the approval of the regulation that allows the establishment of public–private partnerships (PPP) or the Works for Taxes (W for T) exchange for the construction of educational infrastructure. As Uccelli (2011) points out, "a political temptation to favor visible actions" and, in some cases, short-lived in time over more substantive commitments. The One Computer Per Child Program is a clear example of this. Not only did the program lack continuity over time, but also it was not accompanied by the necessary actions to promote an acceptable use of technology in the classroom (Balarin, 2013).

Something worth mentioning for this period is the beginning of the Strategic Program for Learning Achievement of Regular Basic Education Students (PELA, in Spanish) in 2008, within the framework of the gradual transition towards the use of the results-based budgeting mechanism for the management of the sector's financing, promoted by the Ministry of Economy and Finance. The PELA program has been one of the mechanisms that have given greater continuity to the educational policies of the period studied. This program, which has varied over time, consists of articulated interventions and actions that generate a series of products and results through which it is intended to improve the educational achievement of the country's students. The first version of the PELA program (2008–2012) focused on strategies to improve the provision and use of educational materials and improve teaching practice through pedagogical support processes developed parallel to the work of PRONAFCAP. As will be discussed later, this model of budget management and sector policies and the commitment to pedagogical support as the primary strategy for improving teaching practice has become increasingly crucial in MINEDU's policies.

It is worth mentioning that there was a strong continuity in the commitment to learning assessment that was established in the previous government during this period. However, there has been a change in the evaluation agenda and a commitment to the implementation of a Student Census Evaluation (ECE, in Spanish), which evaluates the reading comprehension and mathematics skills of second-grade elementary school students, as well as the reading comprehension skills of fourth-grade elementary school students attending intercultural bilingual education schools. The ECE was first conducted in 2007 and has been repeated annually since then. In 2009, after a six-year interruption, Peruvian students participated in the PISA test again.

2011–2016 – Ollanta Humala: Towards a More Coherent and Articulated Education Policy

During this period, the Ministry of Education was led by two ministers, Patricia Salas (July 2011–October 2013) and Jaime Saavedra (October 2013–December 2016). Although there were some critical continuities between both ministerial administrations, there were also significant differences. Generally, the period was characterized by searching for a more coherent organization of educational policies with clearer management priorities. However, there was a different emphasis between the two ministerial administrations on achieving results, and management was described as more technocratic in the Saavedra administration.

Salas inaugurated his administration by taking up the proposals of the National Education Project (PEN), which, although it had been approved during García's administration, had not been helpful as an accurate reference for the policies of that period. The contributions of the Regional Governments were added to the PEN guidelines, which were embodied in the "Common National-Regional Agenda 2011–2016." These documents became the main reference points for national education policy, prioritizing learning, early childhood, rural and intercultural bilingual education teacher development, and decentralized management. These priorities were reflected in the Multi-annual Strategic Plan (PESEM, in Spanish) 2011–2015.

Decentralized educational management was a clear commitment during the Salas administration, which sought to improve regulatory instruments and strengthen the processes of political coordination and management capacities. At the regulatory level, Salas resumed implementing the General Education Law and discontinued the Municipalization Pilot Plan initiated during the previous period. The commitment to decentralized management resulted in developing a series of instruments that aimed to overcome the gaps and overlapping regulations and improve the delimitation of functions and responsibilities of the different levels of government. These included the Policy for the Modernization and Decentralization of Education Sector Management (2013) and the Matrix and Guidelines for Decentralized Management. The Salas administration mainly emphasized the drafting of the Organic Law of Functions (LOF, in Spanish) of the Ministry of Education as the main instrument that would help clarify the roles of the different levels of government and strengthen the leading role of the Ministry of Education. However, this law has not been discussed or passed so far.

The Salas administration's commitment to decentralization also strengthened intergovernmental coordination spaces between MINEDU and regional and local governments, which led to the signing of a series of Commitment Pacts that should guide educational policies in 2016. Emphasis was also placed on the importance of developing the management skills of the officials of the sector. This commitment resulted in the development of a Strategy and a Capacity Development Plan 2014–2016 for public managers in the education sector, as well as in the implementation of a Public Investment Project (PIP), called "Improvement of the Decentralized Educational Management of IIEE, in Rural Areas of 24 Regions of Peru," which began to be implemented in 2014 in coordination with the 24 GORE.

The other major item on the policy agenda during this government period was improving the teaching career. In 2012, Minister Salas achieved the approval of the Teacher Reform Law (#29944). This law took up the meritocratic orientation of the Public Teaching Career Law but proposed a single and mandatory regime for the teaching career and established mandatory teacher evaluations and a progressive salary structure. The Teacher Reform Law also establishes that access to positions in the institutional management area of the Regional Education Directorates (DRE, in Spanish) and the Local Education Management Units (UGEL, in Spanish) must be through a meritocratic public competitive examination. A significant achievement of the Salas administration in the area of teaching was the approval of the Framework for Good Teaching Performance,[8] which clearly defines the domains, skills and performances that characterize good teaching and has served to guide the teacher assessment processes, as well as the in-service training strategies implemented by MINEDU.

In terms of learning, the Salas administration implemented a series of complementary initiatives. On the one hand, the "Good Start to the School Year" campaign was launched in 2012. It aimed to strengthen intergovernmental coordination and promote the mobilization of all parties (regional and local governments, civil society and families) to ensure that schools start the school year with all the necessary basic conditions. This includes the timely management of teacher recruitment processes, maintenance of school premises, delivery of educational materials and enrollment processes. Since then, the campaign has been established as a regular initiative that takes place every year.

The Salas administration also emphasized improving the curricular policy and moving towards a curricular system that would guarantee the articulation and internal coherence of the different curricular instruments that, according to the analyses carried out, had problems of consistency and clarity in terms of the progression in expected learning (Cueto & Tapia, 2017). The actions developed in this regard took as a starting point the revision of the National Curricular Framework and the work carried out by the Peruvian Institute for the Evaluation, Accreditation and Certification of Educational Quality (IPEBA, in Spanish) to develop learning standards. In addition to these instruments, the so-called Learning Routes were developed to guide the curriculum's implementation in the classroom.

The primary strategy for improving learning, however, was the redesign of the PELA program in 2012. Although the program had been developing pedagogical support activities for teachers in targeted schools throughout the country, the program design had some problems, such as the absence of a conceptual framework and a design incorporating the diversity of different territorial contexts. In addition, there was a lack of a clear implementation strategy to make the management of the necessary processes by the DRE and UGEL easier (Rodríguez et al., 2016). The redesign of the PELA program involved introducing a series of tools that sought to provide pedagogical support to schools of different educational modalities through pedagogical support strategies led by the guidelines of the curriculum system and by the Good Teaching Performance Framework (Balarin & Escudero, 2018). Thus, the

Urban Pedagogical Support, Intercultural Pedagogical Support and Multigrade Pedagogical Support interventions were created.

Salas left his position in 2013. His administration had been affected by a long teacher strike following the passing of the new Teacher Reform Law and evidence of low levels of budget execution and an alleged lack of results during his time in charge of the Ministry. Perhaps Salas' biggest mistake was to place too much emphasis on the ordering of policies and the processes of articulation and dialogue without focusing on the need to achieve measurable results in the short term.

This is the context in which Jaime Saavedra took on the portfolio in October 2013. Although there was continuity with the previous administration, he took over the Ministry with a discourse that emphasized the need to improve efficiency in expenditure and improve results achievement. This led to a strong emphasis on Perfomance Evaluations results and information systems and the introduction of incentive mechanisms to contribute to achieving results.

Saavedra defined four pillars for advancing educational reform: revaluing the teaching career, improving the learning quality for all, effectively managing the school system, and closing the educational infrastructure gap. Although the first two pillars coincided with the priorities of the Salas administration, the emphasis put on infrastructure was something new. In contrast, the lack of emphasis on decentralization in the second pillar could indicate this administration's commitment to more centralized control of education policy.

As regards teaching, Saavedra continued on the same path as his predecessor, although emphasizing the development of actions to revise the teaching career. During her administration, progress was made with the design of new formative teacher performance evaluations. A new remuneration policy was implemented in which salary increases were linked to teaching performance. In 2015, the first teacher appointment and hiring evaluation were carried out within the Teacher Reform Law framework. From the salary policy, differentiated allowances were established according to the type of school. This was an incentive for teachers in rural areas, border areas, or the VRAEM coca-growing area. In bilingual, single-teacher, or multi-grade schools, it was also extended to hired teachers. As of 2014, the School Performance Incentive Bonus "School Bonus" was also implemented, which provides a monetary award to all elementary school teachers and principals whose students have shown good educational results (Cuenca & Vargas Castro, 2018).[9]

Policies aimed at improving learning focused on strengthening pedagogical support programs, in addition to the Full School Day (JEC, in Spanish) and High-Performance Schools (COAR, in Spanish) strategies, which took up and extended to all regions of the country the Colegio Mayor initiative that had been created during the Alan García administration. In curricular matters, Saavedra continued with the revision process initiated by Salas, which materialized with the approval of the National Curricular Design in 2015.

Perhaps the most significant change concerning the previous administration was in terms of educational management policies. Saavedra was emphatic in pointing out that decentralization was not an end but a mechanism to provide educational services better. Thus, the emphasis placed by Salas on political articulation and the importance of territorial management were left behind. Moreover, central control mechanisms on the progress in implementing educational policies were reinforced by developing management indicators and incentive policies. An important initiative implemented during the Saavedra administration was introducing the so-called "School Traffic Light," a monitoring system that allowed the generation of updated information and monthly reports on critical variables such as providing essential supplies and the attendance of teachers and students in schools. Saavedra implemented the School Bonus Program for incentive policies, which granted a monetary incentive to schools with good performance evaluations (León Jara-Almonte, 2016). It also provided for the program of financial incentives to subnational management bodies for compliance with the so-called Teaching Performance Commitments, something that, according to available evaluations, has contributed to ensuring progress in crucial management processes of the system (Sempé, 2017).

The Saavedra administration gave a significant boost to school infrastructure improvement policies. In 2013, the first Educational Infrastructure Census was carried out, making it possible to identify the gaps in terms of premises, classrooms, furniture, technology and complimentary services – food, libraries and sports areas, among others. The Census data made it possible to put figures on the infrastructure gap, estimated at 60 million soles. Within this framework, the National Infrastructure Program (PRONIED) was created in 2014, which established a series of strategies to expand, improve and restore or build various educational spaces. A regulatory framework was designed to deal with the infrastructure needs by taking advantage of Public-Private Partnerships and Works for Taxes mechanisms.

A significant achievement of Saavedra's administration was the approval, in 2016, of the Sectoral Policy for Intercultural Education and Intercultural Bilingual Education and the National Intercultural Bilingual Education Plan to 2021. Both policy instruments focus on improving the access of native members to inclusive and quality education with equity, utilizing diversified service models and improving IBE teacher training and decentralized management with a territorial approach to the educational service.

A key and distinctive element throughout this period of government was the increase in the education budget. Between 2011 and 2015, the sector's budget increased from 3.4% to 4.09% of GDP. This allowed the extension of pedagogical support interventions and the implementation of new initiatives such as the JEC, the establishment of improvements in teacher remuneration, and the implementation of improvements in educational infrastructure.

The challenges of managing a considerably larger budget resulted in a significant change in budget management strategies that led to a gradual recentralization of decision-making power and control of the education budget. This was reflected in the concentration of spending on large-budget programs designed and managed by the Ministry of Education (Balarin & Saavedra, 2021).

In this context, the commitment to decentralized management of education has been strongly weakened. During the period studied, the participation of the central level in the education budget increased, whereas the regional and local governments decreased. In the context of implementing the Budgetary Programs, the UGEL became the operational branch of MINEDU. The role of regional governments in conducting educational policies was considerably weakened. This was justified in a context in which corruption problems and weak management capacities at these levels of government were evident. However, the strategy put forward implied neither a clear commitment to strengthen such capacities nor supervising mechanisms for better decentralized management (Valdivia et al., 2018).

2016–2018 – Pedro Pablo Kuczynski: Political Instability and Confrontations with the Legislative Branch

The 2016–2018 period was marked by significant instability, both in national politics and in the education sector, often at the center of political issues. The term has had two Presidents: Pedro Pablo Kuczynski, who was elected in 2016 and resigned in March 2018 after a series of clashes with an opposition-majority Congress; and his Vice President, Martín Vizcarra, who succeeded him after his resignation. These confrontations had different motivations. On the one hand, there was the questioning of the pardon that Kuczynski gave in favor of former President Fujimori, who was serving a prison sentence for various cases of corruption and crimes against human rights, as well as the evidence that emerged during the investigations of the Lava Jato case regarding the President's involvement in acts of corruption (something that later led to a house arrest order against Kuczynski). However, the parliamentary opposition was also motivated by the rejection of Kuczynski's government by the fujimorista majority and blocking the reforms he proposed, including in higher education.

During this period and to this date, there have been four Ministers of Education: Jaime Saavedra (July–December 2016), Marilú Martens, Idel Vexler and Daniel Alfaro (April 2018–March 2019), who was replaced by Flor Pablo, current Minister of Education, who began her term in March 2019.

The decision to keep Saavedra in MINEDU at the beginning of Kuczynski's government was a commitment to the continuity of the reforms and policies proposed in the previous period. However, Saavedra remained only six months in office. In December 2016, he was subjected to an interpellation process by Congress, which resulted in his censure. The stated reasons for the censure were alleged acts of corruption in the purchase of computers and delays in the Lima 2019 Pan-American Games works. However, several analysts agree that the underlying reason was the university reform implemented by Saavedra, which affected the interests of several economic groups, several with representation in Congress.

After Saavedra's departure, the education portfolio was taken over by Marilú Martens. They had worked in MINEDU during the former minister's administration and proposed a continuity approach with the policies implemented by her predecessor. Martens resigned from MINEDU in September 2017, less than a year after taking office. One of the factors that contributed to her resignation was a more than three-month teachers' strike, in which teachers were demanding, among other things, pay increases and the repeal of the Teacher Reform Law. Although the strike was suspended after agreements were reached on salary increases, the Martens administration was weakened. The rejection by conservative groups compounded this. These groups were supported by Congress's opposition to policies related to incorporating the gender equality approach in the National Curriculum, which had begun to be implemented gradually in 2017. This led to the filing of a lawsuit led by the Parents in Action collective against the ministerial resolution approving the National Curriculum.

After Martens's resignation, the education portfolio was taken over by Idel Vexler, who was Vice-Minister of the area during García's term in office. Vexler's arrival at MINEDU implied a substantial break with the style of previous administrations. It resulted in the departure of many of the ministerial officials linked to the reforms implemented during the Saavedra administration. In a complex political context, Vexler gave priority to negotiations with teachers and the recovery of classes lost because of the teachers strike and the impact of the El Niño weather phenomenon at the beginning of 2017.[10] Regarding the former, Vexler emphasized the importance of improving salaries and created a sectoral commission in charge of preparing a technical study to formulate proposals for the gradual increase of teachers' salaries to one Tax Unit (UIT, in Spanish). It was also established that the assessments for the appointment of teachers would be carried out annually and not every two years, as initially proposed, to provide more significant opportunities for teachers to join the teaching career. On the other hand, priority was given to initial and in-service training, both through pedagogical support programs and the introduction of a Diploma and Second Specialty for school authorities and teachers, through an Induction Program for New Teachers.[11] The other two areas prioritized by Vexler were the improvement of educational infrastructure and higher technical education.

The progress in achieving the objectives set by the Vexler administration was cut short by his departure in April 2018, in the context of Kuczynski's resignation. The successor in the presidency, Martin Vizcarra, began his term with the formation of a new cabinet, in which he appointed Daniel Alfaro as minister of education. Alfaro emphasized teachers and the improvement of educational infrastructure. Regarding the former, his administration managed to show the impracticality of reaching a salary increase of one UIT by 2021. He committed to a policy of progressive improvements according to the fiscal fund. Alfaro faced criticism with incorporating the gender approach into the National Curriculum and initiatives of Congress members who sought to introduce changes in the entry age of students at the initial and primary levels and the reinstatement of school authorities and teachers without prior evaluation. One of the outstanding achievements of the Alfaro administration was the approval, at the end of 2018, of the Educational Assistance Policy for the Population of Rural Areas (DS No. 013–2018-MINEDU), aimed at improving learning achievements, as well as teacher performance and educational infrastructure, in rural areas.

In April 2019, in the context of a change in the conformation of the ministerial cabinet and the appointment of Salvador del Solar as Prime Minister, Alfaro was replaced by Flor Pablo. The teaching issue was one of the main priorities established during the Pablo administration. Emphasis was placed on the need to dignify the profession and the need to resume decentralized management with a territorial approach, and on the importance of rural education. During the first months of his administration, Pablo faced a process of interrogation by the Congress of the Republic, this time focused on the inclusion of allegedly inappropriate content on sexual conduct in educational materials. Regarding the gender equality approach in the National Curriculum, the Judiciary branch ruled in April 2019 in favor of the Ministry of Education, declaring unfounded the lawsuit filed against its inclusion in the National Curriculum (IDEHPUCP, 2019).

Therefore, this period has been one of significant political turbulence, which has hindered substantive progress on important issues such as implementing the New National Curriculum and the consolidation of teacher training.[12]

Conclusion

The period under study in this chapter began with a relatively straightforward education policy agenda, which prioritized teacher career reform, educational decentralization and increased public funding for education. Figure 7.1 illustrates the different periods of educational reform during this time. Although substantial progress was made in critical areas, especially in the reform of the teaching career, education policies during this period have been marked by frequent changes in the sector's management – with some particularly turbulent periods. These changes have not only been associated with alterations in the direction of policies. They have also meant that the cycles during which policies have reached consolidation have been highly protracted. Elements that were expected to generate consensus regarding the main orientations of educational policy, such as the National Educational Project, have not been able to restrain the constant changes in the direction of the educational system, nor have they ensured progress towards the achievement of agreed-upon objectives.

It is not that there have been no significant reforms, but rather the pace at which they have advanced has been extremely slow. The reform of the teaching career and the curricular reform have taken several decades and are not yet fully consolidated. In the case of the teaching career, progress needs to be

146 Balarin

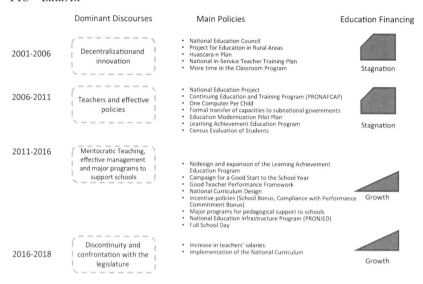

Figure 7.1 Different periods of education reform in Peru

made towards improving teaching practices. There is a need to move away from the compensatory or remedial training that prevails today – which translates into an emphasis on pedagogical support strategies – to comprehensive and continuous training strategies. There are also improvements to be made in the current initial teacher training system and its articulation with the proposed changes at the curricular level and in-service training strategies. In curricular reform, it is urgent to advance in the implementation of the new skills-based curriculum, whose nature and objectives are still not understood by most teachers.

On the other hand, although we find many critical changes during this period, it is possible to say that the main changes constitute first-order reforms, which have focused on "turning the existing system more efficient and effective," but without "disturbing the characteristics of [educational] organizations, nor substantially altering the ways in which adults and children perform their functions [in the context of schools]" (Cuban, 1990, p. 73). There is, therefore, an enormous task ahead in defining what should happen in schools and classrooms and how teachers and students are expected to interact. This is particularly true in secondary education since the main reforms have concentrated on the primary level. Secondary education, on the other hand, shows serious quality problems. Learning assessments have shown that only about 10% of public secondary school students achieve expected learning for their level of study. Strategies such as introducing the Full School Day, which has been implemented in public schools since 2015, have sought to respond to the problems of low quality in secondary education. However, despite its good results (Agüero, 2018), the program has not continued to expand, and additional measures are needed to improve the quality of education at this level.

During the period under study in this chapter, although we find a more significant commitment to rural and intercultural bilingual education, we also see widening learning gaps by socioeconomic level. This is a worrying trend in the Latin American region, in which most countries have advanced somewhat in the opposite direction. In Peru, significant differences persist depending on a student's mother tongue, geographic area and school delivery model. In this sense, there is an urgent need for educational policies and programs to emphasize closing these gaps.

In 2021, Peru begins its third century as an independent republic. The education system has the great challenge – set out in the new National Education Project to 2036 – of promoting citizenship values amongst all students. This implies continuing to advance in the agenda of improving learning, understood not only as results in standardized tests but also in developing capabilities for the exercise of citizenship.

Notes

1 The pillars of decentralization are the Political Constitution of Peru, the Law of Bases of Decentralization (LBD 2002), the Organic Law of Regional Governments (LOGR 2002), the Organic Law of Municipalities (LOM 2003) and the Organic Law of the Executive Branch (LOPE 2007).
2 https://data.worldbank.org/country/peru.
3 According to (CEPLAN, 2016), eight out of ten women, 79.8% of young people between 14 and 29 years old and 78.9% of people with a high school education are informally employed.
4 Later, in October 2018, the Judiciary annulled Fujimori's pardon.
5 This chapter was written before the events that led to the vacancy of Martin Vizcarra by Congress, the inauguration of Manuel Merino de Lama as an illegitimate president, his subsequent resignation after an intense outbreak of citizen protests, and the inauguration of Francisco Sagasti as the new president of the Republic until the elections of 2021, when Pedro Castillo was elected President of Perú.
6 Paniagua was president of the 2000–2001 transition government after the fall of the Alberto Fujimori government.
7 The objectives outlined in the Dakar framework were as follows: (1) early childhood care and education; (2) universal primary education; (3) youth and adult skills; (4) adult literacy; (5) gender equality; and (6) quality of education.
8 See: www.perueduca.pe/documents/60563/cc664fb7-a1dd-450d-a43d-bd8cd65 b4736.
9 The School Bonus has been later expanded to include secondary schools. The bonus is allocated in a differentiated manner to schools grouped into different categories based on fulfilling different requirements.
10 In 2017, the El Niño weather phenomenon caused heavy rains, floods and landslides in the departments of the northern coast of the country. The education sector was one of the most affected, not only because of the schools closing but also because of the severe material damage to the educational infrastructure.
11 www.congreso.gob.pe/Docs/comisiones2017/Comision_de_Educacion__Juventud/ files/20171016-ppt-minedu.pdf.
12 This chapter was completed before the events that led to the departure of Minister Pablo and the fall of the government led by Martin Vizcarra after a constitutional coup carried out by then-President of Congress, Manuel Merino de Lama.

References

Agüero, J.M. (2018). *Logros y temas pendientes de la Jornada Escolar Completa*. Tarea.

Ames, P. (2009). La educación rural: balance del período. In R. Cuenca (Ed.), *La educación en los tiempos del APRA*. Foro Educativo.

Ames, P. (2010). Hacer visible y mejorar la educación rural: una tarea pendiente. In Consorcio de Universidades (Ed.), *Metas del Perú al bicentenario*. Asociación Peruana de Empresas.

Balarin, M. (2013). *Las políticas TIC en los sistemas educativos de América Latina: el caso Perú*. UNICEF.

Balarin, M., & Escudero, A. (2018). *Evaluación del diseño e implementación de la intervención de soporte pedagógico intercultural del Ministerio de Educación del Perú*. GRADE; FORGE.

Balarin, M., & Saavedra, M. (2021). Los caminos encontrados del financiamiento y la descentralización educativa en el Perú. In C. Guadalupe (Ed.), *La educación peruana más allá del bicentenario: nuevos rumbos*. Universidad del Pacífico.

Bigio, S., & Ramírez, N. (2017). *Corrupción e indicadores de desarrollo en el Perú y el mundo: una revisión empírica*. Asociación Peruana de Economía.

Castells, M. (1998). *La era de la información: economía, sociedad y cultura*. Alianza Editorial.

CEPLAN. (2016). *El rostro de la informalidad en el Perú*. Retrieved from www.ceplan.gob.pe/blog/el-rostro-de-la-informalidad-en-el-per/.

Comptroller General of the Republic. (2014). *Estudio del proceso de descentralización en el Perú*. La Contraloría General de la República.

Cuban, L. (1990). A fundamental puzzle of school reform. In A. Lieberman (Ed.), *Schools as Collaborative Cultures: Creating the Future Now*. The Falmer Press.

Cuenca, R. (2011). *La carrera pública magisterial: una mirada atrás para avanzar*. Tarea.

Cuenca, R. (2017). *La educación en los tiempos del APRA: ayuda memoria sobre la política docente 2006–2011*. Retrieved from https://ricardocuenca.lamula.pe/2017/08/20/la-educacion-en-los-tiempos-del-apra/palimpsesto/.

Cuenca, R., & Vargas Castro, J.C. (2018). *Perú: el estado de políticas públicas docentes*. IEP.

Cueto, S., & Tapia, J. (2017). *El apoyo de FORGE al desarrollo del Currículo Nacional de la Educación Básica del Perú*. GRADE; FORGE.

Damonte, G. (2014). El modelo extractivo peruano: discursos, políticas y la reproducción de desigualdades sociales. In B. Gobel & A. Ulloa (Eds.), *Extractivismo minero en Colombia y América Latina*. Universidad Nacional de Colombia; Ibero-AmerikanischesInstitut.

Defensoría del Pueblo. (2009). *Primera supervisión del Plan de Municipalización de la Gestión Educativa: aportes para su implementación*. Defensoría del Pueblo.

Guadalupe, C., León, J., Rodríguez, J., & Vargas, S. (2017). *Estado de la educación en el Perú: análisis y perspectivas de la educación básica*. GRADE; FORGE.

Guerrero, L. (2009). Política docente: balance del período. In R. Cuenca (Ed.), *La educación en los tiempos del APRA*. Foro Educativo.

Hernández, W. (2016). Teorías y evidencias del "dilema urbano" en el Perú ¿Por qué crecimos económicamente con violencia? 2000–2012. *Economía*, 39(77), 145–185.

Herrera, J. (2017). Pobreza y desigualdad económica en el Perú durante el boom de crecimiento: 2004–2014. *International Development Policy, Revueinternationale de politique de développement*, 9(9). https://doi.org/10.4000/poldev.2518.

IDEHPUCP. (2017). *Entrevista a Eduardo Ballón: "La descentralización estaba condenada al fracaso"*. Retrieved from http://idehpucp.pucp.edu.pe/notas-informativas/logro-modelo-regional-sacarnos-del-centralismo/.
IDEHPUCP. (2019). *El enfoque de género en el Currículo Nacional: cuatro preguntas claves para entender la resolución de la Corte Suprema*. Retrieved from http://idehpucp.pucp.edu.pe/analisis/el-enfoque-de-genero-en-el-curriculo-nacional-cuatro-preguntas-clave-para-entender-la-resolucion-de-la-corte-suprema/.
INEI. (2017). *Producción y empleo informal en el Perú: Cuenta pública de la reforma educacional 2007–2016*. Instituto Nacional de Estadística e Informática.
León Jara-Almonte, J. (2016). *Evaluación de impacto del Bono de Incentivo al Desempeño Escolar o "Bono Escuela"*. Fortalecimiento de la Gestión de la Educación en el Perú.
Panfichi, A., & Alvarado, M. (2011). *Corrupción y gobernabilidad*. CIES; PUCP.
Perova, E., & Vakis, R. (2010). *El impacto y potencial del programa Juntos en Perú: evidencia de una evaluación no-experimental*. Programa Juntos, Banco Mundial.
Rivero, J. (2002). *Propuesta: nueva docencia en el Perú*. Ministerio de Educación del Perú.
Rivero, J. (2007). *Educación, docencia y clase política en el Perú*. Ayuda en Acción, Tarea.
Rodríguez, J., Leyva, J., & Hopkins, Á. (2016). *El efecto del programa Acompañamiento Pedagógico sobre los rendimientos de los estudiantes de escuelas públicas rurales del Perú*. GRADE; FORGE.
Sempé, L. (2017). *Balance de la implementación del mecanismo de los Compromisos de Desempeño como impulsor de mejoras en la gestión educativa descentralizada*. Fortalecimiento de la Gestión de la Educación en el Perú.
Trapnell, L., & Zavala, V. (2009). El abandono de la educación intercultural bilingüe en la política educativa del APRA. In R. Cuenca (Ed.), *La Educación en los Tiempos del APRA*. Foro Educativo.
Uccelli, F. (2011). *La política educativa del segundo gobierno de Alan García*. Retrieved from https://iep.org.pe/noticias/francesca-uccelli-la-politica-educativa-del-segundo-gobierno-de-alan-garcia/.
UNESCO. (2000). *Marco de Acción de Dakar. Educación para Todos: cumplir nuestros compromisos comunes (con los seis marcos de acción regionales)*. Paper presented at the Foro Mundial sobre la Educación, Dakar (26–28 de abril).
UNESCO & CNE. (2017). *Revisión de las políticas educativas 2000–2015: continuidades en las políticas públicas en educación en Perú, aprendizajes, docentes y gestión descentralizada*. UNESCO – Oficina de Lima, CNE.
Valdivia, N., Marcos, S., Guzmán, A., Rengifo, W., & Castillo, D. (2018). *La gestión educativa descentralizada en el Perú y el rol de Ministerio de Educación durante el período 2011–2016: un balance crítico desde la perspectiva del Proyecto FORGE*. GRADE.
World Bank. (2019). *Perú: panorama general*. Retrieved from www.bancomundial.org/es/country/peru/overview#1.

8 The Changing Spatial Dynamics of Education Policy in Latin America

Jason Beech

The chapters in this book offer a very detailed and thorough analysis of some of the most critical education policies in the most prominent countries in Latin America during the first two decades of the 21st century. Reading across these chapters, it is possible to identify some common priorities and political strategies in the region and some idiosyncratic elements that characterize education policy approaches in each country.

Another theme that cuts across the above chapters is the complexity of the spatial dynamics of education policy in Latin America during this period. Where is education policy made? Which are the actors that participate in defining policy priorities? Who decides that a particular issue requires public intervention and should become a matter of policy concern and enactment? What state and non-state actors are brought in in the process of creating infrastructures and mechanisms of governance to influence the work of schools and teachers? What kind of networks and heterarchies (Ball & Junemann, 2012) are formed and transformed? How do changing socioeconomic dynamics influence the design and the effects of education policies? To what extent should we consider families and the strategic ways they use the educational system to improve their positions in the social space as key actors of policy processes?

The research that informs this book suggests that policy actors in Latin America have become more aware of the complexity of the trajectories of policies. Changing rules and regulations such as new education laws or the prescribed curriculum do not linearly change what happens in schools and classrooms. Many examples are offered in the chapters of this book of different kinds of governance mechanisms devised to have a more direct influence on the work of schools and teachers in classrooms. As Rivas notes in this book, there was a "race to the classroom" to connect policy decisions with teachers' pedagogic practices and, ideally, the learning of students.

As states attempt to address more complex issues, such as measuring teachers' performance or introducing technologies that can inform stakeholders about the performance of schools in real-time, they get involved in new ways of doing policies. These new forms of policies do not necessarily imply a weakening of the state. Ball (2012) refers to a polycentric state, a state that

DOI: 10.4324/9781003225782-8

uses its power in different ways. On the one hand, the state should not be seen as an indivisible monolithic block. The state is composed of different agencies and levels of government.

Furthermore, political changes and instabilities, which are pretty standard in Latin America, further contribute to power struggles within and across state agencies and levels that can sometimes collaborate and often compete and contradict each other. On the other hand, the state becomes a networked state as it works with other entities at the supranational and subnational levels, from the public and the private sphere, both for-profit and non-for-profit. The notion of heterarchies has been used to denote policy arrangements between hierarchies and networks, based on links between different actors in the policy process. These arrangements are often made to bypass heavy-footed state bureaucracies, and its mechanisms of control are not hierarchical and are usually unstable and flexible (Ball & Junemann, 2012).

The notion of heterarchies as unstable arrangements also introduces the temporal aspects of education policies. When analyzing education policies, we should be aware that we are not taking photographs of stable elements that are once in a while shaken by a given initiative and then tend towards a new equilibrium. Education policies and their trajectories are dynamic phenomena that are constantly changing and becoming. As researchers, we are looking into a world of flux and mobility (Appadurai, 2000; Urry, 2003) in which stability is the exception, not the rule. Even though this is the case for education policy in general, the chapters in this book clearly show that political and economic instability in Latin America contributes to permanent changes with forces that push in very different and often contradictory directions.

Shifting Global Policies

Of course, many of the influences in Latin American education policies come from global actors and global discourses that contribute to defining a language to think about education policies and practices. In the 1950s and 1960s, as international organizations increased their power and activity in education, the focus was mainly on promoting educational planning and increasing access to education. The audience was high-ranking officials that were offered technical tools for governing education by reforming the organizational structures of the macro level, usually the national ministries of education (Ossenbach & Martinez Boom, 2011).

In the 1980s and 1990s, the popularity of concepts of globalization, the information age and knowledge economies contributed to two developments that reinforced the power of international organizations and their capacity to influence education policies. The idea of global challenges that were similar, if not the same, for all countries made the proposals of these organizations especially attractive to governments in times of uncertainty and post-dictatorship in Latin America. Second, the notion that social changes required a new kind of educational system became common sense and widespread at these times. Based on the assumption of a world of permanent changes driven by technological advancements, organizations such as UNESCO, the World Bank and the OCED promoted a universal education model for the information age as the solution to the education challenges of the time (Beech, 2011). This was very influential in most countries in Latin America that initiated significant reforms of their educational systems. What is essential for my argument here is that the proposals of these agencies got into detailed definitions about the content of the curriculum and the kind of pedagogic practices that should be used in classrooms. Global prescriptions got much closer to the level of defining what was an educated person for the *information age*, as they promoted a curriculum based on the development of specific competencies, the notion of teachers as facilitators of learning and child-centered pedagogies (Beech, 2011).

They also tended to promote decentralization, devolution, school autonomy and even some level of autonomy for teachers, which was quite countercultural in the centralist political culture of Latin American education. However, as international organizations tried to influence teaching practices, the complexity of the trajectories of policies become evident. It was much easier to influence high-ranking officials writing regulations in Lima, Mexico City and Brasilia than to change how millions of teachers do their work. Immunological systems at a lower level of the policy cycle blocked and transformed many of these initiatives. Schools and teachers tended to adapt new policy discourses to describe their existing practices rather than change their practices to adapt to new discursive demands (Beech, 2007).

In the 2000s, global policy spaces became even more complex, with the increasing power of large-scale international assessments (notably PISA and its league tables) and the growing participation of for-profit corporations. PISA is probably one of the most influential forces for curricular change in the world, based on quite a detailed notion of what it means to be an educated person that has become a common-sense global definition of quality in education through a powerful logic of governance by numbers (Rizvi & Lingard, 2010; Rutkowski, 2007).

At the same time, both McKinsey and the OECD have been very influential in promoting the idea that teachers are the most critical factor in improving the quality of education (Barber & Mourshed, 2007; OECD, 2005). It is not surprising that in the policies described in this book, so much emphasis has been placed on improving the work of teachers (although with very different mechanisms and political approaches). However, this view also had a strong impact at the level of global actors themselves. The OECD is producing lesson plans for teachers (Vincent-Lancrin et al., 2019). The World Bank offers a classroom observation tool to assess how teachers use their time and the kind of classroom culture and socio-emotional skills they promote (World Bank, 2019).

However, at the same time, as global organizations focus on teachers as a direct target of their initiatives and promote devolution and decentralization, they promote a recentralization of power at the national level. Sellar et al. (forthcoming) argue that PISA has contributed to the emergence of national imaginaries of schooling through its league tables used by the press, public opinion and governments as a national competition that produces new ideas of nationhood as an expression of cultural sovereignty. The desire to perform in PISA based on an image of a national education system conflicts with arrangements in federal countries and others that have devolved power over education to territorial or local entities (Sellar et al., forthcoming).

Changing Scales and Topographies in Education Policy in Latin America

Similar trends of changing spatial dynamics that move between devolution and re-nationalization can be seen in education policies in Latin American countries. In the 1990s, most education systems in the region introduced governance mechanisms that tended to decentralize responsibilities for educational services. At the same time, centralized evaluation systems were devised to connect the policy-producing centers with the policy-practicing peripheries that are granted more autonomy to attain specific goals predefined at the central level (Lingard, 2000).

However, by the end of the century, this logic promoted by global actors and borrowed from New Public Management principles did not result in the expected effects. The use of centralized assessments in the region has been characterized by political instability and technical problems. Neither did the division of labor between state levels contribute to better governance or improve the quality of education, or more equality.

The 2000s, as analyzed in this book, have been times in which Latin American states have been continually reshuffling and adjusting governance mechanisms with shifts in the distribution of power among state agencies and levels. Mexico, for example, started in 2005 with a centralized low stakes assessment with a probabilistic sample, moving in 2006 to a high stakes' assessment for every student in every school. A system that in its peak administered 15 million tests per student, and at some point was associated with performance pay to teachers based on students' results. The strong alliance between the teacher union and the national state weakened, the system was eventually abandoned and the stakes of the exams relaxed. Brazil created the Index of Performance of Basic Education (IDEB). A pretty complex mechanism of governance that combines the measurement of student performance in standardized tests with students' trajectories to create incentives based on quality and equity. The transparency of the system that makes data on the performance of schools widely available has contributed to a recentralization of power at the federal level. In Argentina, while the Kirchner administrations tended to a recentralization of power and initiatives in education at the national level, the government of Macri that replaced them in 2015 tended in the opposite direction, dismantling national programs and transferring funds and initiatives directly to the provinces, while attempting to strengthen the relevance of centralized assessments. The rhetoric about "*Colombia la mas educada*" promoted by Santos in Colombia seems to follow the logic of recentralizing educational power through the kind of nationalistic competitive imaginaries described by Sellar et al. (forthcoming).

These were also times in which philanthropic organizations and for-profit corporations were given significant participation in policy processes. In Brazil, the relationship between the Federal Government and an advocacy coalition for national learning standards, named Mobilization for the National Learning Standards, has been well documented (Avelar & Ball, 2019). In Argentina, new philanthropy has recently gained local influence, primarily through public–private partnerships and an increase of different non-state actors' participation (Feldfeber et al., 2018; Matovich & Cardini, 2019). Furthermore, projects aimed at providing computers or similar technologies for students and schools have opened the way for the influence of many for-profit tech companies on Latin American classrooms (Beech & Artopoulos, 2015; Chapter 2 in this book). Furthermore, many other examples are mentioned in this book of how the heterarchical logic of doing policy is becoming significant in the region.

Socioeconomic shifts and the role of families and civil society add another level of complexity to the spatial dynamics of educational policies in Latin America. Balarin, in this book, documents how improvements in the economic situation of families in Peru resulted in educational demands that could not be satisfied by the state. Enrollments in the private sector grew significantly and became business opportunities for corporations that created successful chains of schools. Even though economic trends were quite different in Argentina, enrollments in private schools have grown in big urban centers. The Catholic Church's role has been crucial in administering many private schools with high state subsidies that cater to low SES families (Narodowski & Moschetti, 2015). Of course, the relevance of the Catholic Church as a compelling policy actor in most of the region should not be ignored. In Chile, social unrest and student movements have pressured the government for significant reform of the system aiming to (to a certain extent) level the field between public and private-subsidized schools and ending with profit-making in subsidized schools (Chapter 4 in this book). The more recent unrest in the country has called for a new constitution that will probably have a much stronger effect in radically changing the Chilean education system. Meanwhile, the closure of schools due to the COVID pandemic brought families and their demands to the fore in education policy decisions.

Conclusion

Latin America is a complex region. It is home to beautiful landscapes and vibrant cultures extending from Tierra del Fuego to the Rio Bravo, and some of the most extreme socioeconomic inequalities in the world, ongoing political and economic instability, and some pressing ecological disasters. At the moment of writing this text, Colombia is experiencing ongoing civil unrest. Chile seems to have channeled social dissatisfaction into an institutional process that will reform its constitution for the first time since the dictatorship. Most countries are being badly affected by the COVID pandemic that exposes the weakness of states and persisting and perverse inequalities.

In education, policy spaces are being created and recreated in dynamic and contradictory ways. In contrast, the panacea of using education as a tool for more equitable and sustainable societies has become an elusive objective. To a certain extent, we are witnessing a technical crisis. Latin American countries struggle to find the best socio-material arrangements to improve education and make educational systems an instrument for social inclusion and equality, rather than mechanisms that contribute to the reproduction of economic inequalities and other associated problems. We need many things to change the dynamics of exclusion in our region. One of them is to understand education policies and how they work in their whole trajectories. In that sense, this book offers an outstanding contribution that can hopefully inspire many more research projects about the complexities of education policies in Latin America in the 2000s.

However, we also need to be aware that what could be seen as a technical challenge is expressing a much more profound moral and political crisis. Goodson (2008) argued that the crisis in education and defining a prescribed curriculum in our era is not so much a technical problem of educational experts that need to improve their knowledge about educational processes. The problem transcends education, and it is related to a generalized crisis of the human narratives on which formal education is based. We need to rethink our political narratives regarding how we want to address the challenge of gender, ethnic and economic inequalities and promote a more sustainable relation to the environment and other species that share the planet with us. The search for alternative education perspectives that can prepare the young to construct a more equitable, safe and sustainable future is growing. Nevertheless, in these changing times, we should be very aware of the challenges of constructing a democratic public sphere. In other words, we have to ask a fundamental question: who is participating in the debate?

References

Appadurai, A. (2000). Grassroots globalization and the research imagination. *Public Culture*, 12(1), 1–19.

Ball, S.J. (2012). *Global Education Inc.: New Policy Networks and the Neoliberal Imaginary*. Routledge.

Ball, S.J., & Junemann, C. (2012). *Networks, New Governance, and Education*. The Policy Press.

Barber, M., & Mourshed, M. (2007). *How the World's Best-Performing School Systems Come Out on Top*. McKinsey & Company.

Beech, J. (2007). La internacionalización de las políticas educativas en América Latina. *Revista Pensamiento Educativo*, 40(1), 153–173.

Beech, J. (2011). *Global Panaceas, Local Realities: International Agencies and the Future of Education*. Peter Lang.

Goodson, I. (2008). Schooling, curriculum, narrative and the social future. In I. Goodson (Ed.), *The Future of Educational Change: International Perspectives*. Routledge.

Lingard, B. (2000). It is and it isn't: vernacular globalization, educational policy, and restructuring. In N. Burbules & C.A. Torres (Eds.), *Globalization and Education*. Routledge.

Narodowski, M., & Moschetti, M. (2015). The growth of private education in Argentina: evidence and explanations. *Compare: A Journal of Comparative and International Education*, 45(1), 47–69.

OECD. (2005). *Teachers Matter: Attracting, Developing and Retaining Effective Teachers, Education and Training Policy*. OECD Publishing.

Ossenbach, G., & Boom, A.M. (2011). Itineraries of the discourses on development and education in Spain and Latin America (circa 1950–1970). *Paedagogica Historica*, 47(5), 679–700.

Rizvi, F., & Lingard, B. (2010). *Globalizing Education Policy*. Routledge.

Rutkowski, D.J. (2007). Converging us softly: how intergovernmental organizations promote neoliberal educational policy. *Critical Studies in Education*, 48(2), 229–247.

Sellar, S., Lingard, B., & Sant, E. (forthcoming). In the name of the nation: PISA and federalism in Australia and Canada. In D. Trohler, N. Piattoeva & W. Pinar (Eds.), *World Yearbook of Education 2022: Education, Schooling and the Global Universalization of Banal Nationalism*. Routledge.

Urry, J. (2003). Social networks, travel, and talk. *British Journal of Sociology*, 54(2), 155–175.

World Bank. (2019). *Teach: Helping Countries Track and Improve Teaching Quality*. Available from www.worldbank.org/en/topic/education/brief/teach-helping-countries-track-and-improve-teaching-quality.

Index

21st century, 1, 6, 9, 19, 29, 97, 150

accountability, 1, 9, 12, 13, 28, 30, 37, 49, 56, 83, 87, 89, 97, 106, 121
assessments, 9, 16, 27, 28, 127, 137, 154
   Evaluations, 17, 101, 141
   measurable, 27, 30, 141
   PISA, 9, 16, 18, 37, 56, 79, 90, 94, 97, 108, 116, 119, 121, 126, 128, 135, 138, 152, 153, 156
   results, 9, 13, 14, 15, 16, 17, 18, 19, 21, 27, 28, 30, 31, 32, 44, 48, 49, 50, 51, 52, 53, 54, 58, 62, 64, 68, 70, 71, 77, 78, 79, 81, 83, 84, 85, 90, 91, 94, 97, 98, 101, 106, 109, 119, 120, 121, 124, 127, 135, 136, 138, 139, 141, 146, 147, 153
   standardized, 1, 13, 14, 15, 17, 18, 19, 21, 27, 28, 58, 64, 82, 83, 84, 88, 90, 98, 101, 102, 103, 120, 121, 124, 125, 147, 153
   tests, 9, 13, 14, 15, 16, 17, 18, 19, 21, 27, 51, 77, 79, 82, 84, 88, 89, 97, 101, 102, 115, 116, 119, 120, 127, 147, 153
agenda. *See* agendas
agendas, 1, 2, 10, 22, 24, 53
Argentina, 1, 2, 3, 4, 5, 6, 7, 9, 10, 22, 23, 24, 25, 26, 27, 28, 29, 30, 33, 34, 37, 38, 39, 40, 41, 42, 43, 44, 45, 46, 47, 48, 49, 51, 53, 54, 55, 56, 57, 95, 153, 154
   Cristina Fernández, 10, 37, 39, 41, 57
   Mauricio Macri, 3, 11, 40, 48
autonomy, 12, 20, 25, 28, 49, 64, 71, 81, 97, 103, 105, 106, 123, 125, 127, 131, 152, 153
   school autonomy, 28

basic, 6, 13, 14, 15, 19, 27, 28, 41, 42, 45, 46, 50, 54, 58, 60, 62, 63, 65, 66, 67, 68, 69, 70, 71, 72, 79, 83, 86, 97, 99, 100, 101, 103, 104, 107, 116, 117, 119, 120, 121, 137, 140
Bolivia. *See* Latin America
Brazil, 1, 2, 3, 4, 5, 6, 7, 9, 10, 12, 13, 14, 22, 23, 24, 25, 26, 27, 28, 29, 30, 34, 58, 59, 61, 62, 63, 64, 65, 66, 67, 68, 69, 71, 72, 73, 153, 154
   Common Curricular National Base, 14
   Dilma Rousseff, 3, 13, 14, 62, 67, 68
   FUNDEB, 12, 13, 64, 66, 67, 70, 71, 72
   IDEB, 13, 64, 153
   Jair Bolsonaro, 3, 14, 69
   Lula da Silva, 2, 3, 13, 66
   SAEB, 12, 13, 64, 65
challenges, 10, 34, 47, 48, 51, 54, 72, 84, 103, 106, 122, 132, 142, 151, 152, 155
Chile, 1, 2, 3, 4, 6, 7, 9, 10, 14, 22, 23, 24, 25, 26, 27, 28, 29, 30, 33, 34, 36, 38, 75, 76, 77, 78, 79, 80, 81, 82, 83, 84, 85, 86, 87, 89, 90, 91, 92, 93, 94, 95, 154, 155
   Augusto Pinochet, 14, 15, *See* dictatorships
   Concertación, 3, 15
   Michelle Bachelet, 16, 36, 94, 95
   Sebastián Piñera, 3, 91
   SIMCE, 15, 30, 77, 79, 83, 88, 90, 91
Colombia, 1, 2, 4, 6, 7, 9, 10, 17, 18, 23, 24, 25, 26, 27, 28, 29, 30, 36, 38, 96, 97, 98, 99, 100, 101, 102, 103, 104, 105, 106, 107, 108, 148, 154, 155
   Álvaro Uribe, 17, 97, 98
   SABER, 17, 18, 102

Index

SENA, 17
Comparative, 3, 5, 9, 11, 13, 15, 17, 19, 21, 23, 25, 27, 29, 33, 35, 37
competencies, 14, 15, 17, 19, 20, 43, 50, 69, 98, 99, 100, 106, 107, 120, 152
connectivity, 20, 99
conservative, 10, 14, 69, 105, 144
constructivism, 20
corruption, 2, 3, 19, 20, 40, 96, 111, 126, 130, 131, 132, 133, 143
COVID-19, 2, 5, 58, 91, 97
curricular, 9, 10, 11, 13, 15, 16, 17, 19, 20, 21, 22, 26, 30, 34, 41, 43, 49, 50, 51, 52, 55, 76, 78, 79, 82, 83, 88, 91, 99, 103, 104, 120, 123, 140, 141, 145, 146, 152, *See* reforms
curricular regulation, 17, 30

deficit, 6, 12
   fiscal deficit, 13, 39, 40, 134
democracies, 1, 2, 30
dictatorships, 1, 2
disadvantaged. *See* marginalized

economic crisis. *See* poverty
economic growth, 1, 5, 8, 9, 10, 20, 22, 25, 47, 69, 110, 111, 132
economic indicators, 6
Economic recovery, 6
Ecuador. *See* Latin America
education reforms. *See* reforms
education system, 11, 12, 14, 16, 17, 19, 22, 26, 29, 41, 42, 43, 47, 50, 51, 52, 75, 76, 83, 84, 85, 87, 88, 98, 104, 111, 114, 115, 119, 121, 153, 154
educational material, 11
   computer labs, 15
   didactic materials, 15, 78, 117
   textbooks, 11, 13, 16, 17, 18, 21, 26, 29, 30, 42, 43, 78, 115
educational policies, 1, 14, 17, 18, 20, 24, 42, 43, 44, 52, 53, 54, 55, 62, 69, 71, 76, 77, 78, 79, 80, 86, 88, 89, 92, 112, 118, 119, 130, 133, 134, 138, 139, 143, 147, 154
election, 3, 98, 109, 130
employment, 5, 104, 132
enactment, 14, 21, 23, 43, 58, 62, 63, 67, 68, 134, 150
evaluating teachers. *See* accountability
export, 5, 6, 132

GDP, 5, 6, 7, 8, 10, 14, 22, 23, 24, 39, 40, 42, 55, 59, 69, 132, 134, 142

Gini coefficient, 6, 8, 40, 97, 132
governance, 9, 11, 22, 30, 31, 32, 33, 36, 37, 48, 54, 56, 65, 67, 87, 97, 99, 103, 104, 117, 127, 131, 132, 133, 150, 152, 153
governments, 2, 3, 6, 9, 15, 20, 22, 25, 29, 33, 44, 54, 62, 63, 65, 77, 78, 81, 96, 114, 115, 121, 126, 130, 131, 132, 136, 137, 139, 143, 146, 151, 153

ideological, 3, 9, 70, 101
improvement, 5, 6, 15, 16, 17, 20, 22, 25, 51, 58, 78, 79, 80, 81, 82, 87, 88, 89, 90, 91, 99, 100, 102, 103, 104, 119, 123, 134, 135, 136, 137, 142, 144
inclusion, 5, 13, 19, 33, 44, 48, 55, 66, 68, 120, 123, 124, 126, 145, 155
instability, 14, 16, 20, 30, 39, 69, 103, 133, 134, 143, 151, 153, 154
Intercultural Bilingual Education, 21, 135, 142
international agencies, 1

kindergarten, 15, 50, 98

Latin America, 1, 2, 5, 6, 8, 9, 22, 29, 33, 34, 36, 37, 38, 55, 91, 93, 96, 97, 100, 102, 125, 150, 151, 152, 153, 154, 155, 156

management, 15, 17, 18, 21, 27, 28, 30, 48, 52, 60, 64, 70, 71, 77, 79, 81, 83, 84, 87, 89, 91, 99, 100, 102, 114, 115, 116, 122, 125, 131, 132, 133, 134, 135, 137, 138, 139, 140, 141, 142, 143, 145
marginalized, 9, 13, 24, 29, 103
market, 2, 3, 14, 15, 16, 17, 18, 25, 29, 46, 59, 76, 77, 78, 79, 80, 82, 83, 84, 85, 87, 88, 89, 90, 91, 92, 93, 94, 101, 102, 106
Mexico, 1, 3, 6, 7, 9, 10, 18, 19, 23, 24, 26, 27, 28, 29, 30, 34, 36, 108, 109, 110, 111, 112, 113, 114, 115, 116, 117, 119, 120, 121, 122, 123, 125, 126, 127, 128, 129, 152, 153
ENLACE, 19, 119, 127
Enrique Peña Nieto, 3, 19, 110, 121
EXCALE, 19, 116, 127
Felipe Calderón, 3, 110, 118
INEE, 19, 20, 30, 111, 116, 120, 121, 123, 124, 125, 127, 128

PRI, 3, 109, 110, 111, 112, 113, 117, 118, 126
RIES, 19, 117
SNTE, 19, 112, 113, 114, 117, 118, 121, 122, 125, 126
Minister, 10, 11, 17, 18, 21, 41, 49, 61, 98, 100, 134, 136, 139, 143, 144, 145, 147
municipal. *See* municipalities
municipalities, 15, 61, 71, *See* subnational

neoliberal reforms. *See* reforms

Peru, 1, 2, 3, 4, 7, 8, 9, 10, 20, 23, 24, 25, 26, 27, 28, 29, 30, 35, 130, 131, 132, 133, 135, 136, 137, 139, 141, 143, 145, 146, 147, 149, 154
Alan García, 3, 21, 136, 141, 149
COAR, 22, 141
PELA, 21, 138, 140
polarized, 3
policies, 1, 2, 3, 6, 9, 10, 12, 13, 14, 15, 16, 18, 20, 21, 22, 24, 25, 26, 27, 28, 29, 30, 31, 32, 33, 34, 39, 40, 42, 43, 44, 45, 46, 47, 49, 51, 52, 54, 58, 59, 60, 61, 62, 64, 66, 67, 68, 69, 71, 72, 77, 78, 79, 84, 89, 90, 91, 93, 97, 99, 100, 101, 103, 104, 105, 106, 109, 110, 111, 118, 125, 126, 130, 131, 135, 136, 137, 138, 139, 141, 142, 143, 144, 145, 146, 150, 151, 152, 153, 155
policy agendas. *See* agendas
population, 5, 6, 8, 17, 24, 41, 59, 71, 72, 75, 76, 104, 130, 132, 137
poverty, 5, 6, 7, 8, 20, 34, 39, 40, 46, 97, 102, 119, 132
private, 15, 16, 17, 18, 23, 26, 27, 28, 29, 47, 60, 75, 76, 77, 78, 79, 80, 82, 84, 85, 86, 87, 88, 89, 93, 102, 112, 113, 115, 120, 121, 135, 138, 151, 154, 156
professional, 11, 13, 15, 16, 21, 25, 29, 47, 50, 62, 77, 78, 81, 86, 87, 102, 107, 112
public investment, 6
public spending, 6, 12, 14, 22, 23, 40, 41, 52, 69

recentralization, 20, 30, 133, 153
reforms, 1, 2, 9, 10, 11, 14, 15, 16, 20, 25, 26, 29, 30, 33, 38, 42, 58, 77, 82, 83, 88, 89, 90, 91, 96, 100, 105, 106, 109, 110, 111, 112, 113, 114, 117, 119, 120, 121, 122, 123, 124, 125, 126, 130, 131, 132, 133, 143, 144, 145, 146, 152
resistance, 10, 17, 19, 25, 26, 30, 85, 86, 122

secondary, 7, 11, 12, 13, 14, 15, 18, 23, 27, 28, 29, 41, 43, 44, 45, 46, 47, 48, 49, 50, 51, 52, 54, 55, 58, 60, 62, 63, 66, 69, 72, 76, 78, 79, 80, 91, 100, 102, 103, 104, 115, 116, 120, 121, 122, 124, 125, 127, 134, 135, 138, 146, 147
social inequalities. *See* marginalized
socio-emotional, 20, 123, 152
stagnation, 6, 10, 11, 39, 40, 41, 48, 84, 125
standards, 16, 17, 21, 26, 29, 30, 31, 63, 82, 89, 91, 99, 100, 102, 105, 106, 120, 140, 154
state terrorism, 2, *See* dictatorships
subnational, 12, 25, 31, 32, 42, 54, 58, 62, 63, 64, 65, 68, 70, 109, 111, 130, 131, 137, 142, 146, 151, *See* Latin America
subsidy, 14, 15, 27, 76, 78, 82, 85, 100

tax, 8, 67, 85, 91, 120, 132
teacher training, 11, 15, 19, 25, 26, 31, 43, 44, 45, 47, 49, 50, 51, 52, 53, 78, 86, 101, 102, 115, 117, 118, 134, 137, 142, 145, 146
Teacher unions. *See* unions
teaching career, 15, 16, 18, 19, 21, 25, 26, 30, 43, 48, 53, 54, 85, 86, 114, 117, 121, 122, 134, 136, 139, 140, 141, 144, 145
teaching practices, 10, 16, 21, 26, 137, 146, 152
technology, 19, 20, 27, 97, 107, 116, 119, 135, 138, 142
television, 11, 45

unions, 10, 17, 25, 43, 54, 104, 105, 127
Uruguay. *See* Latin America

Venezuela. *See* Latin America

wages, 25
working conditions, 25, 45, 77, 79, 90

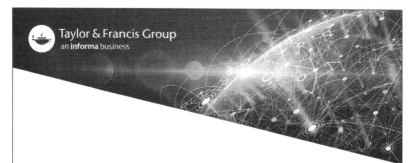

Printed in the United States
by Baker & Taylor Publisher Services